TEXAS SOMEWHERE
SOMEWHERE IN TEXAS

DRAW
THEM IN
PAINT
THEM OUT

DRAW THEM IN PAINT THEM OUT

TRENTON DOYLE HANCOCK CONFRONTS PHILIP GUSTON

REBECCA SHAYKIN

With contributions by Trenton Doyle Hancock, Valerie Cassel Oliver, and Art Spiegelman

JEWISH MUSEUM, NEW YORK
Under the auspices of the Jewish Theological Seminary of America

YALE UNIVERSITY PRESS
NEW HAVEN AND LONDON

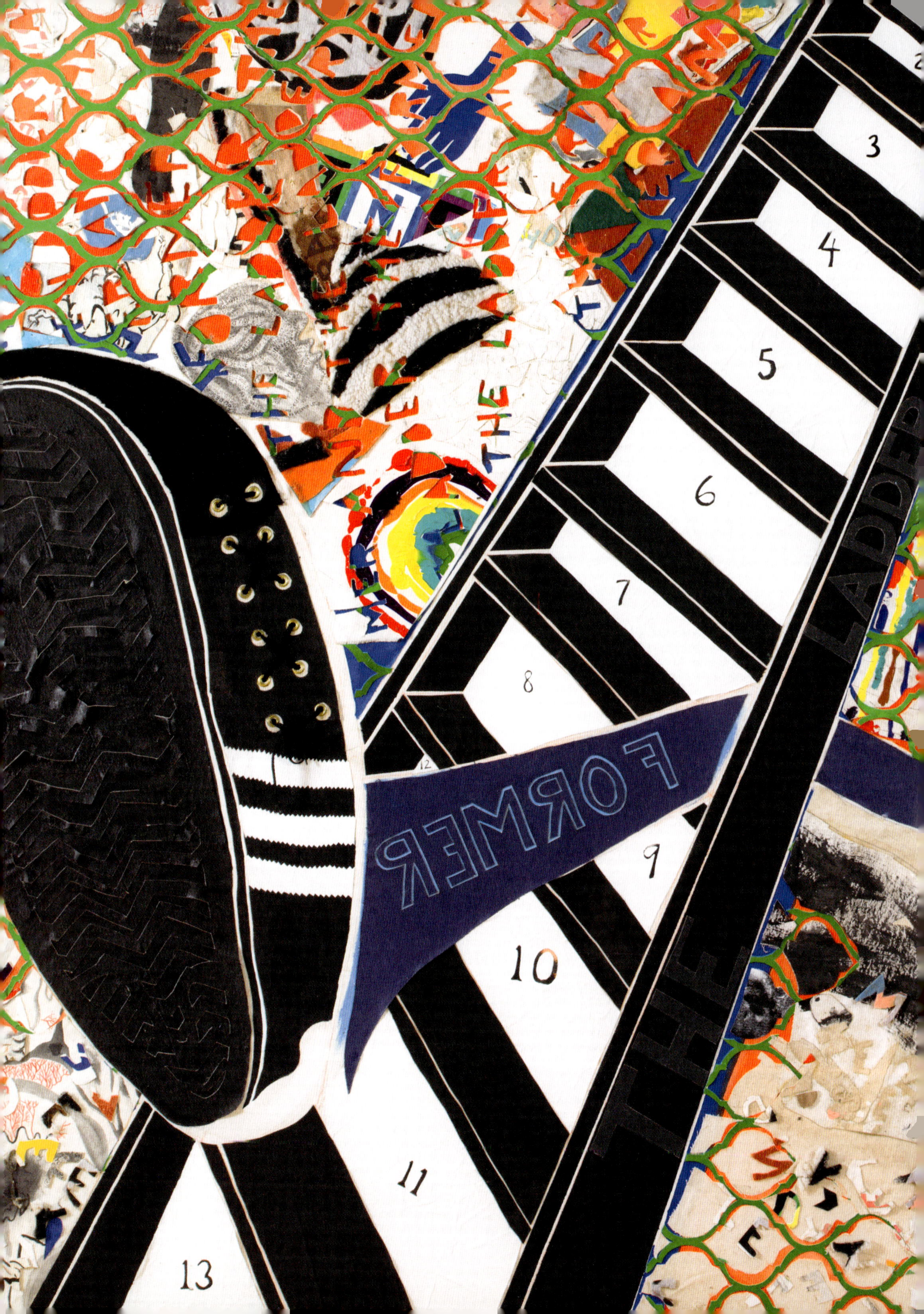

THE LADDER
THE LADDER
FORMER
3
4
5
6
7
8
9
10
11
12
13

CONTENTS

Trenton Doyle Hancock, *The Former and the Ladder or Ascension and a Cinchin'*, 2012 (detail; see p. 34); previous spread: *Globetrotters*, 2023 (detail; see p. 119)

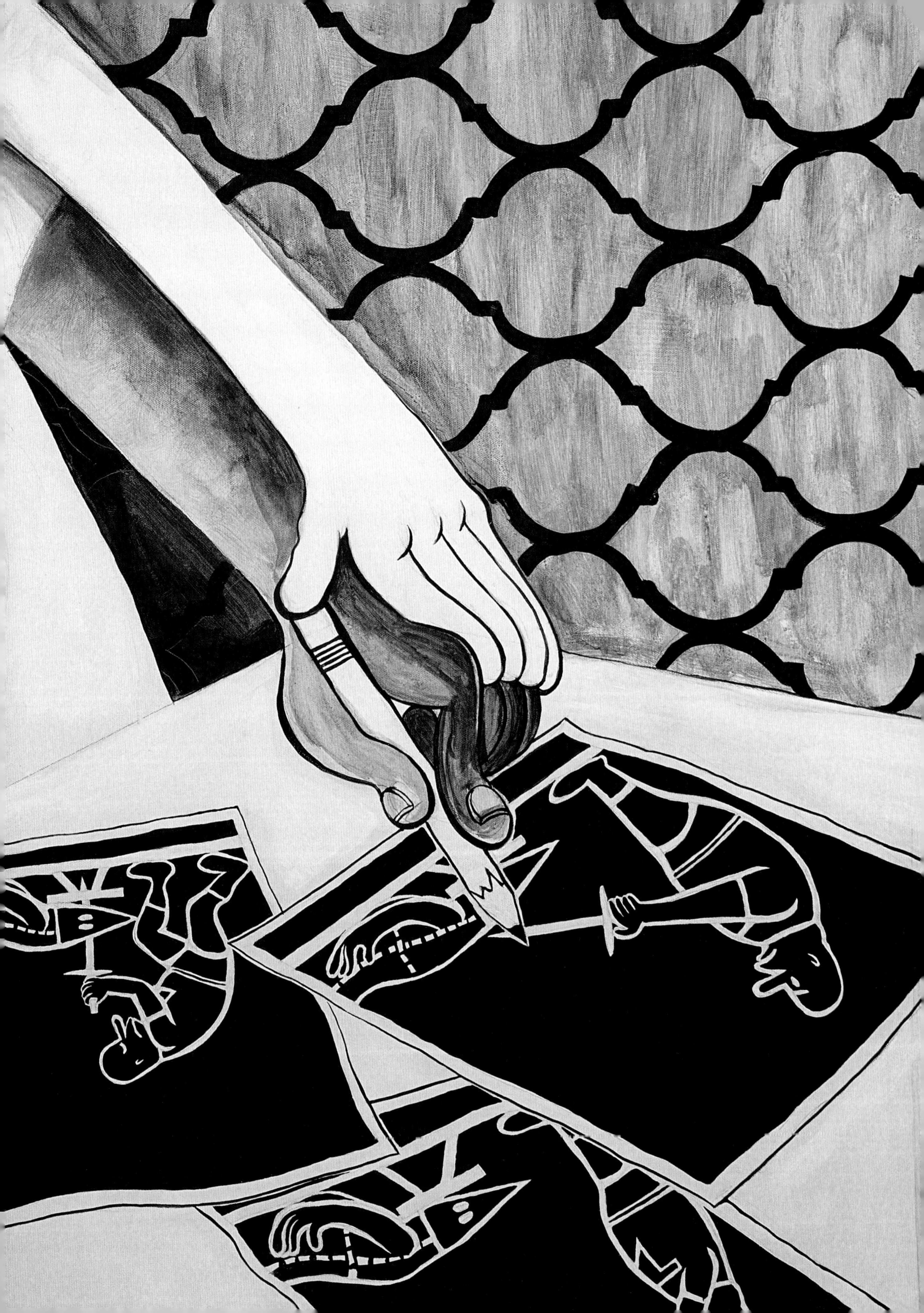

DONORS TO THE EXHIBITION

Draw Them In, Paint Them Out: Trenton Doyle Hancock Confronts Philip Guston is made possible by The Guston Fund; the Ford Foundation; the National Endowment for the Arts; the Knapp Family Foundation; Art Mentor Foundation Lucerne; Hedy Fischer and Randy Shull; Agnes Gund; James Cohan, New York; the Shulamit Nazarian Foundation; Nazarian / Curcio Gallery, Los Angeles; and other generous donors.

Ford Foundation

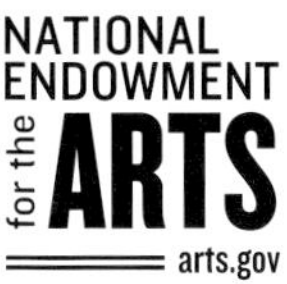

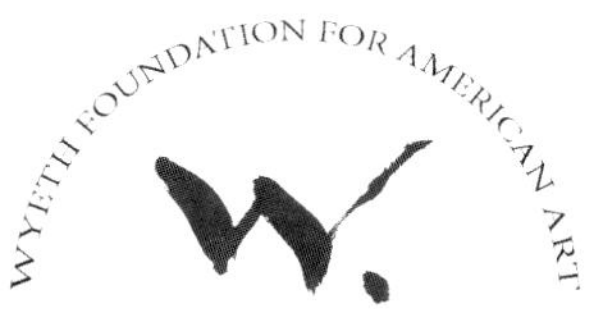

The publication is made possible by the Wyeth Foundation for American Art.

LENDERS TO THE EXHIBITION

Anonymous
Mandy and Cliff Einstein, Los Angeles
Hedy Fischer and Randy Shull, Asheville,
    North Carolina
Lisa and Stuart Ginsberg, New York
Trenton Doyle Hancock
Stephanie and Tim Ingrassia, Brooklyn
Jewish Museum, New York
JKiZ, Lisbon, Portugal
Musa Guston Mayer
Menil Collection, Houston
Metropolitan Museum of Art, New York
Amanda and Donald Mullen
Museum of Fine Arts, Boston
National Gallery of Art, Washington, DC
Pizzuti Collection, Columbus, Ohio
Ariel Roger-Paris, Antwerp, Belgium
Thomas Rom
Virginia Museum of Fine Arts, Richmond
Whitney Museum of American Art, New York

Trenton Doyle Hancock, *The Boys in the Hoods Are Always Hard,* 2023 (detail; see p. 120); next page: *Step and Screw: The Star of Code Switching,* 2020 (detail; see p. 107)

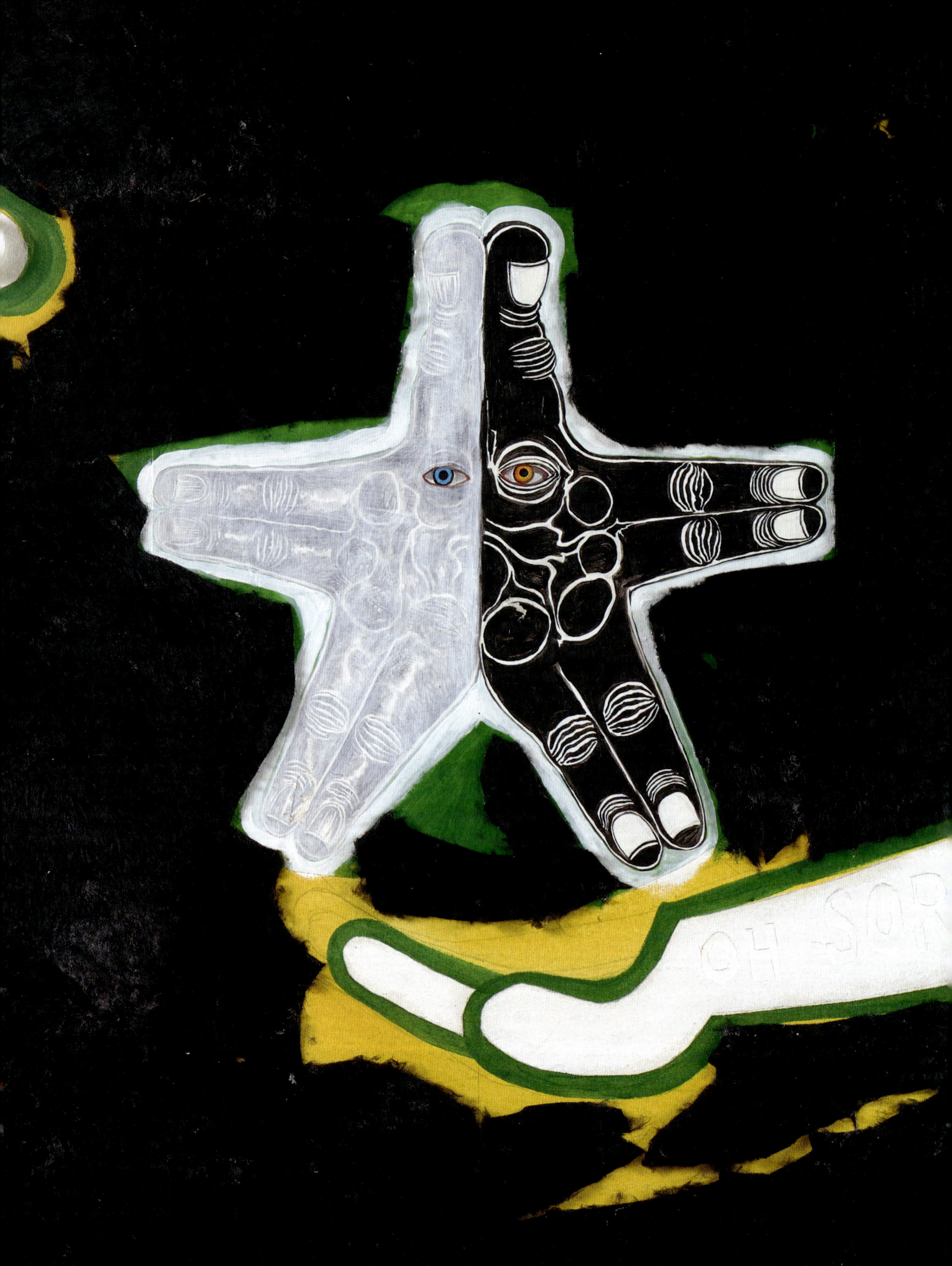
OH SORRY

FOREWORD

Draw Them In, Paint Them Out: Trenton Doyle Hancock Confronts Philip Guston brings together two trailblazing American artists, separated by half a century and yet presented here in dialogue with each other for the first time in a museum setting. The unexpected resonances between these artists build on the Jewish Museum's long history of exhibitions that illuminate Black and Jewish relations both within and beyond the art world. The Museum's landmark exhibition *Bridges and Boundaries* (1992), co-organized with the NAACP, examined the parallel trajectories of African American and American Jewish communities in their struggles for social justice, explored through artworks by Black and Jewish contemporary artists. *Kehinde Wiley/The World Stage: Israel* (2012) featured Wiley's vibrant large-scale portraits of young Israelis from diverse ethnic and religious heritages, each embedded in a unique backdrop drawn from depictions of Jewish ritual objects. *From the Margins: Lee Krasner/Norman Lewis, 1945–1952* (2014–15) revealed previously unexplored dimensions of Abstract Expressionism through the work of two artists whose gender and race had precluded their presence in canonical histories of the era. And, more recently, *Edith Halpert and the Rise of American Art* (2019–20) investigated the way in which Halpert, a Jewish art dealer, pioneered efforts to desegregate the American art world in the early 1940s by supporting Black American artists such as Jacob Lawrence and Horace Pippin.

Draw Them In, Paint Them Out continues to mine this rich field of underappreciated cross-cultural encounters and alliances, offering a rare opportunity to consider Guston—whose solo exhibition at the Jewish Museum took place in 1966, just before the emergence of his late and iconic antiracist work with Klan imagery—in resonance with Hancock, a prominent contemporary Black artist who, in discussions with peers and colleagues, reflects on his own use of Klan imagery. Bringing renewed focus on the role that artists can play in advocating for social justice, Hancock cites as one of his goals for this project "to examine the relationship between Jewish and Black cultures, which have been linked historically through resonant experiences with trauma and achievement, oftentimes managing to cope through a symbiotic relationship with one another." Underscoring this point, Musa Mayer, President of the Guston Foundation, has said that Hancock's vision for this exhibition "carries forward the social conscience" of her father's work. Given the Jewish Museum's mission to promote understanding through education, engagement, and dialogue, this exhibition is especially urgent now, in the wake of an unprecedented rise in anti-Black and antisemitic violence across the United States that has been fueled by the challenges of these times both in the United States and globally.

We are deeply grateful to Curator Rebecca Shaykin for her powerfully insightful work on this project. Museums exist to be custodians of the creative production of artists like Trenton Doyle Hancock, and our greatest thanks go to him for his generous partnership in realizing this exhibition. We also thank James Cohan and Paula Naughton at James Cohan, and Musa Mayer and Sally Radic at the Guston Foundation. Darsie Alexander, Senior Deputy Director and Susan and Elihu Rose Chief Curator, deserves our appreciation for her help and support, as do all of the Museum's staff who have contributed to the production and realization of this timely exhibition and its accompanying publication.

Finally, our profound gratitude goes to the exhibition's many generous lenders and donors. For their major support of *Draw Them In, Paint Them Out*, we thank The Guston Fund, the Ford Foundation, the National Endowment for the Arts, the Knapp Family Foundation, and Art Mentor Foundation Lucerne. For making possible this beautiful publication, we thank the Wyeth Foundation for American Art. As ever, we also extend our gratitude to the Jewish Museum's Board of Trustees, under the visionary leadership of Chairman Robert A. Pruzan and President Shari Aronson, and to the Board's Exhibitions Committee, cochaired by Andrew E. Lewin and Aaron Malinsky. During these challenging times, it is evermore important for museums to demonstrate how they can explore cultural dialogue as a pathway to greater clarity in brighter times ahead, and we could not be more grateful to our leadership, donors, and friends for their unwavering support in doing so.

James S. Snyder
Helen Goldsmith Menschel Director
Jewish Museum

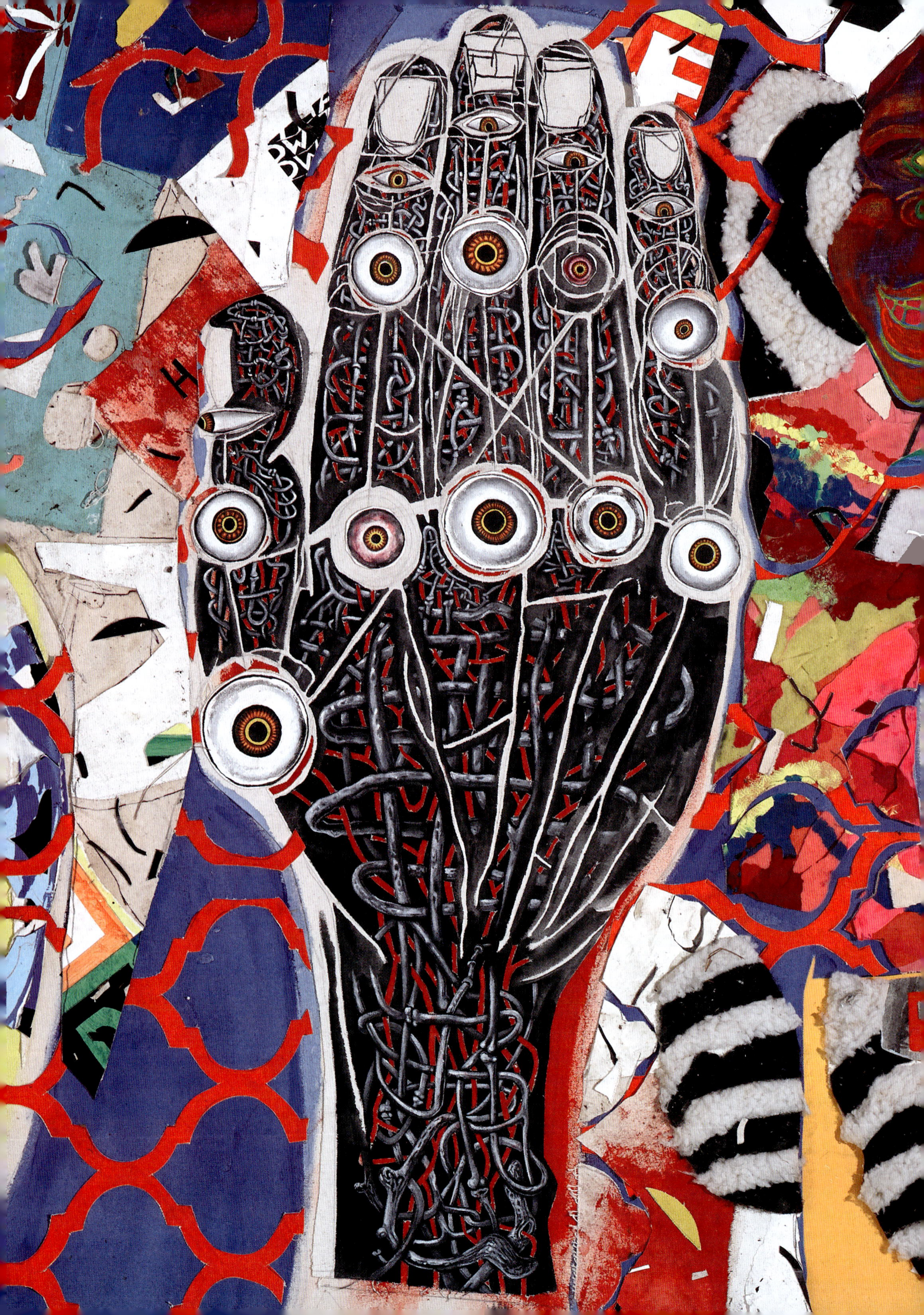

ACKNOWLEDGMENTS

It is a remarkable privilege to have one's curatorial idea given the necessary space and time to grow into a fully realized exhibition. I owe an enormous debt of gratitude to so many people who have helped *Draw Them In, Paint Them Out* come into being over these past seven years.

First and foremost, I thank Trenton Doyle Hancock for entrusting me with his story and so generously allowing me into his wondrous Moundverse. He has been an ideal coconspirator, from conception to execution. Paula Naughton, who sets the gold standard for artist advocacy, has been an invaluable partner to us both. I am indebted to her, as well as to James Cohan, David Norr, Sarah Stengel, and the rest of the team at James Cohan. Shulamit Nazarian and Seth Curcio at Nazarian / Curcio Gallery also provided critical support and assistance with loans, as did Sasha Gomeniuk at Hales Gallery. For their early encouragement, I am grateful to Denise Markonish, curator of *Trenton Doyle Hancock—Mind of the Mound: Critical Mass* (2019) at MASS MoCA; and to Edouard Kopp and Michelle White at the Menil Collection, Houston, where *Contemporary Focus: Trenton Doyle Hancock* was presented in 2019.

I extend my heartfelt gratitude to Musa Mayer, President of the Guston Foundation, for her open embrace of and genuine interest in deepening the artistic dialogue between Trenton Doyle Hancock and her father. It has been an honor to partner with her on Guston's return to the Jewish Museum. In addition to Musa's steadfast support, collaboration, and guidance, Sally Radic at the Guston Foundation and Anders Bergstrom at Hauser & Wirth each gave indispensable feedback and facilitated key loans.

Along with those named above, I am grateful to the many curators who welcomed Trenton and me into the greater Guston family during the runs of *Philip Guston: On Edge* at Hauser & Wirth (2021); *Philip Guston Now* (2022–24), which toured multiple venues; and *Philip Guston: What Kind of Man Am I?* (2023) at the Metropolitan Museum of Art, New York. They include David Breslin and Brinda Kumar at the Metropolitan Museum; Kelly Baum at the Des Moines Art Center, Iowa; Harry Cooper at the National Gallery of Art, Washington, DC; Ethan Lasser at the Museum of Fine Arts, Boston, along with his curatorial collaborator in that endeavor, Kate Nesin; Alison de Lima Greene at the Museum of Fine Arts, Houston; and Michael Wellen at Tate Modern, London.

This publication would not be nearly as compelling without Valerie Cassel Oliver's historical insights and Art Spiegelman's singular voice; I thank them both for providing vital cultural context for the subject at hand. The text benefited immensely from Marcie Muscat's deft editorial skills. The striking book design and exhibition graphics represent the impressive creative talents of Morcos Key; thanks to Jon Key and Chuck Gonzales for making it look effortless. I am grateful to Andy Chen and Waqas Jawaid at Isometric Studio for their collaborative and playful approach to exhibition design and for sharing their expertise and perspectives.

In addition to our external creative team, I benefited each day from an incredible cast of colleagues at the Jewish Museum. Claudia Gould, our former director, was an indomitable champion of contemporary art and artists, as well as a great admirer of Guston's paintings. I am forever grateful to her for greenlighting this exhibition and for entrusting me with its realization. Many thanks to our current director, James S. Snyder, for his subsequent endorsement of this project and for his leadership during these challenging times. A million thanks to Susan Weiss and Sari Weisenberg in the Director's Office for all that they do. I am especially honored to count myself in the same curatorial company as Shira Backer, Stephen Brown, Rebecca Frank, Mason Klein, Liz Munsell, Claudia J. Nahson, Kristina Parsons, Abigail Rapoport, and Aviva Weintraub, a brilliant team led by Senior Deputy Director and Susan and Elihu Rose Chief Curator Darsie Alexander—my work is better because of them. I am indebted to Danielle Byerley, Shoshanna and David Wingate Curatorial Intern, and María Wilson Núñez and Collin Robinson, Blanksteen Curatorial Interns, for their capable research assistance. Caroline Harvey keeps our department running, while Jody Heher and Maureen Merrigan ensure that our exhibitions go up without a hitch. Many thanks to Katherine Danalakis, Ellen Croisier, and Mimi Reeves for helping to bring Trenton's *Step and Screw: The Star of Code Switching* into our physical and digital collections. Registrars Julie Maguire and Jennifer Roberts, along with a dedicated crew of operations staff, art handlers, and preparators, guaranteed that all loans arrived on site safely and were expertly installed. Thanks, as ever, to Eve Sinaiko and Amelia Kutschbach for managing all publications-related logistics and to Rebecca Merriman for making quick work of image gathering and rights clearance. Nelly Silagy Benedek and her incredible staff in Education, particularly Jenna Weiss and Demily Soler-Alemañy, who manage our public programs and audio guides, are to be commended. I am grateful to Sarah Supcoff, Anne Scher, Daniela Stigh, Paige Caldwell, Yael Miller, and Katherine Flores for helping this exhibition reach a wide audience, and to our Visitor Experience team, led by Lyndsey Anderson, Jack O'Neill, and Frazier Braverman-Greenberg, for welcoming the public to our museum on Fifth Avenue. Katie Hollander, Collin Garrett, Genesis Mullis, and Ella Parker undertook the momentous task of fundraising for this project; I thank them for their collective efforts. I likewise thank our many generous lenders and funders, without whom this exhibition would not have been possible.

Thank you to my friends and family, who give me guidance and keep me grounded—Samuel Ashworth, Layla Bermeo, Ruthie Birger, Caitlin Condell, Elena Derkits, Ruthie Dibble, Rachel Furnari, Alison Hokanson, Sheryl Kaskowitz, Emily Knapp, Diana Nawi, Sam Sackeroff, Benjamin Shaykin, Gabriel Shaykin, Leonard Shaykin, Norah Shaykin, Alison Smith, and Sarah Van Anden.

This book is dedicated to my children, Lila and Jacob. Like Trenton, they have taught me the importance of maintaining a sense of awe and wonder about the world, as well as a profound sense of justice. And finally, to my husband, Nathaniel Walton: there is no one I would rather confront life with.

Rebecca Shaykin
Curator
Jewish Museum

My heartfelt gratitude goes out to Musa Mayer and everyone at the Guston Foundation, without whose generosity and knowledge this exhibition would not be possible. It means the world to have been given your blessing to pair my voice with Philip Guston's. He will always be a fixture in my pantheon of great artists, and it is such an honor to be exhibited alongside him. Thank you so much—dreams do sometimes come true! To Sally Radic at the Guston Foundation, thank you for your time and generosity. I sincerely appreciate your guidance through the archives.

Thanks to the Jewish Museum for its institutional support and for granting me the opportunity to exhibit on its walls; it has truly been an honor. It was an extreme pleasure to partner with curator Rebecca Shaykin in realizing this exhibition and catalogue. I am beyond appreciative of your illuminating perspectives, and I will cherish the many conversations we had while crafting our project and bringing this unique vision to life.

To Valerie Cassel Oliver and Art Spiegelman: I thank you both for rich and engaging dialogues and for lending your insights and expertise on important cultural themes and matters of creativity.

Special thanks to James Cohan and Paula Naughton. Your guidance and input have been invaluable. Thanks as well to everyone at Hauser & Wirth for your help in moving this exhibition forward.

I am truly grateful to all the lenders and supporters of this exhibition and catalogue. If not for you, then this project would not have been possible.

To my loving wife, JooYoung, thank you for your continued faith in me.

Finally, thank you to Philip Guston. I wish we had met. Let this exhibition be evidence that our spirits certainly have.

Trenton Doyle Hancock
Artist

Trenton Doyle Hancock, *I Want to Be at the Meeting After the Separation,* 2014 (detail; see pp. 52–53); previous spread: *Referee,* 2014 (detail; see pp. 50–51)

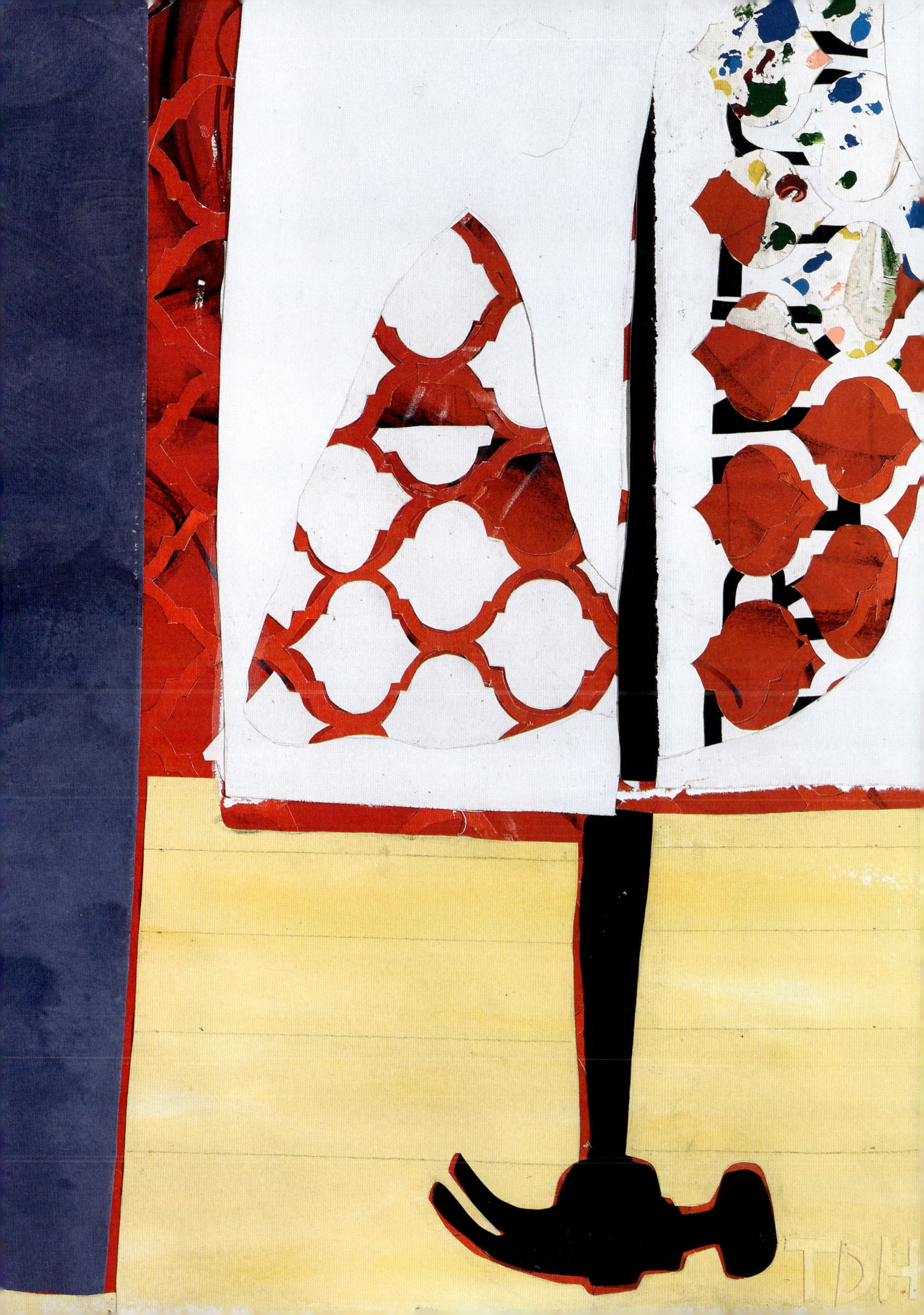

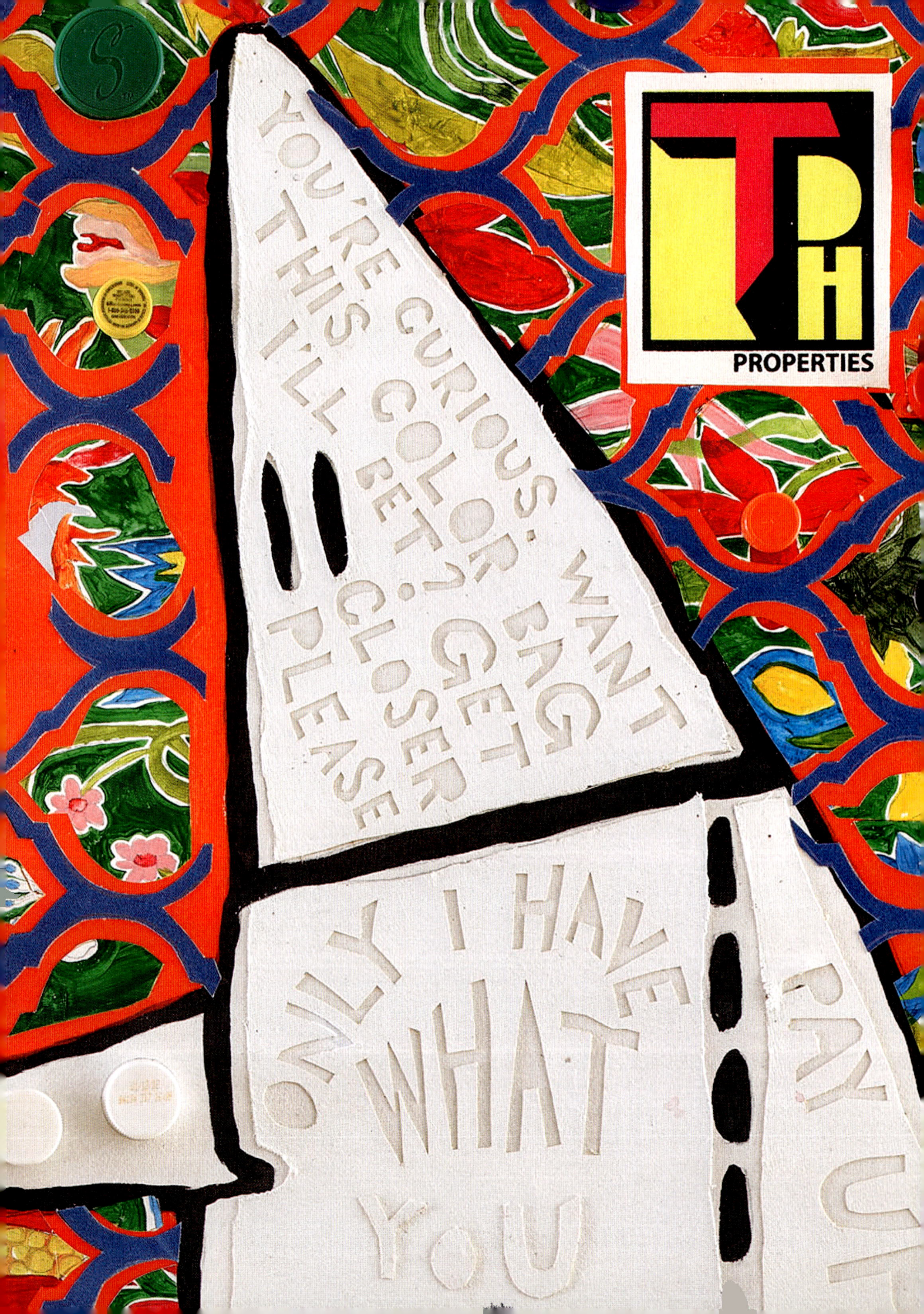
YOU'RE CURIOUS. WANT THIS COLOR? BAG
BET? GET CLOSER PLEASE
ONLY I HAVE WHAT YOU
PAY U
TPh
PROPERTIES

DRAW THEM IN PAINT THEM OUT

REBECCA SHAYKIN

Trenton Doyle Hancock, *Schlep and Screw, Knowledge Rental Pawn Exchange Service*, 2017 (detail; see p. 103)

The idea for this exhibition came to me in a flash. It was December 2017 and I happened upon a new painting by Trenton Doyle Hancock (see p. 103). I was drawn in immediately by its oversized red apple and lush floral background overlaid with a trellis pattern, reminiscent of a patchwork quilt. A red ouroboros wound its way along the border. So here was Eden, the forbidden fruit, the snake in an American garden. I looked closer. The serpent carried a message incised on its body: "SCHLEP AND SCREW," it repeatedly intoned, half in Yiddish. And then I noticed another devil in disguise: a Klansman. And not just any Klansman but Philip Guston's Klansman, pillowy and buffoonish. The reference was unmistakable.

Philip Guston was very much on our minds at the Jewish Museum at the time. A revered Jewish painter of the twentieth century, he had been something of a sleeping giant of art history since his last major retrospective traveled to the Metropolitan Museum of Art in 2003, cropping up occasionally around town in concise gallery presentations and surveys of his works on paper. Then, the acclaimed *Philip Guston and the Poets* exhibition at the Gallerie dell'Accademia in Venice, timed to coincide with the 2017 Biennale, generated a fresh wave of excitement for Guston and his work, and we knew it was time for a major reassessment in New York. At first we thought we might examine our own institutional history with the artist. Guston had had a solo exhibition at the Jewish Museum in 1966, curated by then-director Sam Hunter, in which he had presented some sixty paintings and twenty drawings, all in somber tones of black and gray. About fifteen years earlier, Guston had abandoned his social-realist roots to pursue abstraction, then the dominant style among the downtown avant-garde. Although he was close with key figures of the New York School and showed his work in defining exhibitions of the period, he never felt quite at ease in the movement. His Jewish Museum exhibition attempted to reassert his claim that, as a people, "We are image-makers and image-ridden."[1] His paintings coalesced around central forms—ragged squares of black emerging out of a silvery abyss. Assigning them titles like *Painter* (1959–60) and *Portrait II* (1965), he was clearly pushing against the constraints of abstraction, insisting on figuration in its crudest form while looking to find himself in his own creations.

The critics were unimpressed, calling the work dull and repetitive, and Guston, a "minor lyricist who occupies himself with a very narrow range of feeling."[2] Worst of all, his painting was considered rearguard when compared with the ascendant trends of Minimalism, Pop, and Op art. Dejected, and repelled by an art world that now favored gloss over substance, Guston gave up painting for two years and retreated to Woodstock, New York, where he would maintain his studio in relative isolation for the

Philip Guston, untitled, 1969, charcoal on paper, 18 × 24 in. (45.7 × 61 cm). Private collection

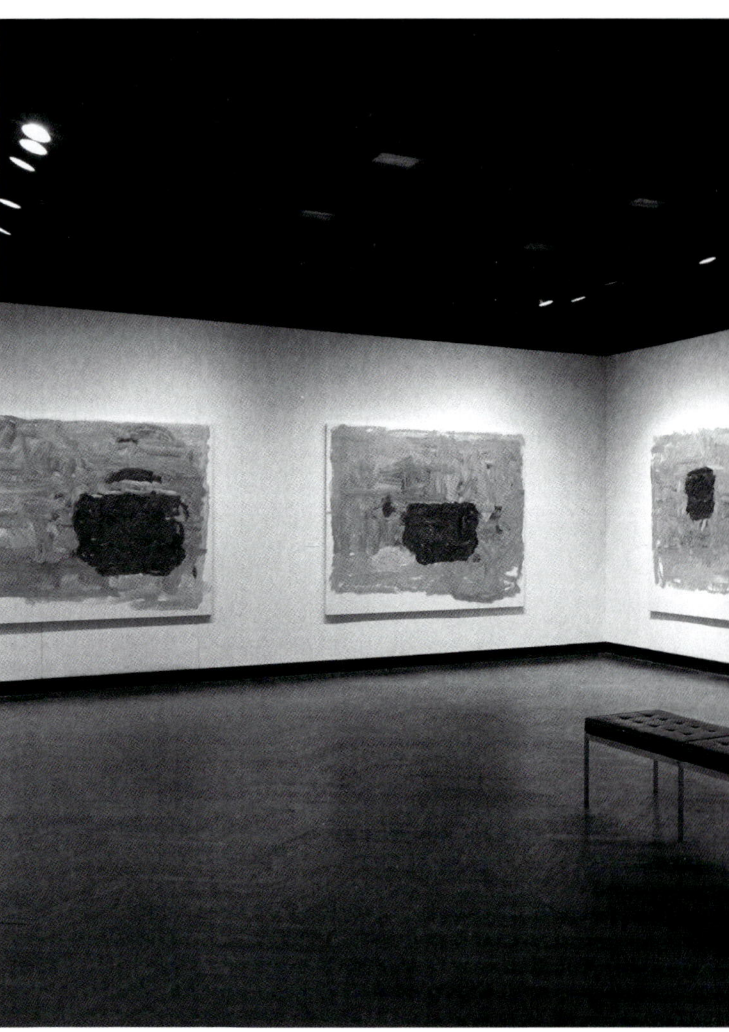

Installation view of *Philip Guston: Recent Paintings and Drawings* at the Jewish Museum, 1966

remainder of his career. Though these raw, brutish canvases would, in retrospect, come to be better understood as an important turning point for the artist, this unfortunate chapter of Guston's career was hardly one the Jewish Museum wanted to focus on now.[3]

By late 2017, about a year into Donald J. Trump's presidency, there was growing alarm over the abrupt shift in the American political climate and the steady dilution of the hard-won social progress of the mid-2010s. The extent of our country's problem with racially motivated violence was thrust into the national spotlight following the heinous murders of Trayvon Martin, Michael Brown, Eric Garner, Rekia Boyd, and so many other Black Americans at the hands of the police. MAGA hats soon blended with Confederate flags and swastikas, all part of the historically conflated visual culture of the white supremacists and neo-Nazis who turned out for the Unite the Right rally in Charlottesville, Virginia, in August 2017 chanting "Jews will not replace us." As an identity-based institution dedicated to art and Jewish culture, we felt an urgent responsibility to address the disturbing rise of antisemitism in the United States, as well as anti-Black violence, both of which stem from white-supremacist ideology.[4] As always, but especially in times of crisis, we look to artists to help make sense of the world around us. Our thoughts returned to Guston, whose earliest forays into art making, in addition to his late, iconic works, were laden with images of hooded figures and their victims, indicating a fixation on the toll of white supremacy in his adopted homeland.

Guston was born Phillip Goldstein in Montreal, Canada, in 1913 to working-class Jewish immigrants from Odessa.[5] The Goldstein family relocated in 1919 to Los Angeles, where the Ku Klux Klan had an active presence. A vigilante hate group founded by Confederate veterans in Tennessee in 1865, the Klan began as a campaign of anti-Black terror aimed at keeping the newly emancipated Black population from voting and holding office, and to uphold white supremacy by any means necessary. D. W. Griffith's *The Birth of a Nation* (1915), the phenomenally popular silent film that glorified KKK atrocities, helped the Klan surge into a nationwide, white Protestant fraternal order that targeted not only Black communities but also Jews, Catholics, immigrants, Communists, and union workers—anyone it deemed "un-American." It was during this resurgence that the iconography of the Klan—white hoods and robes, burning crosses—was established. At its peak, in

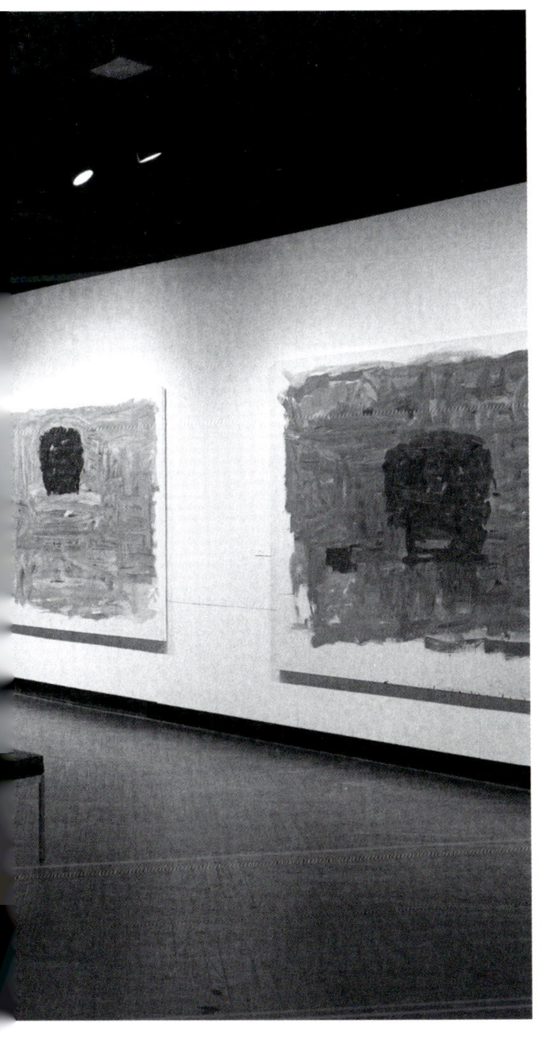

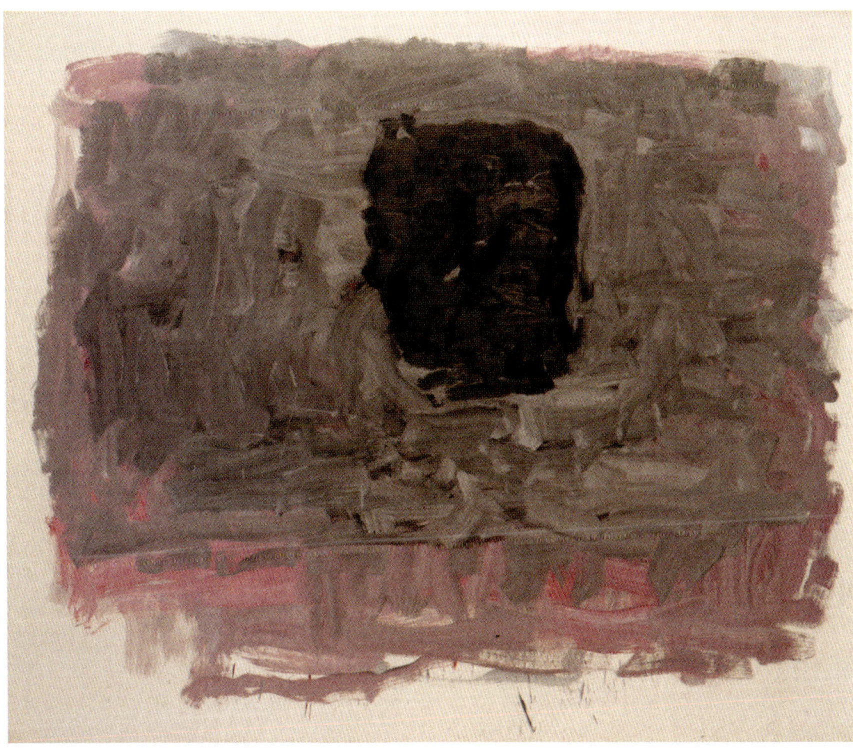

Philip Guston, *Portrait II*, 1965, oil on canvas, 65 × 78 in. (165.1 × 198.1 cm). Art Institute of Chicago

1924, the organization boasted at least four million members. That same year, Klan members were elected to city council in Anaheim, just outside Los Angeles. While its political reign there was short-lived, the Klan's swift rise to power, local rallies, and initiation ceremonies, not to mention its large-scale march on Washington, DC, in 1925, must have been terrifying for the Goldsteins to witness, having so recently escaped the pogroms of Eastern Europe and still reeling from the death of Guston's father, who, having struggled to find work in such a hostile environment, hanged himself in 1923 (Guston, then ten years old, discovered his body).

Guston channeled his rage, grief, and trauma into art. He began drawing at a young age, often in the privacy of a closet, his "sanctuary," lit only by a dangling lightbulb, a motif that would recur in compositions throughout his life, and a symbol that cannot help but be tangled up with his father's tragic end (see pp. 28, 33, 59). With the exception of a correspondence course in cartooning, a year at Manual Arts High School, and three months at Otis Art Institute, Guston was self-taught, but by the age of twenty, he had studied enough of the Renaissance masters, European Cubists and Surrealists, and Mexican muralists to earn commissions for public projects. His first was for the Los Angeles headquarters of the John Reed Club, a national Marxist organization that believed, as Guston did, that art had the potential to promote social change. The assignment was to illustrate the plight of "Negro America." A central panel, painted by Murray Hantman, depicted the Scottsboro Boys, the nine Black teenagers who had been falsely accused of raping two white women in Alabama in 1931 and were summarily sentenced to death by an all-white jury. Two additional panels depicted lynching scenes—Reuben Kadish's showed a Black man hanging from a tree, while Guston's victim was tied to a post and whipped. In both instances, the violence was meted out by hooded Klansmen. In February 1933, the murals were vandalized by the anti-Communist Red Squad of the Los Angeles police, aided by members of the American Legion and the KKK.

The following year, Guston began work on another, equally polemic mural, this time a monumental fresco for the Palacio de Maximilian in Morelia, Mexico. Again, Guston worked alongside Kadish, as well as their friend Jules Langsner. They produced a multilevel, architectonic composition populated by muscular giants surrounded by instruments of oppression and punishment: iron shackles, spiked paddles, and whips. Notably, three hooded figures are pictured with a Bible, a cross, a cat o' nine tails, and a swastika, a jumble of transhistorical iconography connecting flagellant priests of the Spanish Inquisition—a time of brutal antisemitic violence—with the Klan's fascist ideology in the United States and the rise of Nazism in interwar Europe.

Only one of Guston's early Klan images, *Drawing for Conspirators* (1930; see p. 42), veered away from such heavy-handed political messaging. In this preparatory drawing for a now-lost painting, the artist steps back from a KKK meeting beneath a lynching scene to focus on a single Klansman, set apart from the huddled group. An imposing figure in the foreground, his head downturned, he appears to be contemplating the consequences of his actions. The rope he holds seems heavy, a symbol, perhaps, for the weight of his conscience. Here, we see the artist beginning to grapple with the nature of evil, to question the interiority of a person who commits violence, and to consider the boundaries of empathy. It was this approach to depicting the Klan—less illustrative and didactic, more personalized and complex—that burst forth with clarity in Guston's work of the late 1960s. Following his Jewish Museum exhibition, Guston reinvented himself, beginning with a series of small, "pure" drawings

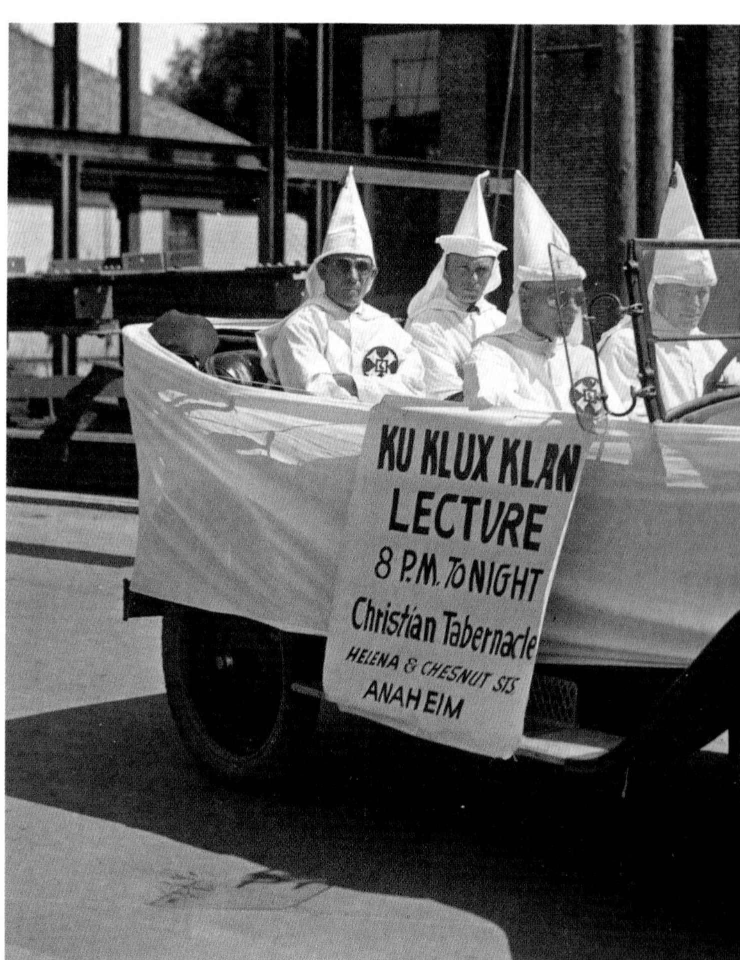

Members of the Ku Klux Klan advertising a lecture at the Anaheim Christian Tabernacle, ca. 1924

of simple lines and geometric forms that ultimately morphed into a visual vocabulary that included the mundane stuff of life (buildings, books, a cup, a clock), the detritus of the studio (paint cans, brushes, easels), evidence of his well-documented vices (cigarettes, liquor bottles), and, somewhat unexpectedly, the Klan, now reduced to lumpy and comical triangular forms (see pp. 22–23).

Guston described having at the time a "strong need to cope with tangible things," indicative of an imperative to make art that was grounded in the realities of the world around him.[6] The Civil Rights movement, having led to critical advancements for Black Americans by the mid-1960s, was continuously being met with resistance and hostility. A third resurgence of Klan activity followed suit, including, among many other horrific incidents, the 1963 bombing of the 16th Street Baptist Church in Birmingham, Alabama, which killed four Black girls, and the 1964 murders in Mississippi of James Chaney, Andrew Goodman, and Michael Schwerner, the Black and Jewish student activists targeted for their voter registration work. In 1968, the year Guston took up painting again, the assassination of

Dr. Martin Luther King Jr. led to a period of national mourning and unrest. Riots erupted across the country, joining other demonstrations against the Vietnam War and for the burgeoning Black Power and Women's Liberation movements in a chorus of opposition against the status quo. In August 1968, thousands of antiwar and civil rights protesters were teargassed and beaten by police outside the Democratic National Convention in Chicago, a televised event that triggered for Guston memories of his own run-ins with the LAPD as a young artist. As he explained, "When the 1960s came along I was feeling split, schizophrenic. The war, what was happening in America, the brutality of the world. What kind of man am I sitting at home, reading magazines, going into a frustrated fury about everything—and then going into my studio *to adjust a red to a blue.* I thought there must be some way I could do something about it."[7]

It is perhaps no surprise, then, that Klansmen reemerged as his protagonists, though reimagined through the lens, stylistically speaking, of one of the artist's other early obsessions: the comic strips he had loved in his childhood, in particular, George Herriman's *Krazy Kat* (see p. 139) and Bud Fisher's *Mutt and Jeff*, with their lovable losers and violent antics played for laughs. In 1968, when he returned to painting, Guston's ruddy cityscapes and domestic interiors were overrun with bumbling Klansmen, alternately self-flagellating and blinking in innocent disbelief when an accusatory hand (godlike, but gloved like that of Herriman's Offissa Pupp) pointed out their bad behaviors from on high (see

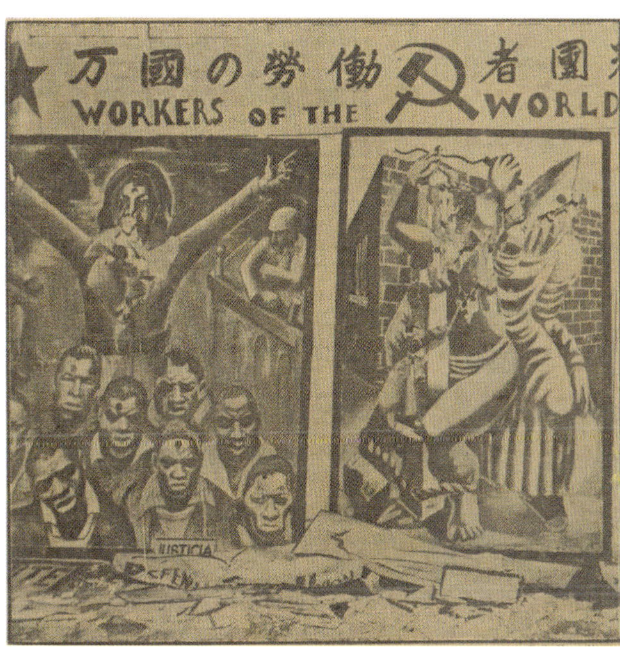

"Where Vandals Wrecked Paintings," *Los Angeles Illustrated Daily News,* February 13, 1933

p. 61). Indoors, the hoods convened to smoke, talk, and look at art, contemplating the finer points of what, exactly? Aesthetics? Their murderous sprees? The absurdity of these situations and the ridiculous manner in which the Klansmen are portrayed did much to deflate the hateful symbolism of their organization, the masks and robes of which were always intended to instill fear and respect. The disconnect, too, between the group's violent tendencies and otherwise mundane activities served

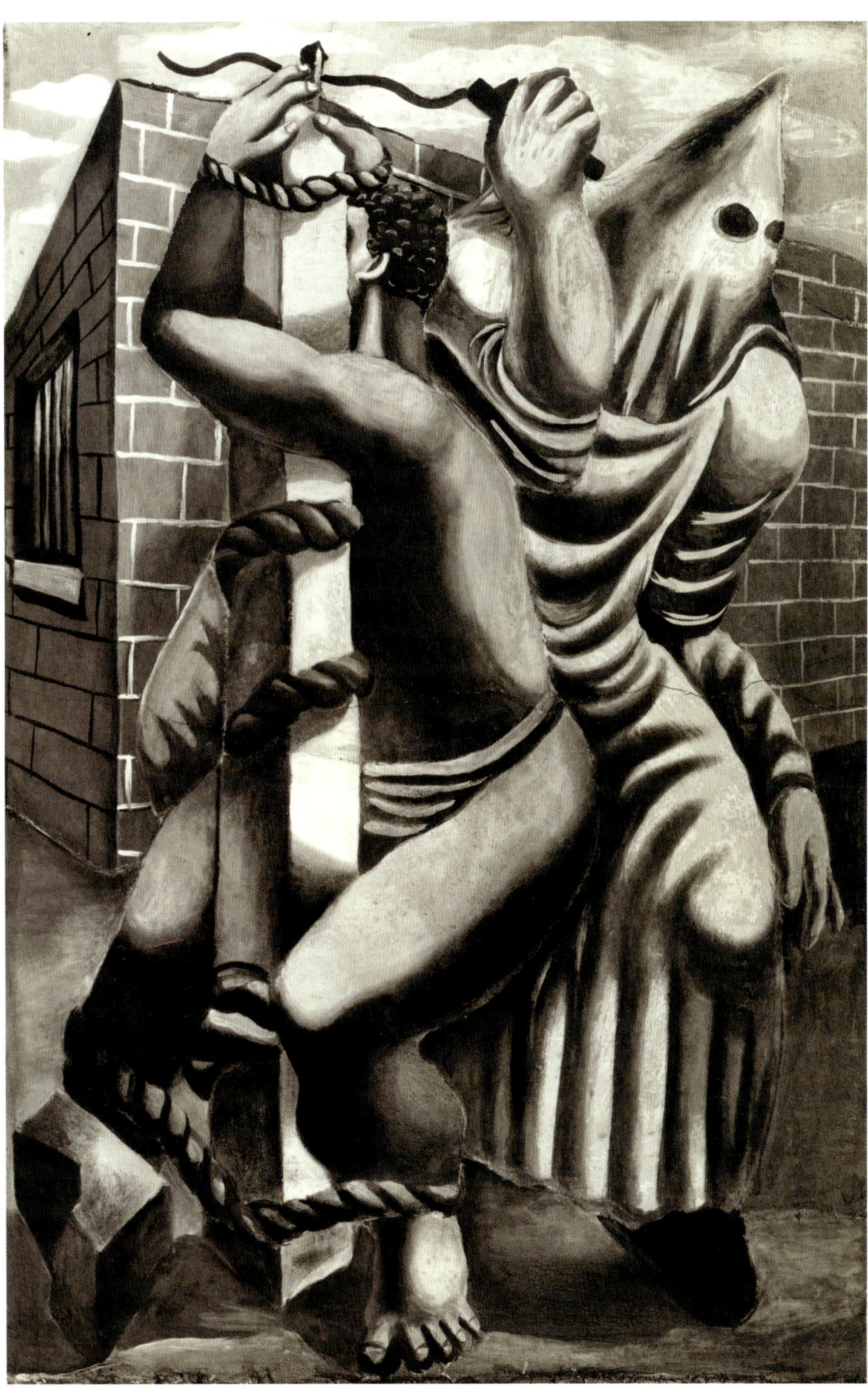

Philip Guston's mural for the Los Angeles headquarters of the John Reed Club, ca. 1931

as a reminder that the real-world KKK was composed of average citizens. There was nothing special about their monstrosity.

As a whole, the Klan paintings are a meditation on the banality of evil, a concept that had then been recently introduced by the Jewish political philosopher Hannah Arendt in her 1963 report on the trial of Adolf Eichmann, one of the chief organizers of the Holocaust. Guston, too, was fascinated by how tormentors and their victims can become

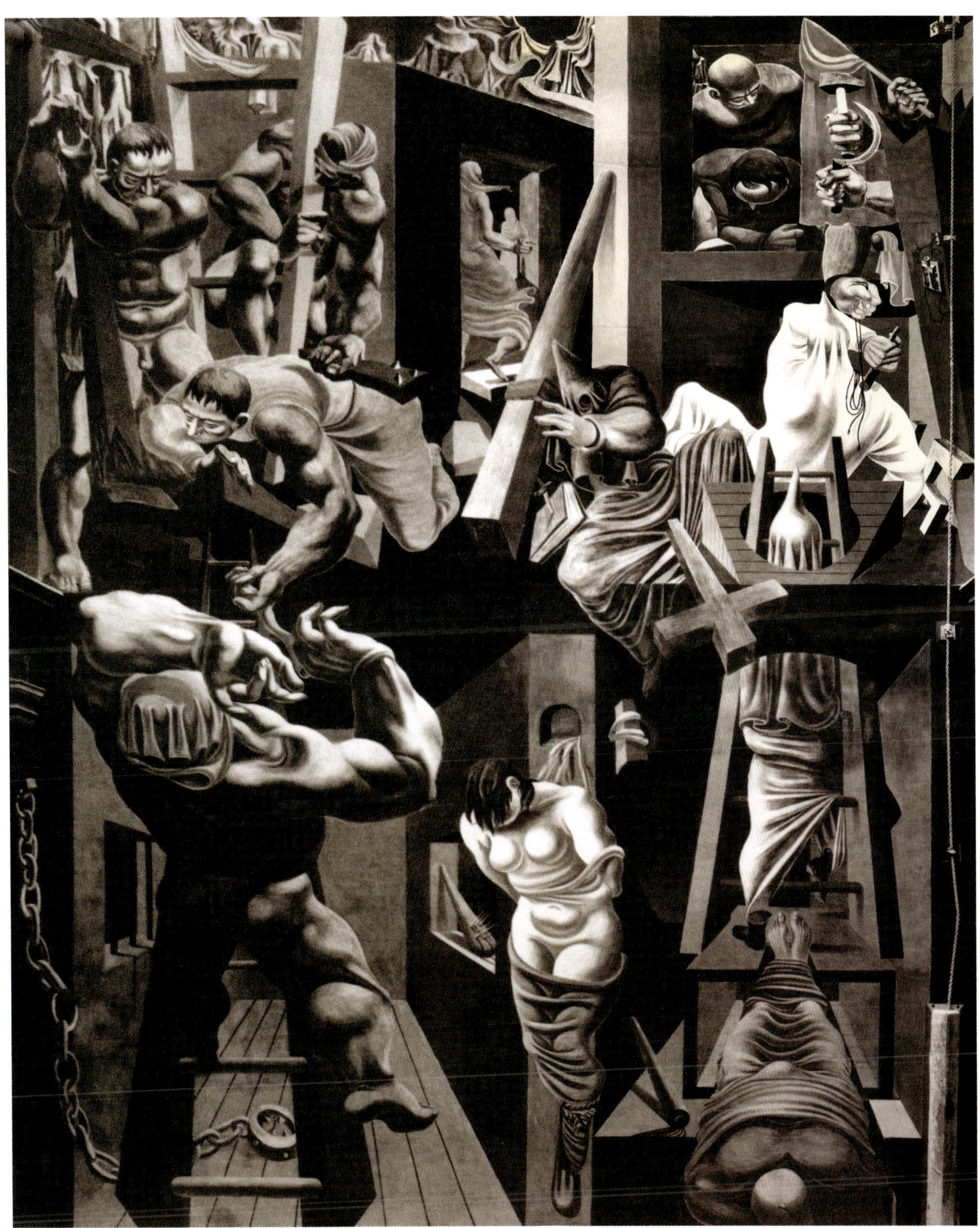

Philip Guston, Reuben Kadish, and Jules Langsner, *The Struggle against Terrorism*, 1935, fresco, 480 × 318 in. (1219.2 × 807.7 cm). Palacio de Maximilian, Morelia, Mexico

inured to the violence they inflict and receive, and how whole societies can become complicit in wrongdoing through inaction. "The only reason to be an artist," he asserted in 1968, is "to bear witness."[8] While direct references to the Holocaust would also emerge in his work—notably, the piles of legs that allude to the mass graves of the extermination camps (see p. 132)—it would be the hoods that largely occupied his paintings at first. Humor was needed not just to mock the Klan but also to startle people out of their numbness to the violence inherent in American life.

According to the artist, his interest in exploring the Klan was a radical expression of self-identification. "They are self-portraits," he proclaimed to a group of University of Minnesota students during a slide lecture in 1978. "I perceive myself as being behind the hood."[9] This idea is expressed clearly in *The Studio* (1969; see p. 59), perhaps Guston's most acclaimed work in the series. Here, we see the artist as Klansman, painting a self-portrait of the artist as a Klansman—an intimate, iterative scene that pulls back the curtain, literally and metaphorically, on his true identity. He is caught red-handed, not with a gun but with a smoking brush, playacting at being evil. The painting betrays a hint of equivocation, an implication that the role of the artist as witness is insufficient or even dangerous in its futility. Guston

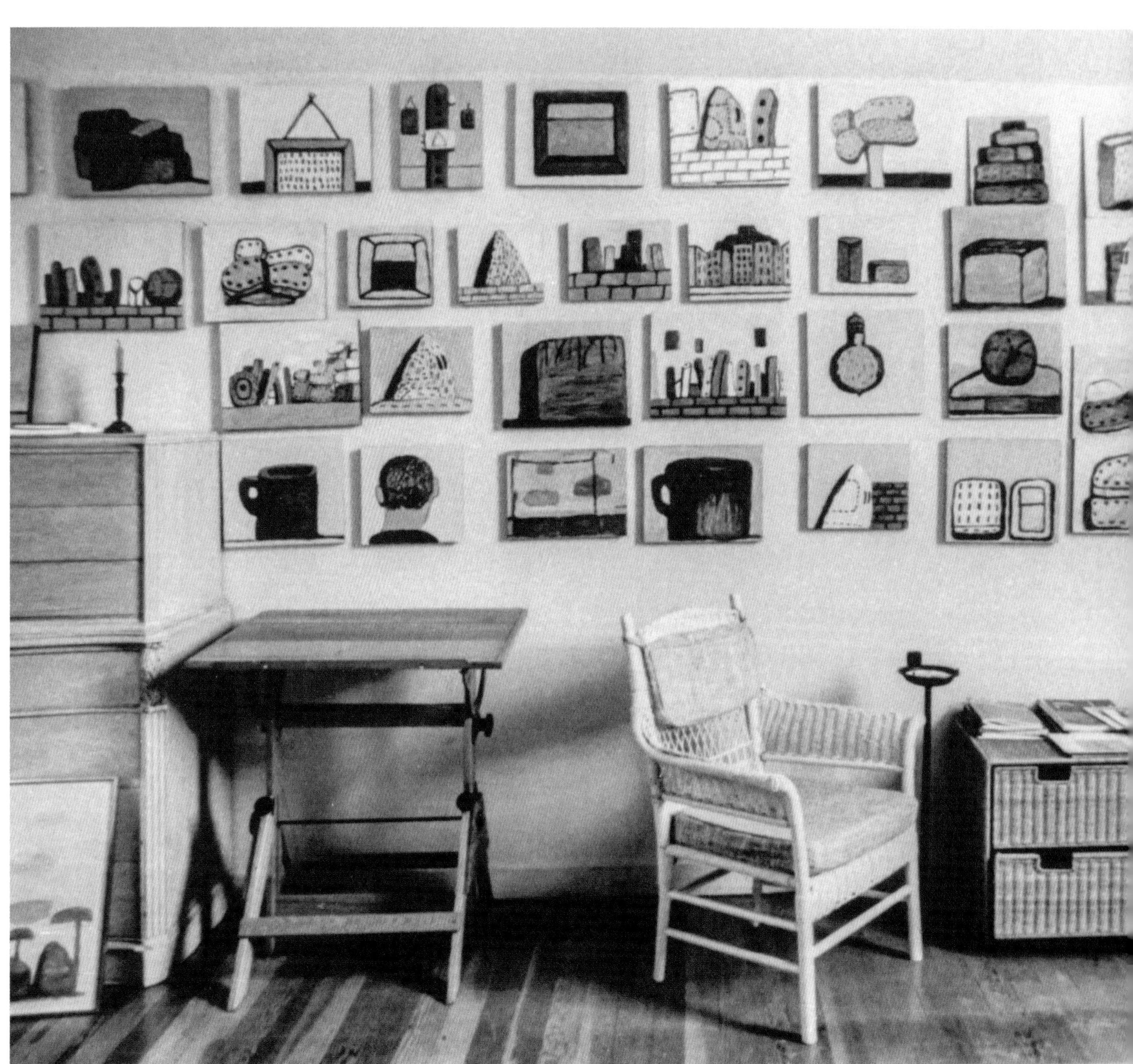

Paintings by Philip Guston in his Woodstock, New York, studio, 1975

himself understood the limitations of socially minded art. "I have no illusions that I could ever influence anybody politically," he admitted. "That would be silly."[10]

Guston's masquerade reveals not only this politically minded ambivalence but also his inner conflict about his proximity to whiteness as an assimilated Jew. He had changed his name in 1935, removing an "L" from his first name and trading the identifiably Jewish "Goldstein" for the seemingly French "Guston." It was, perhaps, a means of distancing himself from the overtly political work of his youth as he transitioned to alternative modes of expression. There was also his soon-to-be wife,

Musa McKim, whose parents he may have felt the need to placate by suppressing his Jewish identity. It was a decision he would come to regret. Guston's assumption of a white identity may have felt like a necessary step toward self-preservation and social acceptance, but three decades on, when it was finally possible to be recognized as both white and Jewish in America, it felt like a betrayal of the self. Worse, it made him complicit in a system that rewarded whiteness while causing harm to so many others. By midcentury, however, given the professional reputation he had built for himself as Guston, it would have been impossible to revert back to his given name. His Jewish origins, and his name change, were not publicly disclosed until the last major retrospective of his work in his lifetime, less than a month before his death at sixty-six in 1980. It was a secret that clearly preoccupied a large part of his artistic output in the last decade of his life—hiding behind the hood.[11] His Klan paintings take his white identity to its logical conclusion, forcing him to confront his desire to assimilate in the first place.

The Klan work debuted at the Marlborough gallery in midtown Manhattan in 1970, and the critical response was harsh. Although the paintings traded in comic illustration (like Roy Lichtenstein's) and drew on imagery ripped from the headlines (Andy Warhol's *Jackie* and *Race Riot* series come to mind), they were much too clunky and enigmatic to be considered Pop. Guston's irreverent, hieroglyphic canvases were uncategorizable and as such made

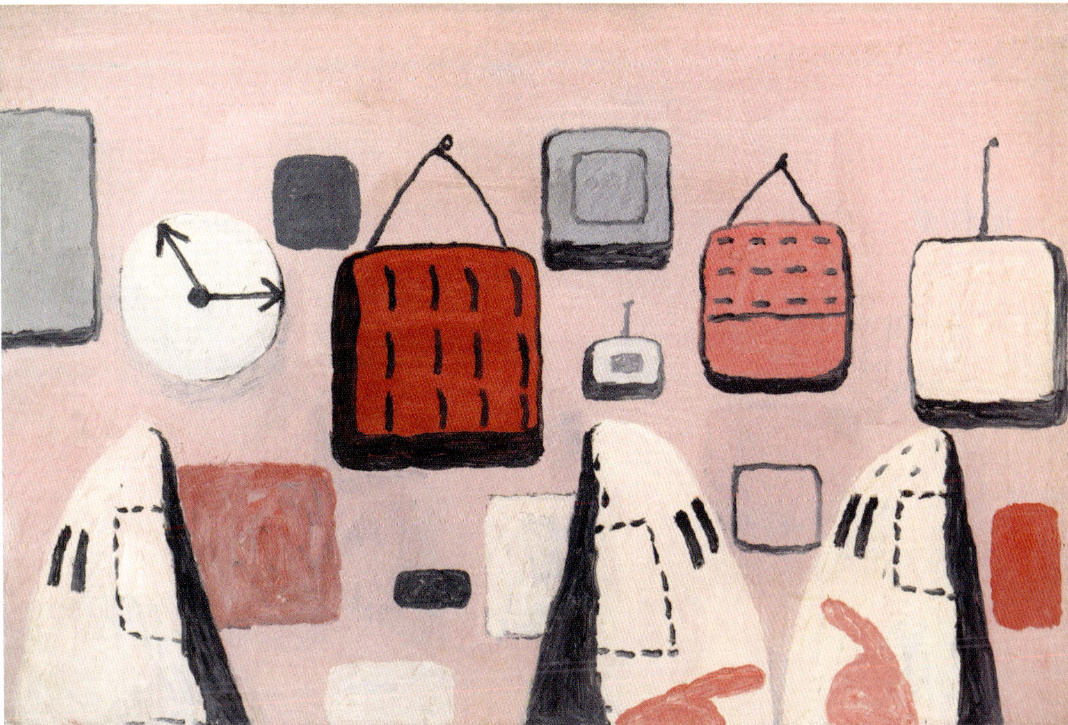

Philip Guston, untitled, 1969, oil on panel, 26 × 40 in. (66.0 × 101.6 cm). Private collection

23

for uneasy viewing. Harold Rosenberg, the rare critic who supported the artist's transition, understood that his "new crudeness" had "an important expressive function: it enables him to give a simple account of the simple mindedness of violence."[12] Yet most critics had the opposite reaction. Robert Hughes, in a scathing review in *Time* titled "Ku Klux Komix," declared, "As political statement, they are all as simple-minded as the bigotry they denounce."[13]

Guston's Klan paintings continue to provoke and unsettle, as became abundantly clear in the lead-up to *Philip Guston Now*, a major multicity retrospective that had been scheduled to open in 2020 but was postponed by both the Covid-19 pandemic and the intense moment of racial reckoning that followed the murder of George Floyd, an unarmed Black man, by the Minneapolis police. Spurred by the Black Lives Matter movement, millions of people across the United States took to the streets in protest, calling for an end to anti-Black violence in everyday life and to the systemic racism inherent in American institutions. Museums were no exception. Questions arose about the propriety of a team of white curators mounting an exhibition of potentially triggering iconography. The Klansman—that *ur*-symbol of racial terror—painted in a satirical manner by a white Jewish artist might be misinterpreted. There was also the specter of Guston's Klansmen being misread by the far right as a demented seal of approval. A four-year proposed delay, however, was met with a swift and resounding backlash from the art world, led by Guston's daughter, Musa Guston Mayer. Guston "dared to hold up a mirror to white America, exposing the banality of evil and the systemic racism we are still struggling to confront today," she wrote in an excoriating statement. The Klansmen, she clarified, "are us. Our denial, our concealment. . . . These paintings meet the moment we are in today. The danger is not in looking at Philip Guston's work, but in looking away."[14] Her sentiments were echoed by hundreds of artists, critics, and scholars who admonished the organizers for renouncing their duty to engage the public in a dialogue that might lead to much needed self-reflection. The exhibition ultimately opened in May 2022, to great acclaim.[15]

This outpouring of support for Guston affirmed our conviction that bringing him back to the Jewish Museum was apposite. But instead of retreading the past, we sought to move the conversation into the present by giving a platform to a leading Black voice in the contemporary art world. We invited

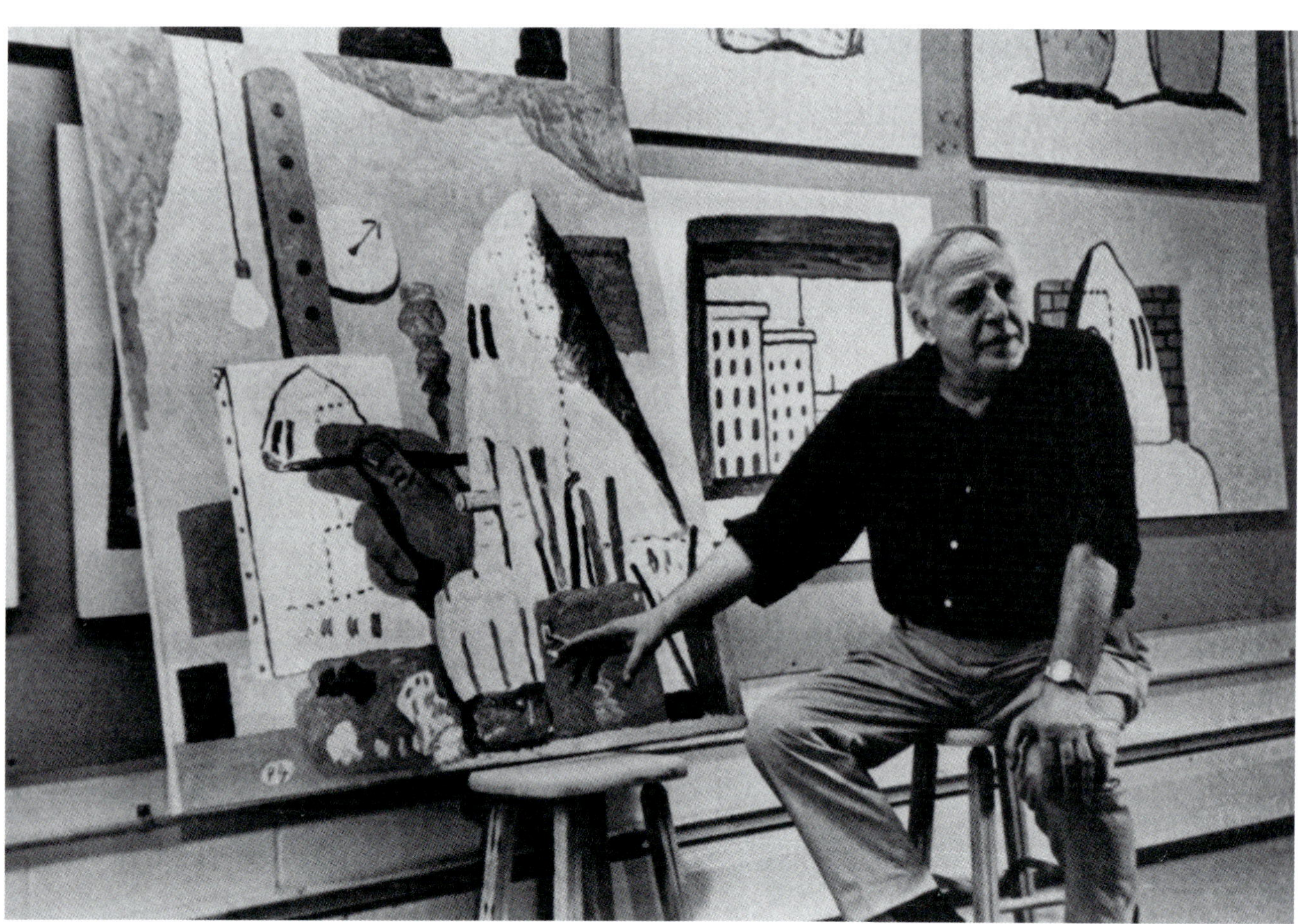

Philip Guston with his painting *The Studio,* 1969

Trenton Doyle Hancock to be a contributing artist and curatorial collaborator so we might examine Guston through his eyes and offer audiences a deeply personal, twenty-first-century account of who Guston was as an artist and what he means today. Hancock, a multifaceted artist, cartoonist, illustrator, and wordsmith, has a voracious appetite for aesthetic influences, from comics, video games, horror films, and science fiction to biblical legends, Greek myths, and art-historical imagery spanning centuries. In densely layered canvases, he hoards the world around him, cannibalizing even

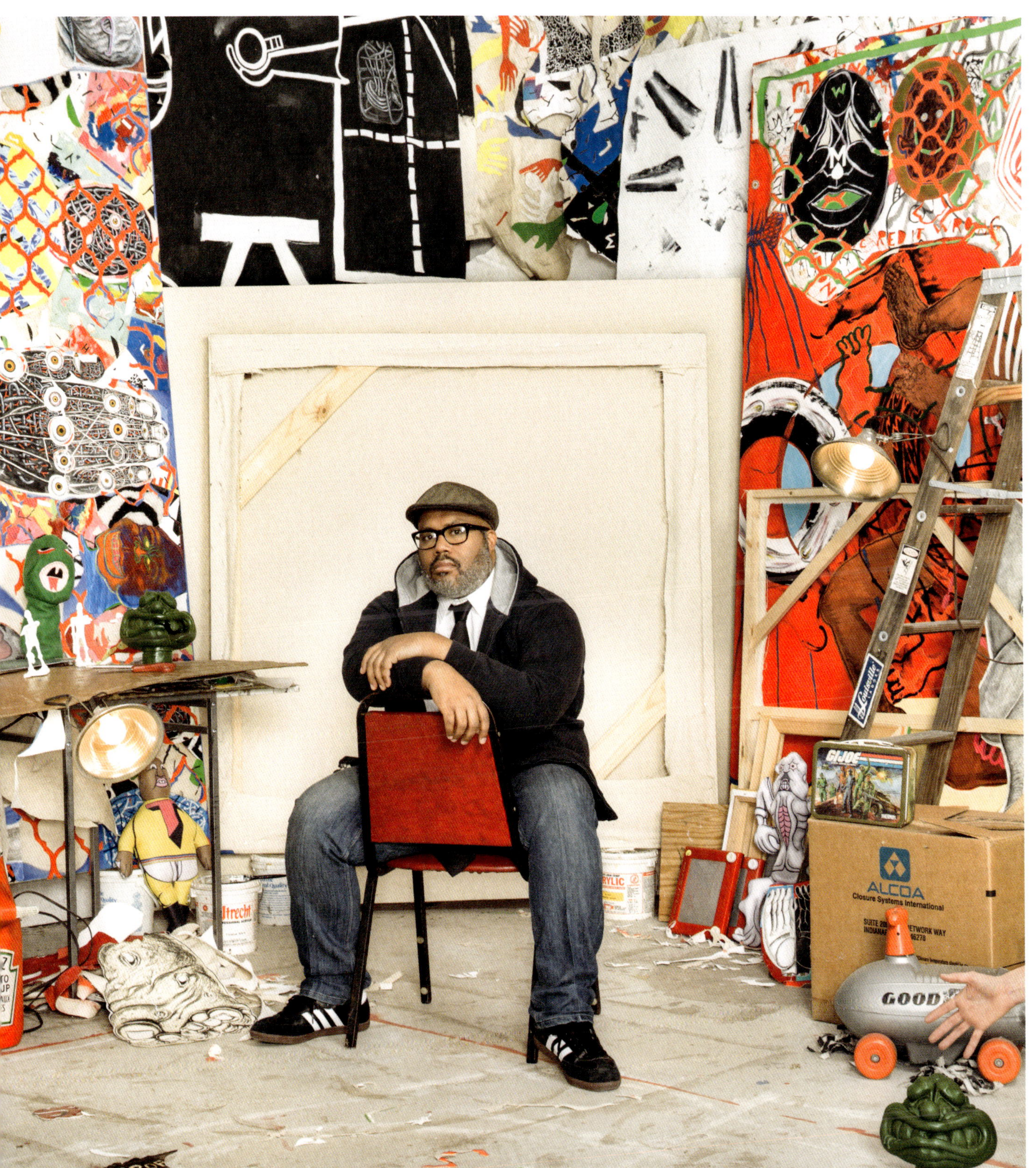

Trenton Doyle Hancock in his studio, 2015

his own work to create something new and fantastical. Emerging from this heterogeneous sea is the undeniable stamp of Philip Guston, who has been a recurring source of inspiration for the artist for three decades. In fact, in 1997, on a paper tacked to his wall on which he scribbled random thoughts and doodles, Hancock wrote in all caps, "LIKE GUSTON BUT BLACKER AND WORSE," articulating as a college student what would become a career-defining thesis statement, imbued with the critical introspection and dark, self-deprecating humor he shares with his predecessor.

Hancock's engagement with Klan imagery began in 1994, in his late adolescence, just as Guston's had. A year prior, while attending junior college, he had produced a harrowing self-portrait, titled *The Properties of the Hammer* (1993; see p. 43). Hancock photographed himself sitting in a bare room with a white sheet draped over his body and a noose around his neck, the remainder of the rope wound around his arms and legs. He holds a hammer in his right fist, his forearm and face partially exposed, revealing his Black skin. A final, unnerving detail: the figure still wears his glasses,

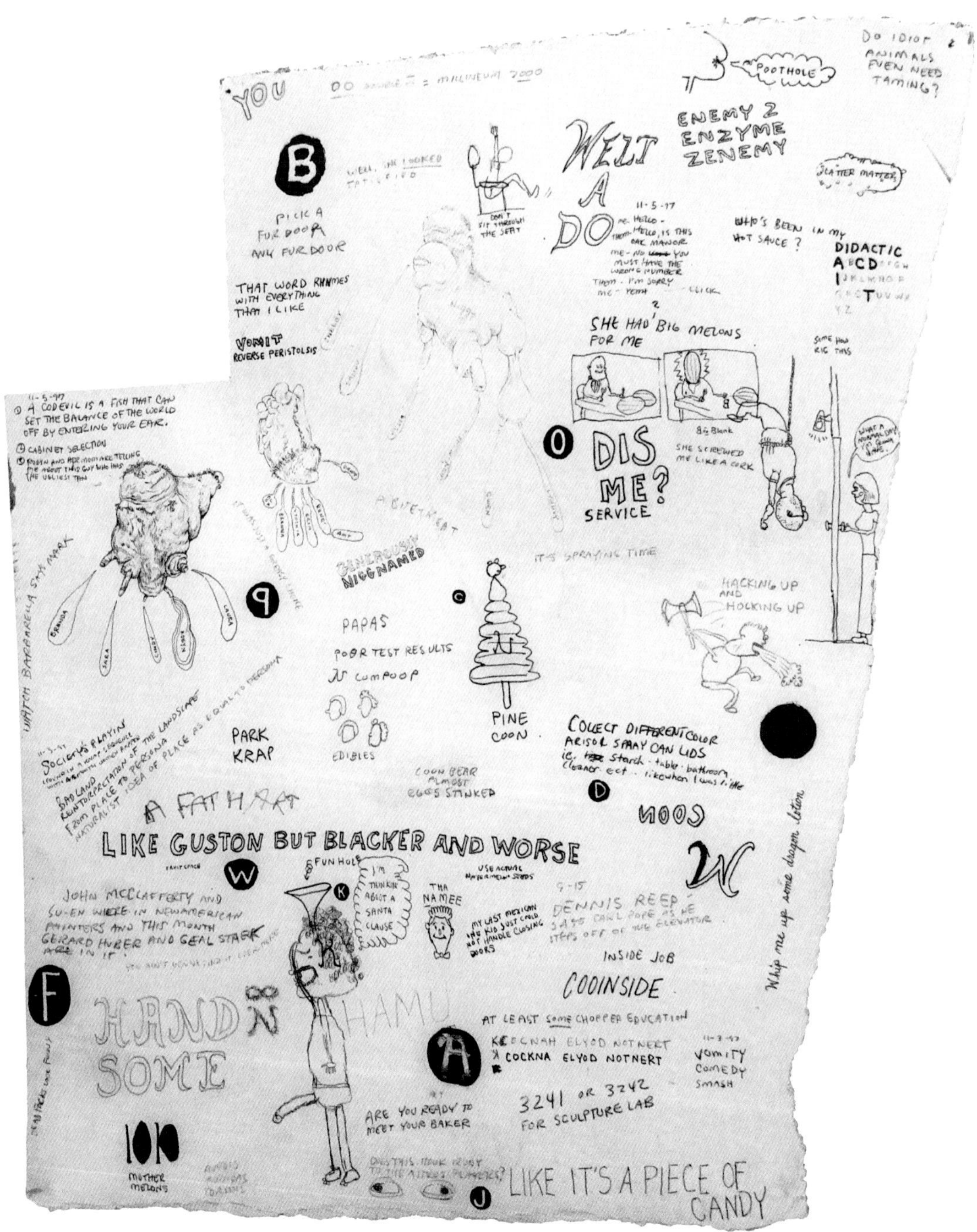

"LIKE GUSTON BUT BLACKER AND WORSE," a note that Trenton Doyle Hancock scribbled to himself in 1997, would become something of a mission statement for his subsequent career.

despite the fact that his face is obstructed by the sheet on one side. Half Klansman, half Klan victim, it is unclear if he is alive or dead, real or merely an apparition. "This character was, in a direct way, showing that I didn't feel whole as a person," Hancock explains. "I didn't feel like I was fully seen as a person or as a creative being."[16]

Growing up, Hancock often felt misunderstood. Born in 1974 in Oklahoma, and raised in a devoutly Christian home in Paris, Texas, he enjoyed a quintessential Black American childhood in many ways. He played football at school and was a junior deacon at church, where he led the congregation in call-and-response prayers each Sunday. But in 1985, his mother, Carolyn Joyce Twitty, and maternal grandmother, Alma Twitty, consumed by the fearmongering of televangelists, became convinced that literal demons might infiltrate their homes. Certain toys and media were deemed conduits for these unholy spirits. In a series of events Hancock now refers to as the "three trials by fire," he and his younger brother were forced to watch as their mother burned their Dungeons and Dragons gaming manuals, their He-Man action figures, and, finally, their prized Garbage Pail Kids trading cards. The purge was humiliating and destabilizing for Hancock, who was also dealing with the recent death of his beloved great-aunt Fannie Mae Twitty Rollerson, whom he called Fan Fan. Hancock retreated into art, just as Guston had done after his own familial trauma. He continued to develop the character of Torpedoboy, a superhero alter ego he had created at the age of ten, whose godlike powers he modeled on Superman's and who allowed him to gain control on the page, if not in life. His penchant for drawing was accepted at home only up to a point. While his mother recognized that making comics kept him off the streets and out of trouble, his flights of fantasy were a perpetual concern, and she continued to monitor his output, tearing up pictures she feared might summon the devil.[17]

Hancock grew increasingly disillusioned with religion. While his self-portrait at nineteen might read as an indictment of his oppression as a Black man in white America, his sense at the time was, in his own words, that "the noose around my neck had more to do with the Black church interfering with my individuality."[18] At the same time, *The Properties of the Hammer* is predicated on a familiarity with the iconography of the Klan and with a subconscious understanding of the racism his family and community had experienced throughout their lives. As he left home and entered predominantly white spaces—academia, the art world—he became increasingly aware of his own "double-consciousness," a term W. E. B. Du Bois had coined in 1903 to describe the dual self-perception Black people often experience in mainstream society. Caught between being viewed as too Black by some, not Black enough by others, Hancock created the hooded character as a way to understand his surroundings and to express how lonely and trapped he felt.[19]

Klan imagery resurfaced in his work a few years later. As he pursued a BFA at East Texas State (now Texas A&M University–Commerce), Hancock continued to draw cartoons, including a weekly comic strip for *The East Texan* student

Trenton Doyle Hancock, *Judgment #1*, 1998, ink and marker on paper, 25½ × 24 in. (64.8 × 61.0 cm). Collection of the artist

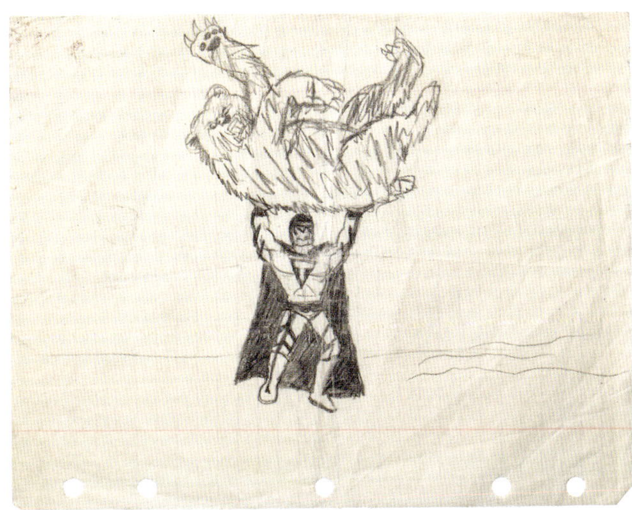

"Torpedoboy Fights a Bear," one of Trenton Doyle Hancock's earliest renderings of his alter ego Torpedoboy, drawn in 1984, when the artist was ten years old

newspaper (see p. 144). *Epidemic!*, as it was later called, featured a number of recurring characters, including a hooded figure, which he would draw occasionally "as an expression of frustration."[20] As with many of Hancock's characters who populate his endlessly inventive world known as the Moundverse, the hooded figure grew in depth and meaning as time went on. A course titled The Art of the Book, co-taught by Lee Baxter Davis and Michael Miller, introduced Hancock to the cut-up technique, a Dadaist literary style in which new works are created from preexisting texts by excising and rearranging words based on the principles of chance. Thus, an illustrated medical textbook on the rare disease lichen amyloidosis led to "Loid,"

the name Hancock assigned to his hooded character. From there, a backstory developed: Loid was a Black sharecropper of the 1950s who was publicly hanged for having a white girlfriend. He came to symbolize the vengeful spirit of a victim of Klan violence. Emmett Till was front of mind for the artist as Loid developed. Till had haunted Hancock since he had learned about the fourteen-year-old Black boy's horrific lynching in 1955 following accusations that he had flirted with a white woman. Hancock was in middle school when he first saw the image of Till's brutalized body, presented in an open casket. Hancock understood that, as a young Black man in America, he "had to attend the funeral," describing a metaphorical rite of passage through which

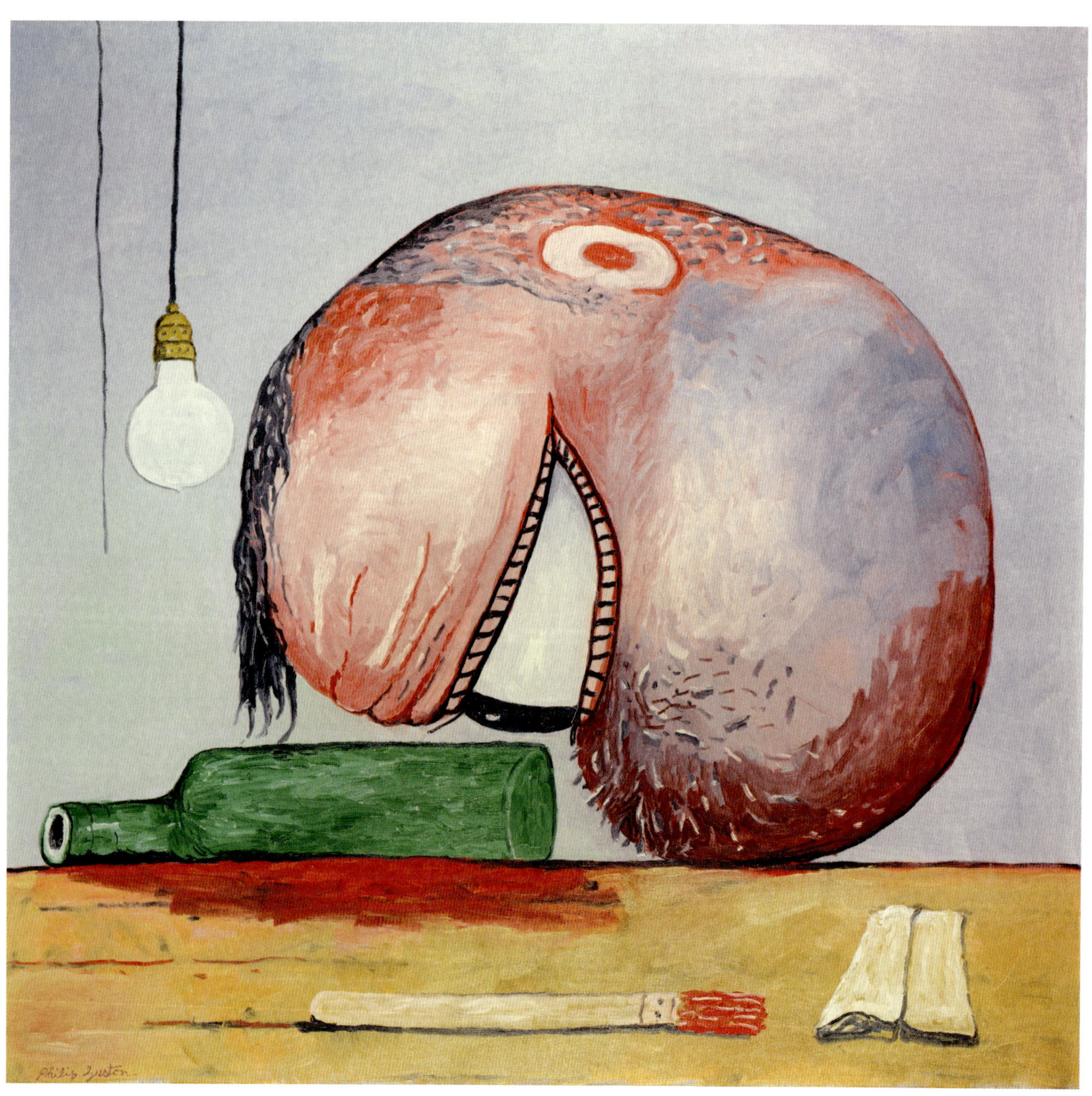

Philip Guston, *Head and Bottle*, 1975, oil on canvas, 65 ½ × 68 ½ in. (166.4 × 174 cm). Private collection, New York

he recognized that he "had the potential to be this character."[21]

Hancock's political consciousness expanded further through his understanding of history and how lynchings persist into the present day, even if the violence now goes by a different name. Making those historical connections imbued his Klan character with a new sense of purpose. "I started to feel more like myself," he says. "At that point, Loid became closer to who he is now, a harbinger of vengeance. . . . He became the idea of judgment."[22] In drawings like *Judgment #1* (1998) and *Judgment #2* (2000; see p. 44), Loid batters rich and poor, young and old, women, men, Black, white, human, and mythological creatures alike with his mantra, "You deserve less." The phrase derives from the Christian emphasis on humility as a virtue. "There's something within all that language I grew up with," Hancock explains, "that keeps you down, makes sure you stay down so that you can be controlled."[23] Religion, he realized, was just one of several social constructs in America, along with capitalism, racism, and gender

inequality, designed to reinforce this degrading mantra. The words form a drumbeat of dread as Loid's speech bubbles morph into ropes and tentacles, an early indication of Hancock's facility in blending historical imagery with science-fiction, comic-book, and body-horror tropes.

It was Hancock's printmaking teacher, Thomas Seawell, who first recognized an art-historical precedent in his use of hooded, Klan-like imagery. Seawell lent Hancock his copy of Robert Storr's 1986 monograph on Guston, a book that, Hancock says, he slept with under his pillow for the next two years. It features Guston's iconic *Head and Bottle* (1975) on its cover, and one might be tempted to imagine that, through this tilted image, Guston's ideas poured themselves into Hancock's mind, melding osmosis-like with his own dreams in the night. Over time, Guston has wound his way subconsciously into paintings by Hancock, such that decades later, the ear of Guston's stubbled bean head reemerged as the third eye of a mythic life form in Hancock's *Knowledge from Samantha* (2015),

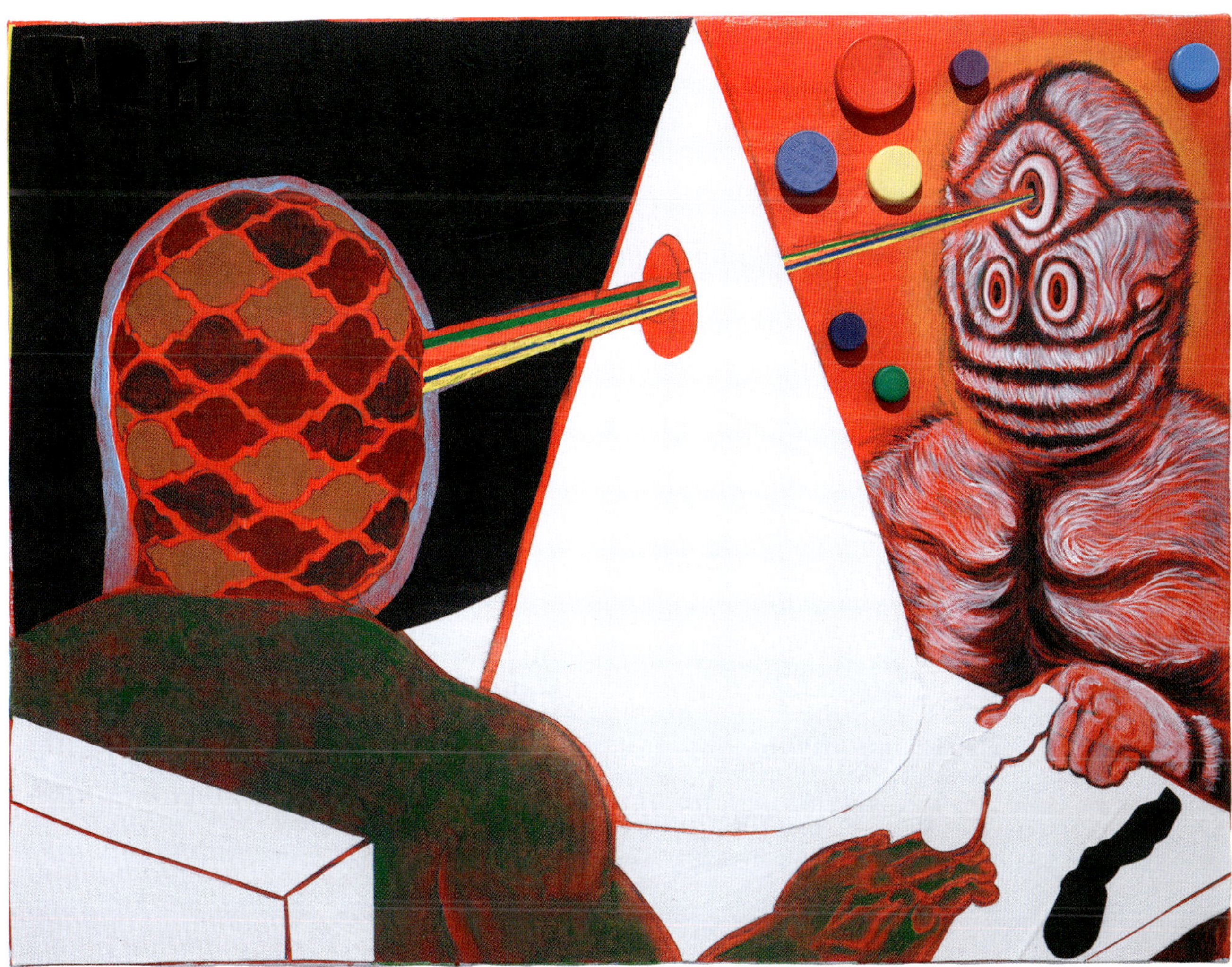

Trenton Doyle Hancock, *Knowledge from Samantha*, 2015, acrylic and mixed media on canvas, 30 × 42 in. (76.2 × 106.7 cm). John and Mable Ringling Museum of Art, Sarasota, Florida

and his unzipped eyeballs and baggy hoods inform Hancock's use of white cones as mystic symbols. Hancock often gravitates toward a palette reminiscent of Guston's as well. His iconic Mounds and Bringback creatures, with their black-and-white-striped fur accentuated by fleshy pinks (see pp. 136, 139), relate to Guston's limited color selection, particularly in the mid-1960s.

Hancock remembers responding to Guston's work at first on a visceral level, luxuriating in the multisensory experience of his first encounters with these paintings. His gut reaction: "I want to eat these."[24] Hancock describes being consumed by the images and wanting to consume them in turn, mouth first, like a newborn. It is no wonder, then, that Hancock has considered Guston to be an artistic father figure ever since. "I fell in love with the forms, and how he used comedy to take the wind out of the sails of the KKK," Hancock says. "He helped me understand where I could take my character Loid, how I could embody that character."[25]

In 2000, the year Hancock completed an MFA at the Tyler School of Art and Architecture at Temple University, and again in 2002, his work was selected for the Whitney Biennial in New York. He was one of the youngest artists to be included in the prestigious survey at the time. The exposure catapulted him to fame but also clued him in to the segregated nature of the art world, where his work about injustice writ large was supported by white collectors (many of them Jewish), while his concerns about real-world racial inequities were routinely ignored or dismissed.

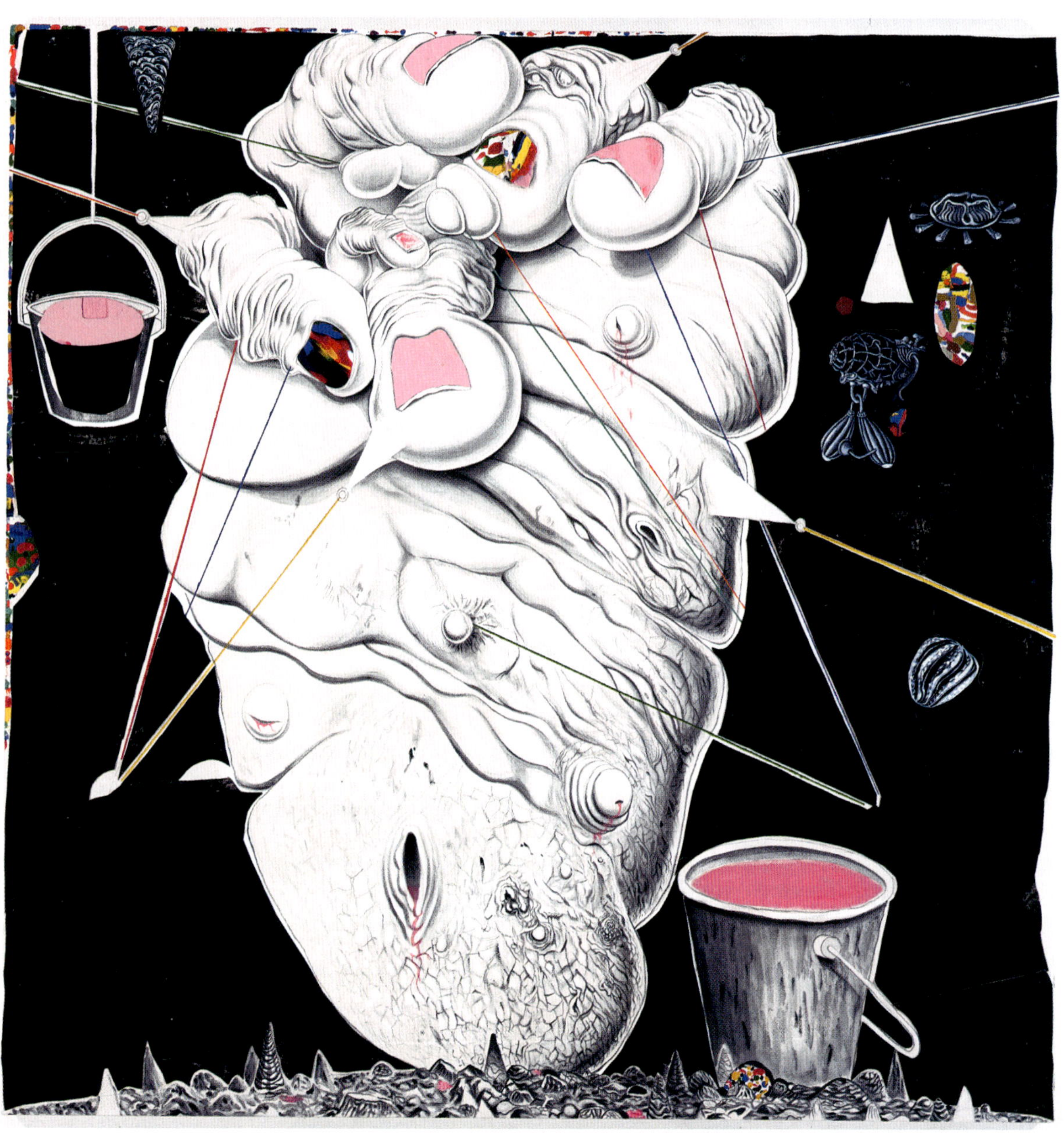

Trenton Doyle Hancock, *Give 'em an Inch and They'll Take a Foot*, 2006, mixed media on canvas, 60 × 60 in. (152.4 × 152.4 cm). Collection of Hedy Fischer and Randy Shull, Asheville, North Carolina

Certain people seemed capable of seeing his value as a commodity—*Might he be the next Basquiat?*—but not as a whole human being.[26] Guston, whose influence on Hancock had gone dormant for a time, reemerged in his work at this point, once again providing an avenue for the young artist to channel his rage. "The timing of Guston coming back into my life was perfect," he explains. "It's like how folks talk about Christ. He may not come when you want Him, but He's always right on time."[27] Hancock's paintings of the period deliberately align with Guston's visual strategies through enigmatic, monolithic forms that are simultaneously "concrete and evasive."[28] Pictures abound of bodies, in whole or in part, their skin peeled back, being pulled and prodded and extracted for profit, a coded commentary on the machinations of the art world, as in *Give 'em an Inch and They'll Take a Foot* (2006), a grotesquery that Hancock insists would slip right into Guston's polymorphous *Sculptor's Shoe* (1975). Hancock has stated that it was Guston who inspired him to "refocus my work with an inward-pointed lens and really paint my own skin for the first time. It was Guston's relentlessness towards depicting the 'self' that permitted me to become adamant about my visibility, and ultimately grow into a more politically aware being."[29]

As Hancock's career continued to flourish, the curator Valerie Cassel Oliver included his work in *Radical Presence*, her groundbreaking survey of Black performance art that originated at the Contemporary Arts Museum Houston in

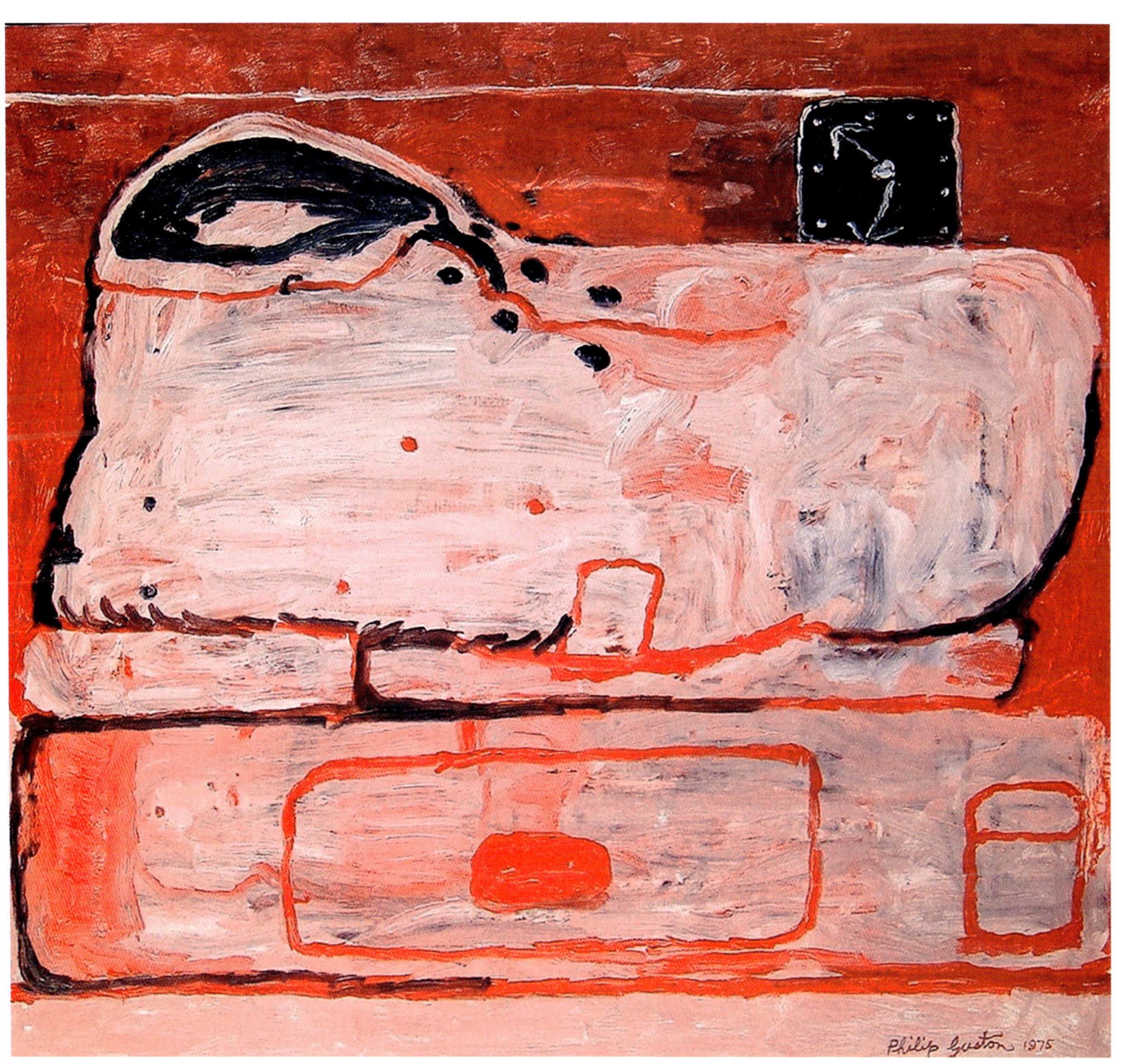

Philip Guston, *Sculptor's Shoe*, 1975, oil on canvas, 45 × 48 in. (114.3 × 121.9 cm). Private collection, New York

2013. He presented *Devotion*, a meditation on ritual and remembrance, in which he led the audience in singing hymns that he had learned from his recently deceased stepfather, Thomas Lee Johnson, and step-grandmother, Earline Johnson (see p. 124). Later that year, he was invited to be the keynote speaker at the annual NAACP meeting in Paris, Texas, where he spoke about "the legacy of *Blackness* in the fine art world and connected that history with the plight of all who may be underrepresented."[30] The homecoming allowed for a frank conversation with his family about their lives in northeast Texas, a region Hancock describes as "proudly racist."[31] Stories he had never heard before came pouring forth, about how his mother and grandparents carried the psychological burden of having witnessed or lived through lynchings firsthand.[32] By this point, Hancock had begun to research the history of race relations in his hometown and knew, for example, about the Klan-led execution of Henry Smith, a Black seventeen-year-old whom they paraded through town, tortured, and burned alive before a crowd of ten thousand onlookers, who then scavenged his remains for mementos (see pp. 126–27). What the artist had not realized was that the lynching, which made national headlines in 1893, had been staged on the site that would become the local fairgrounds, a place of wonder and joy he had visited many times as a child. Suddenly, the pleasures of the county fair were blurred with the carnivalesque horrors of America's haunted past.[33]

Needing an outlet for his anger, Hancock set to work on a surreal graphic memoir, this time with Guston front and center. *Epidemic! Presents: Step and Screw!* explored what would happen if Torpedoboy met Guston's own alter ego, the Klansman. In thirty black-and-white cartoon panels (see pp. 68–97), KKK members lure Hancock's avatar into a shed to change a lightbulb, only to reveal that he is destined to be their next victim. Torpedoboy's name encapsulates a series of contradictions—he is omnipotent but also incompetent, morally compromised, and capable of extraordinary feats of self-sabotage. At the same time, he embodies Hancock's defiant attitude toward the impossible standards of Black excellence while also throwing racist tropes back in the face of white America. (In other words, as Hancock puts it, Torpedoboy is a real "Gen X piece of shit.")[34] As he climbs onto the stool, his shoulders slumped, Torpedoboy recalls both Stepin Fetchit, a vaudeville-era stereotype of Black servility, and the dimwitted cat from the animated cult classic *Ren and Stimpy*. In the end, he does not seem particularly concerned that he is surrounded by violent racists (after all, he is immortal). Instead, he is horrified to discover a different aspect of their identities. "Oh shit you didn't tell me you were, you didn't tell me you were ... were ... were ... PAINTERS," he blurts out, a punchline that undercuts politically motivated art while mocking those who view it as dangerous. Like Guston, Hancock uses humor as a coping mechanism and the visual language of cartoons to describe the darker aspects of the American condition.

A sobering, if at times fantastical, timeline below the panels, rendered in hand-cut white-on-white lettering, blends Hancock's biography with

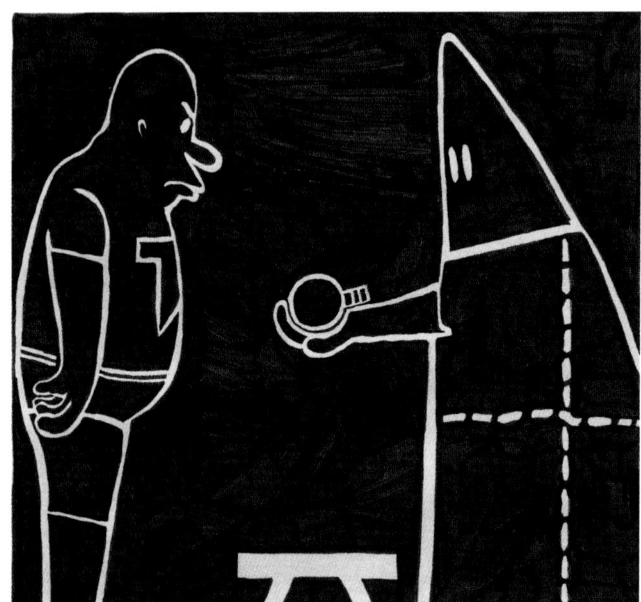

Trenton Doyle Hancock, panel no. 18 from *Epidemic! Presents: Step and Screw!*, 2014 (detail; see p. 85)

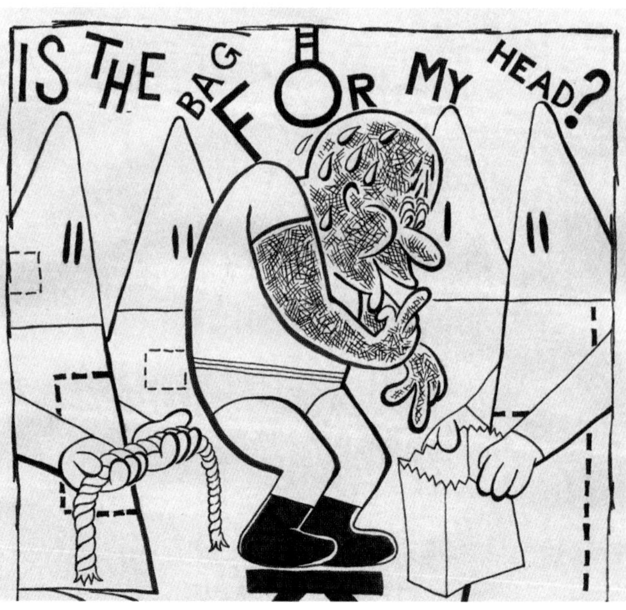

Trenton Doyle Hancock, panel no. 28 from *Epidemic! Presents: Step and Screw!*, 2014 (detail; see p. 95)

Guston's, delving into their respective traumas and motivations for grappling with white supremacy. Intertwined with key dates from his family's history and his artistic development are events related to the life of the anti-lynching crusader Ida B. Wells and to the tragic story of Henry Smith. We learn that, on the eve of his eighteenth birthday, in 1992, Hancock's mother discovered his trove of pornography, an embarrassing incident made serious by her concern over his seeming interest in white women. Earlier in the timeline, Hancock had noted that even consensual relationships between Black men and white women were common justifications for lynchings in the nineteenth century. Hancock also recounts the time, in the spring of 1996, that he and a Jewish student journalist, Vince Leibowitz, were targeted at East Texas State for criticizing Greek life. One fraternity retaliated by hosting an "anti-Leibowitz-Hancock" newspaper-burning party reminiscent of KKK cross- and book-burning intimidation tactics, and not dissimilar to the Klan's destruction of Guston's murals some sixty-three years prior. Interspersed among these hard truths are whimsical details about Torpedoboy's imagined past as the consciousness of the Jewish American helicopter pioneer Henry Adler Berliner and his eventual transference into a new host, Hancock, upon his birth. These anecdotes situate the entire enterprise in the realm of historical science fiction, leaving readers to question whether the horrors

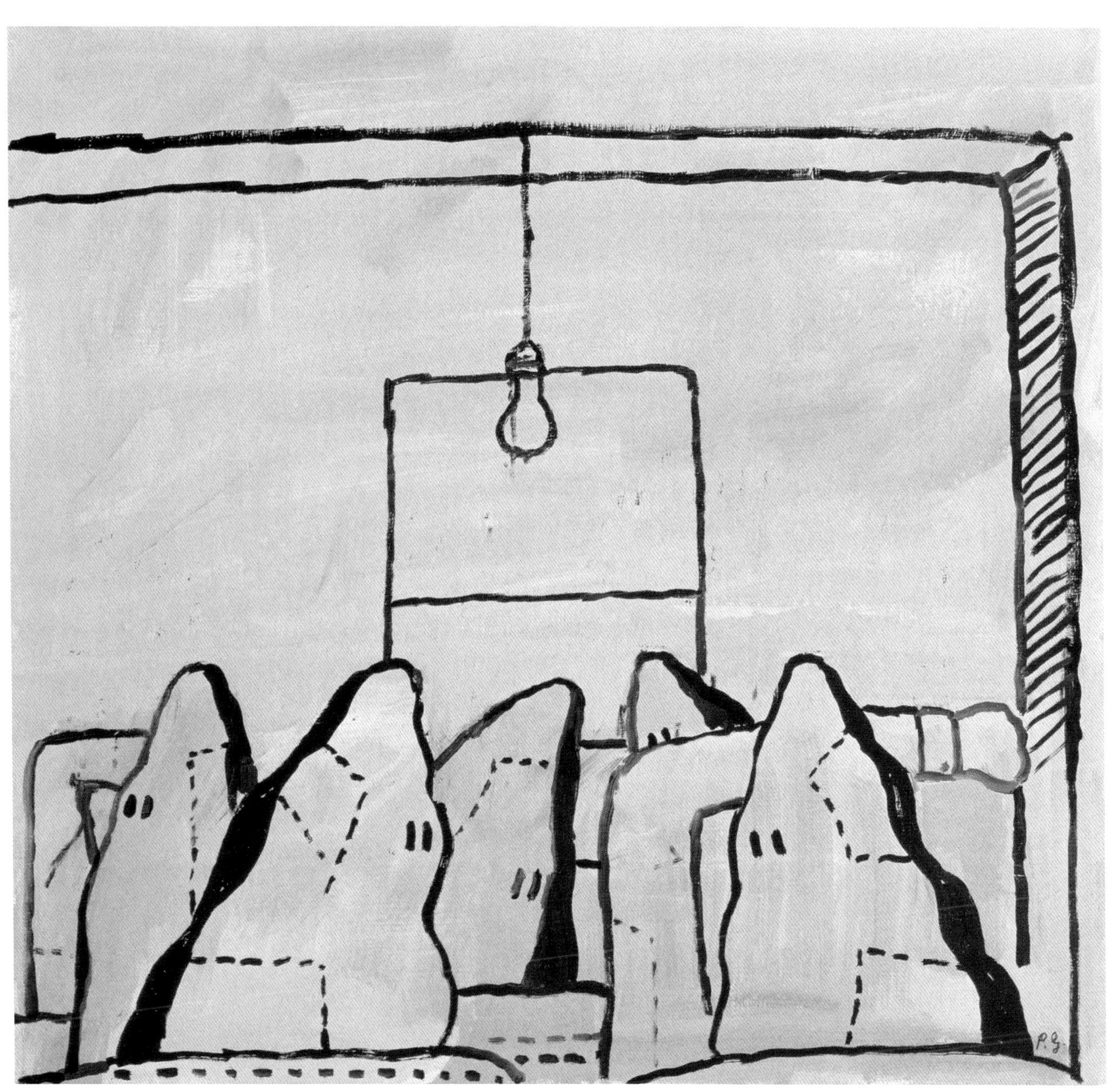

Philip Guston, *Meeting*, 1969, acrylic on panel, 30 × 32 in. (76.2 × 81.3 cm). Private collection

detailed in the rest of the timeline are true. What *Step and Screw!* makes clear is that, like Torpedoboy, racism functions as a sentient being, time traveling and shapeshifting so as to rear its head in every era.

While *Step and Screw!* is a complex work, Hancock conceived and completed it in under two weeks, in time for it to be included in *Skin and Bones, 20 Years of Drawing*, his first major drawings retrospective, in 2014, also organized by Cassel Oliver. Hancock knew he had to get the idea out of his system, "so there was a sense of urgency and sharpness to this work."[35] The result is a master class in economical line and lettering. In panel 23, the hoods and eyes of the Klansmen blend seamlessly into the jumble of A's and H's that form Torpedoboy's scream (see p. 90). The lightbulb above his head appears both bright and hollow, its resemblance to a noose reinforced by the Klansman at far left who holds a piece of rope, a direct and ridiculous nod to the ambivalent figure in Guston's *Drawing for Conspirators*. Working fast, Hancock claims that there was no intended correlation between the comic strip above and the calendar below, and yet the central panel, number 18 in the series, depicting the exchange between Torpedoboy and the Klansman, coincides with the recording of Guston's death on June 7, 1980, when Hancock was

six years old (see p. 85). This data point suggests that the contract being negotiated by the two avatars reflects a spiritual transference of knowledge, power, responsibility, and perhaps even consciousness between Guston and Hancock. "There's something about making art that isn't just about painting," Hancock has said. "I use the term 'séance,' where you're conjuring up the spirit of the dead in order to have a conversation, and have that person speak through you again, and come back alive."[36]

Since completing *Step and Screw!*, Hancock has sustained his engagement with his imagined mentor, making a number of paintings, many of them on an ambitious scale, focusing on the "pregnant" moment of exchange between the Klansman and Torpedoboy. In each, the characters participate in a suspicious trade, with the hooded figure offering the skeptical superhero an object associated with wisdom, be it a lightbulb, apple, star, or head (see pp. 102–7). These collaged interactions sometimes fuse image and text, with words incised directly into the characters. They appear to be locked in a battle of wills, the episodic nature of their confrontation influenced as much by cartoon rivalries like that of Tom and Jerry—where the setup is always the same, but the hijinks are different—as it is by the architectural templates of Renaissance paintings

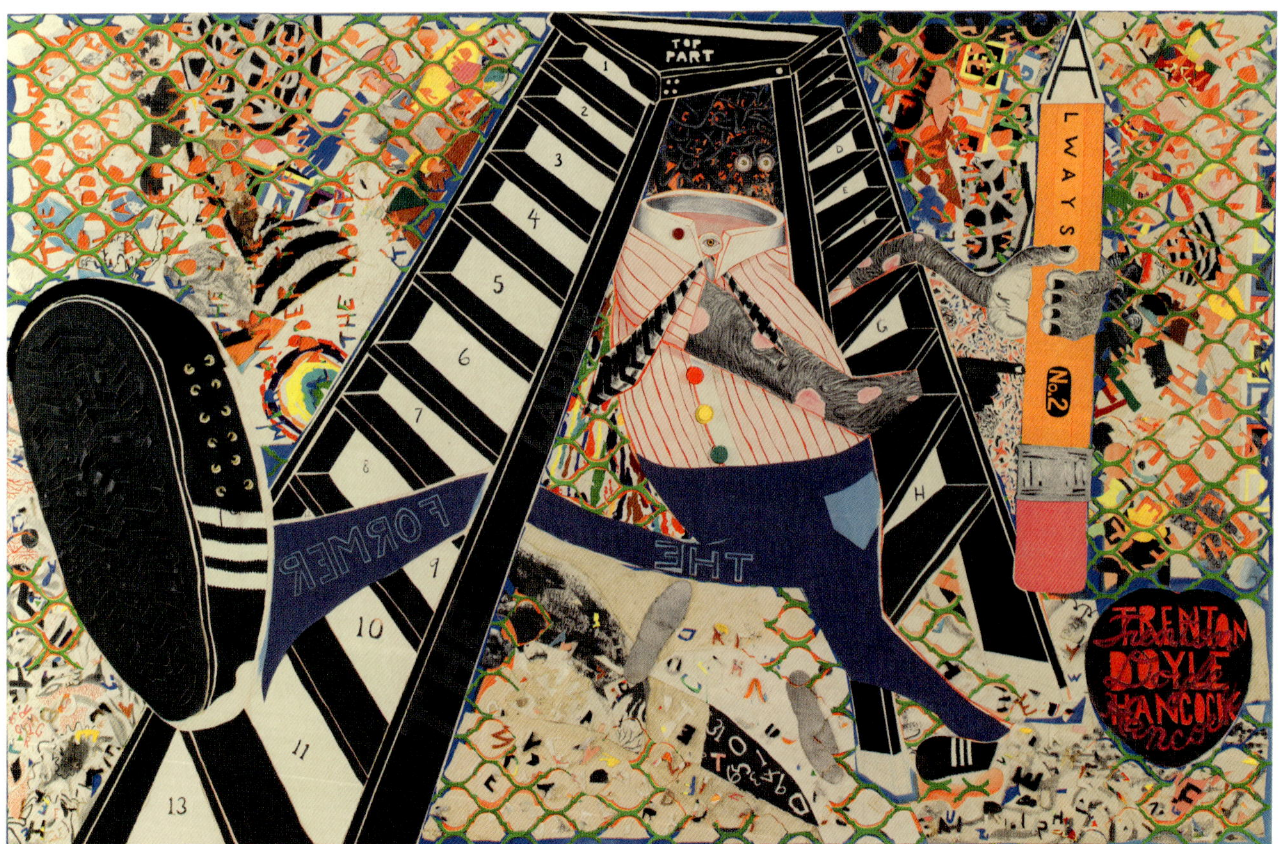

Trenton Doyle Hancock, *The Former and the Ladder or Ascension and a Cinchin'*, 2012, acrylic and mixed media on canvas, 84 × 132 × 3 in. (213.4 × 335.3 × 7.6 cm). Virginia Museum of Fine Arts, Richmond

of, for example, Annunciation scenes, which, in their duplicative formats, become less about the specific biblical story and more about the transmission and reception of knowledge and beliefs.

Overall, these exchanges act as a metaphor for "America's contract with white supremacy, especially how that contract is negotiated with Black Americans."[37] In *Schlep and Screw, Knowledge Rental Pawn Exchange Service* (2017; see p. 103), Torpedoboy's understanding of this contract is inflected with self-awareness. "Wait! You are seriously trying to sell me something I already own?" he scoffs, insulted by the Klansman's suggestion that he implicate himself in the coopting and rebranding of Black culture. (On another level, there is an undercurrent of resistance to the idea that Hancock has anything meaningful to gain from Guston. After all, there is nothing Guston's Klansman can teach him about white supremacy that Hancock did not know already—that knowledge was always his to begin with.) The antagonism continues in *Step and Screw: The Star of Code Switching* (2020; see p. 107). Here, Hancock recognizes Guston's assimilation as a form of code switching, a term used to describe how people might change their patterns of speech and appearance to conform to the dominant culture, whether for self-protection, material gain,

or both. "When people talk about code switching, it's often just along racial lines, about Blackness," Hancock explains. "But my understanding of what code switching is runs deep[er than that.] . . . It becomes a superpower at the end of the day, to be able to weave in and out of a range of social situations."[38] In this painting, we see Guston's Klansman holding out a five-pointed "star of code switching," a heterochromic creature made of Black and white fingers and two eyes, one brown and one blue. The talisman is so potent that, without even touching it, Torpedoboy already looks "white as a ghost." The Klansman claims that the token will help him live longer and also grant the ability to get "back to your own color in no time flat." Incredulous, Torpedoboy asks for a mirror, to which the Klansman simply responds, "You're looking at it."

In subsequent paintings, Torpedoboy wrestles with his conditional whiteness, at times quite literally, taking on the guise of a Klansman himself. In the storyboarded background of *Let's Try the Yellow Triangle Angle or The Return of Piss Christ* (2022; see p. 114), Torpedoboy rubberbands between racial extremes. His metamorphosis, however, remains incomplete; no matter how hard he tries, he cannot make his Klan persona stick, and he snaps back to Blackness. It is "the same logic that

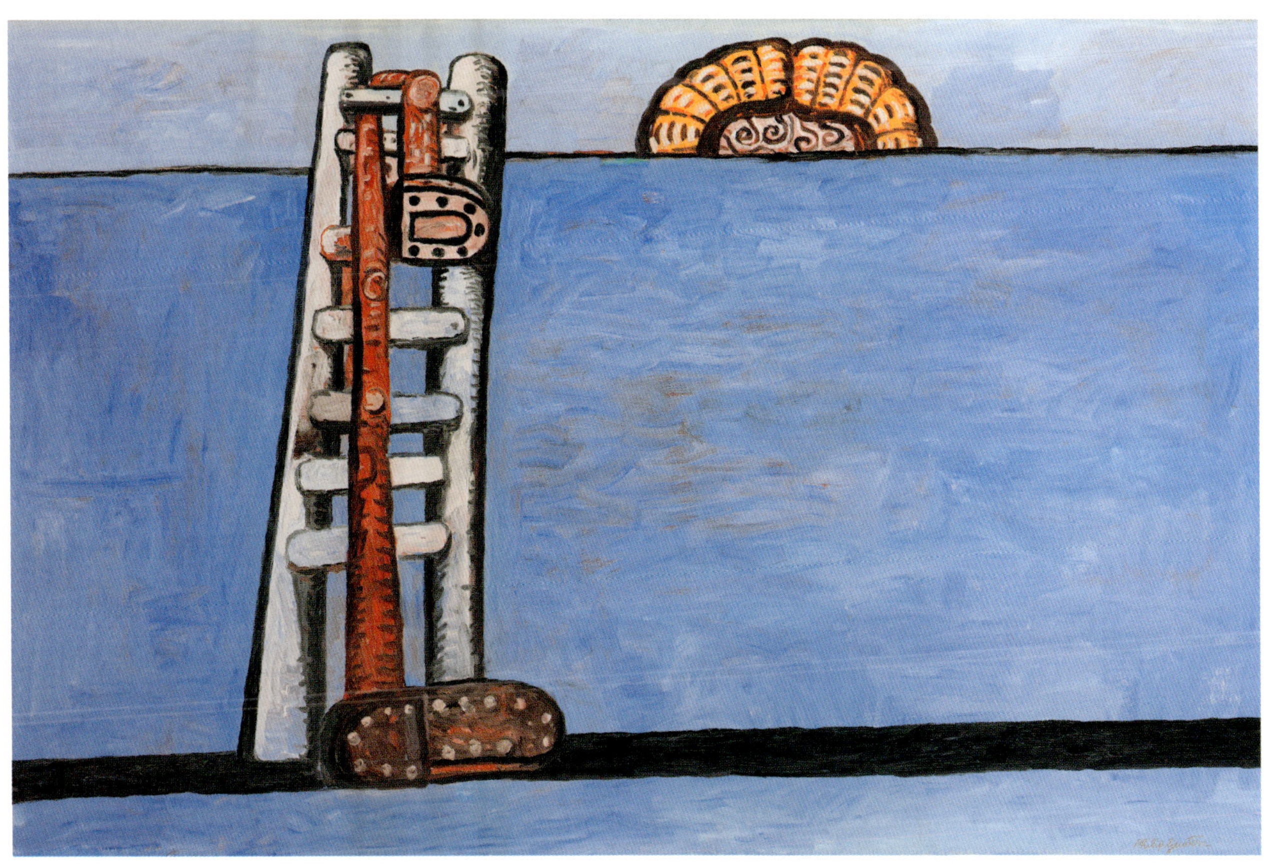

Philip Guston, *The Ladder*, 1978, oil on canvas, 70 × 108 in. (177.8 × 274.3 cm). National Gallery of Art, Washington, DC

Guston followed," Hancock explains. "Torpedoboy goes inside the hood, to try to get into the mind of the enemy," but there is trepidation there. "We are always in danger of slipping past the point of no return, where we become the very thing we're fighting against," Hancock acknowledges.[39] In the subsequent standalone painting *Globetrotters* (2023; see p. 119), it seems as if Torpedoboy has stopped oscillating and has finally tuned in to the white supremacy station. But to what end?

It is clear that Hancock will continue to honor what he calls his "umbilical connection" with Guston.[40] There is a synchronicity between them, one that defies all temporal logic, whereby ideas that Guston put forth in the world years ago, even beyond the Klan, wind up surreptitiously altered and transfixed in Hancock's studio, and vice versa. Hancock has long been interested in Carl Jung's theories of the collective unconscious, or the "lattice of coincidence," as it is described in one of his favorite films, *Repo Man* (1984). In his monumental *The Former and the Ladder or Ascension and a Cinchin'* (2012), Hancock's Artist, headless, steps through a ladder, his legs elongated with a dramatically foreshortened foot. The painting was meant as an homage to his stepfather, who had passed away in 2010, the ladder being a potent stand-in for his trade as a carpenter. It was also a portentous symbol in Hancock's early life. To a child with a vivid imagination, a tall ladder might appear as awe-inspiring as a temple, imbued with mystical significance. The idea that a ladder might hold magical properties was reinforced by his stepfather, whose superstitions led him to warn Hancock not to walk under them. Here, the Artist disobeys that order in a bold attempt to reach him in death. In a different dimension, the ladder is also a portal to his other father figure, Guston, who similarly alighted on the symbol of the ladder to work through feelings of loss, mortality, and grief.[41] Guston painted *The Ladder* (1978) just two years before his death, at a time when his health and that of his wife were failing. The disembodied legs, tangled on the steps, stand in for the elder artist as he desperately attempts to reach his wife, whose head is only just visible beyond the blank blue wall. Both Guston's and Hancock's paintings operate under a kind of dream logic—perhaps even the same dream. If Hancock's *The Former and the Ladder* conveys a subconscious communion with Guston, could it be that Guston unknowingly summoned Hancock's spirit when he painted *The Ladder*? It may not be possible to reach any proof about this particular lattice (ladder) of coincidence, but "I like to think," Hancock says, "that I'm in Guston's pantheon, just as much as he's in mine."[42]

1   As quoted in Ross Feld, *Guston in Time: Remembering Philip Guston* (New York: New York Review of Books, 2023), p. 16.

2   Hilton Kramer, "Art: Abstractions of Guston Still Further Refined; Works Made Since '62 at Jewish Museum," *The New York Times*, January 15, 1966.

3   Moreover, the history of this particular point in the artist's evolution had just been examined in *Philip Guston: Painter, 1957–1967*, an installation at Hauser & Wirth in New York from April 26 to July 29, 2016.

4   According to the Anti-Defamation League (ADL), antisemitic attacks in the United States have been rapidly increasing in recent years. In 2016, nearly 1,300 antisemitic incidents were reported nationwide. That number nearly tripled in the span of six years, with 3,700 incidents recorded in 2022, the highest level since the ADL began its reporting in 1979. These incidents have involved all manner of harassment, vandalism, and assault, including a mass shooting at the Tree of Life synagogue in Pittsburgh, Pennsylvania, in October 2018; another at a Jersey City kosher supermarket in December 2019; and the hostage crisis at Congregation Beth Israel in Coveyville, Texas, in January 2022. For more details on these and other incidents, see https://www.adl.org/adl-tracker. See also Krystina Shveda, "Antisemitic Incidents in the US Are at the Highest Level Recorded since 1970s," *CNN*, March 23, 2023, https://www.cnn.com/2023/03/23/us/antisemitism-report-unprecedented-rise-dg/index.html. The FBI reported 2,755 incidents of attacks on Black people in the United States in 2020; this number rose to 3,421 in 2022. See "FBI Reports Hate Crimes at Highest Level in 12 Years," *Equal Justice Initiative*, September 9, 2021, https://eji.org/news/fbi-reports-hate-crimes-at-highest-level-in-12-years/. See also https://www.justice.gov/crs/highlights/2022-hate-crime-statistics.

5   For further insight into the Goldstein family's history in Odessa, see Harry Cooper, "Guston Then: Telling Tales," in *Philip Guston Now* (Washington, DC: National Gallery of Art, 2020), p. 5.

6   As quoted in Dore Ashton, *Yes, But . . . : A Critical Study of Philip Guston* (New York: Viking, 1976), p. 154.

7   As quoted in Jerry Talmer, "'Creation' Is for Beauty Parlors," *New York Post*, April 9, 1977.

8   In a conversation with his close friend the musician Morton Feldman at the New York Studio School in 1968, Guston spoke at length about a memoir he was reading, written by a French Jew whose parents had been murdered at Treblinka. He was fascinated to learn about the processes by which the Germans and their victims became inured to the violence they inflicted and received, to the point where prisoners needed to be convinced by a fellow inmate that there was a genuine need for them to escape, not just to save their lives but in order to bear witness. "I began to see all of life really as a vast concentration camp. And everybody is numbed, you know. Then I thought, 'Well, that's the only reason to be an artist: to escape, to bear witness to this.'" Philip Guston, "Conversation with Morton Feldman," in *Philip Guston: Collected Writings, Lectures, and Conversations*, edited by Clark Coolidge (Berkeley and Los Angeles: University of California Press, 2011), p. 80.

9   Philip Guston, "Philip Guston Talking," in Musa Mayer, *Night Studio: A Memoir of Philip Guston* (New York: Hauser & Wirth, [1988] 2023), p. 204.

10 Philip Guston, "On Drawing," lecture given at the Yale Summer School, 1974, as quoted in Robert Storr, *Philip Guston: A Life Spent Painting* (London: Laurence King, 2020), p. 259.

11 The art critic Ross Feld, whose catalogue essay exposed Guston's Jewishness, was one of three Jewish friends Guston requested to recite Kaddish for him at his funeral (the other two were the writer Philip Roth and the musician Morton Feldman). For more on Guston's Jewishness, see especially Mark Godfrey, "Jewish Image-Maker," in *Philip Guston Now* (Washington, DC: National Gallery of Art, 2020), pp. 193–203.

12 Harold Rosenberg, as quoted in Mayer, *Night Studio*, p. 218n25.

13 Robert Hughes, "Art: Ku Klux Komix," *Time* 96, no. 19, November 9, 1970.

14 As quoted in Sarah Cascone, "Philip Guston's Daughter and Other Critics Speak Out Against Four Museums' Decision to Postpone a Major Retrospective on the Artist," *Artnet*, September 25, 2020, https://news.artnet.com/art-world/philip-guston-retrospective-postponed-1910658.

15 Taylor Dafoe, "Nicole Eisenman, Martin Puryear, and 100 Other Artists and Intellectuals Call on Museums to Reinstate the Postponed Philip Guston Retrospective," *Artnet*, September 30, 2020, https://news.artnet.com/art-world/open-letter-philip-guston-postponement-1911865.

16 Trenton Doyle Hancock, interview with the author, August 4, 2023.

17 Ibid.

18 Trenton Doyle Hancock, interview with the author, April 21, 2023.

19 Trenton Doyle Hancock, interview with the author, August 4, 2023.

20 Ibid.

21 Trenton Doyle Hancock, in discussion with the author, Musa Mayer, Sally Radic, and Paula Naughton, October 19, 2023, and in an interview with the author, August 4, 2023.

22 Trenton Doyle Hancock, interview with the author, August 4, 2023.

23 Ibid.

24 Trenton Doyle Hancock, interview with the author, October 13, 2023.

25 Trenton Doyle Hancock, interview with the author, August 4, 2023.

26 Trenton Doyle Hancock, interview with the author, August 18, 2023.

27 Ibid.

28 Trenton Doyle Hancock, "Fort Worth Review: Philip Guston Retrospective, Modern Art Museum of Fort Worth," *ARTL!ES* (Summer 2003), p. 67.

29 Trenton Doyle Hancock, letter to Musa Mayer, February 8, 2022.

30 Trenton Doyle Hancock, *EMIT: What the Bringback Brought* (Sarasota, Fla.: John and Mable Ringling Museum of Art, 2015), p. 14.

31 Trenton Doyle Hancock, video contribution to "Philip Guston: On Edge," a hybrid symposium organized by Hauser & Wirth, September 10, 2021.

32 Between 1890 and 1920, white lynch mobs claimed the lives of nine Black men in Paris, making it one of the most violently racist Texas towns in that era. See Katie Nodjimbadem, "Can the Black Lives Matter Movement Heal Paris, Texas?," *Texas Monthly*, August 2020, https://www.texasmonthly.com/news -politics/black-lives-matter-movement -paris-texas/.

33 A second lynching, of the brothers Irving and Herman Arthur, occurred at the same fairgrounds in 1920. Trenton Doyle Hancock, interviews with the author, August 4, 2023, and September 22, 2023.

34 Ibid.

35 Trenton Doyle Hancock, interview with the author, August 4, 2023.

36 Trenton Doyle Hancock, interview with the author, August 25, 2023.

37 Trenton Doyle Hancock, interview with the author, August 4, 2023.

38 Ibid.

39 As quoted in "Musa Mayer and Trenton Doyle Hancock in Conversation," moderated by Harry Cooper, Museum of Fine Arts, Houston, October 22, 2022.

40 Trenton Doyle Hancock, interview with the author, April 21, 2023.

41 Trenton Doyle Hancock, interview with the author, August 18, 2023.

42 Ibid.

Trenton Doyle Hancock, *Schlep and Screw, Knowledge Rental Pawn Exchange Service*, 2017 (detail; see p. 103)

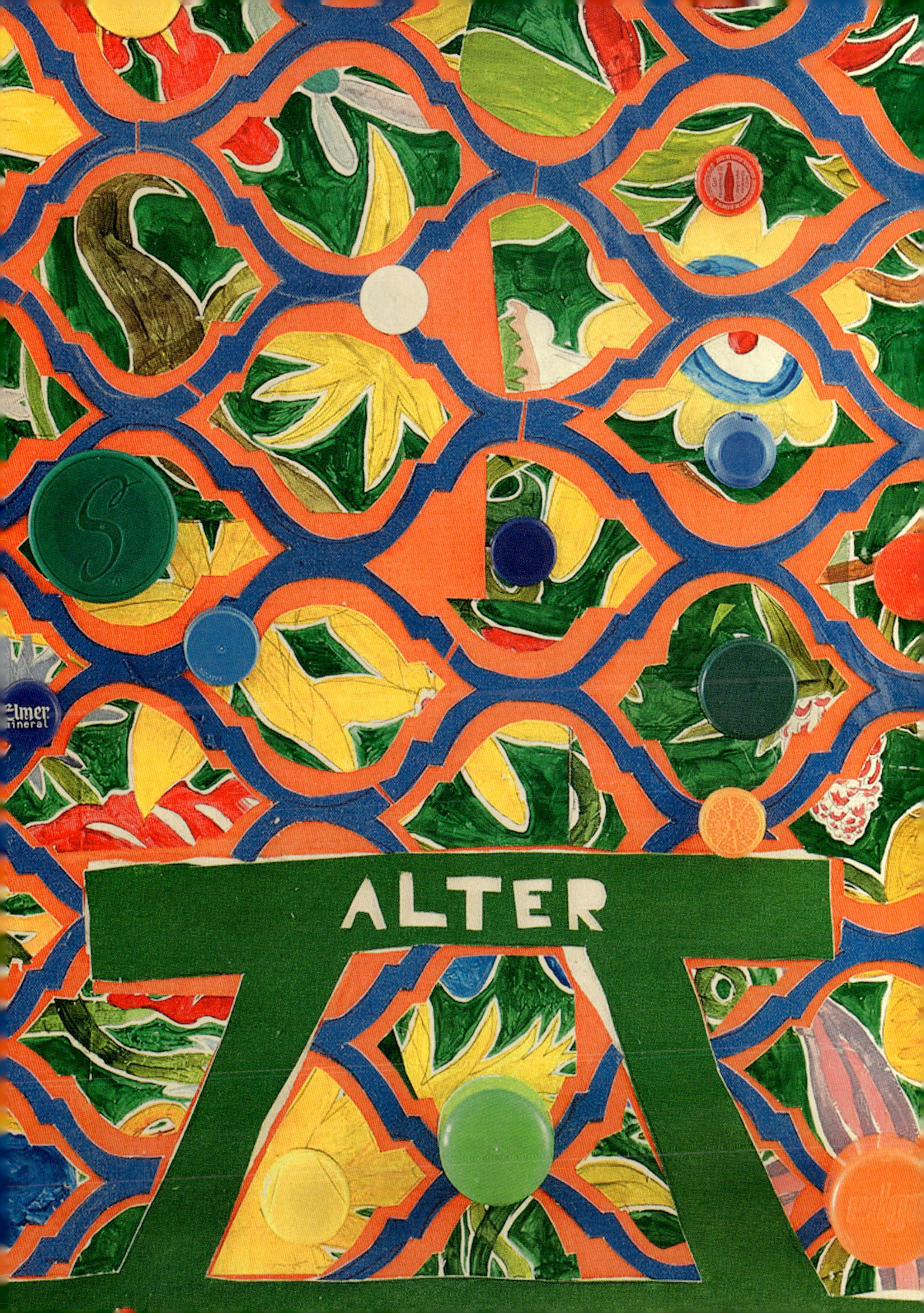

ALTER

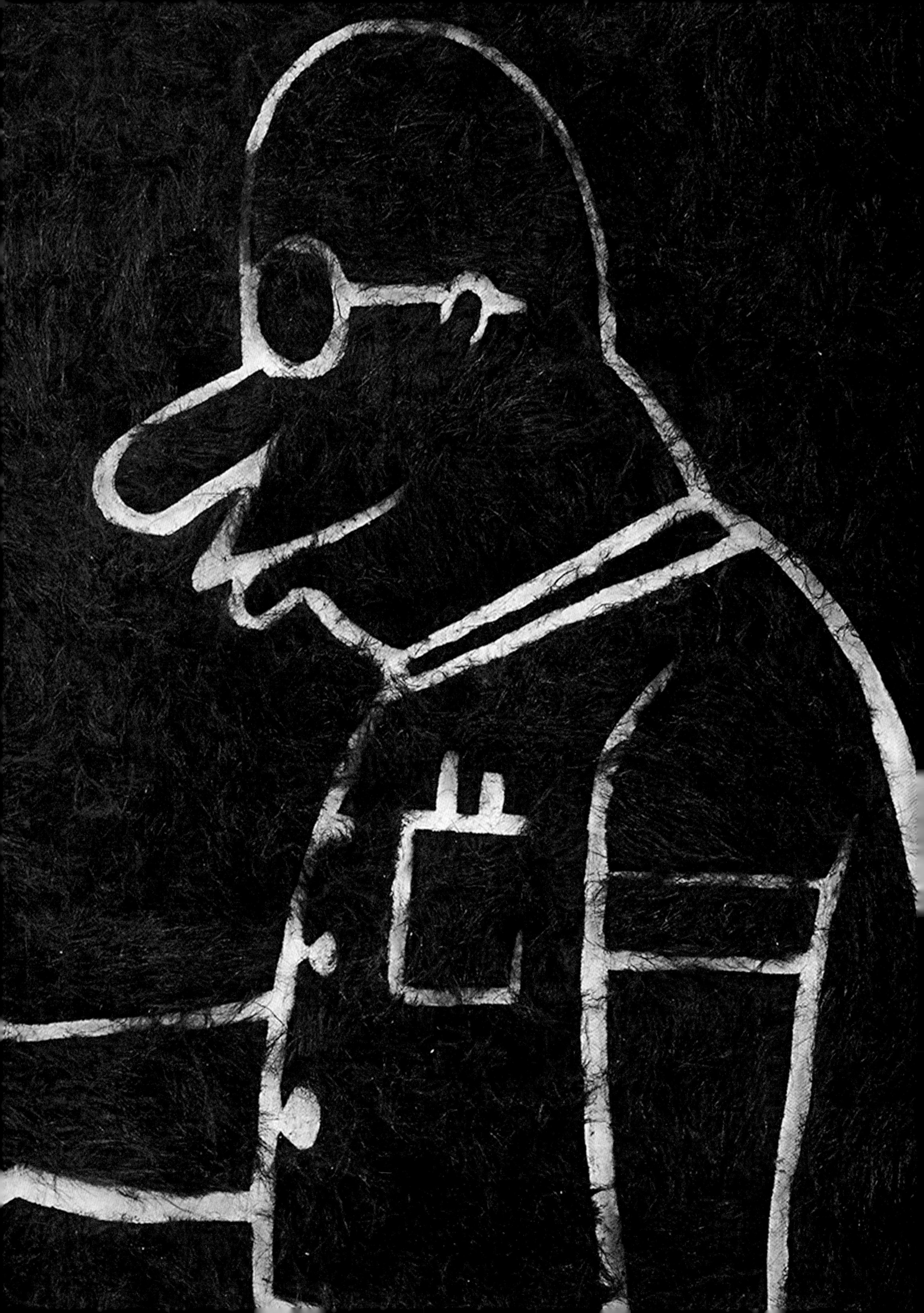

THE ARTWORKS

Trenton Doyle Hancock, *Step and Screw:
West End Scrap (Four Foot Furry
Face Off)*, 2021 (detail; see p. 118)

Philip Guston
Drawing for Conspirators, 1930
Graphite pencil, ink, colored
pencil, and wax crayon on paper,
22⅝ × 14⅝ in. (57.6 × 37 cm)
Whitney Museum of American Art,
New York

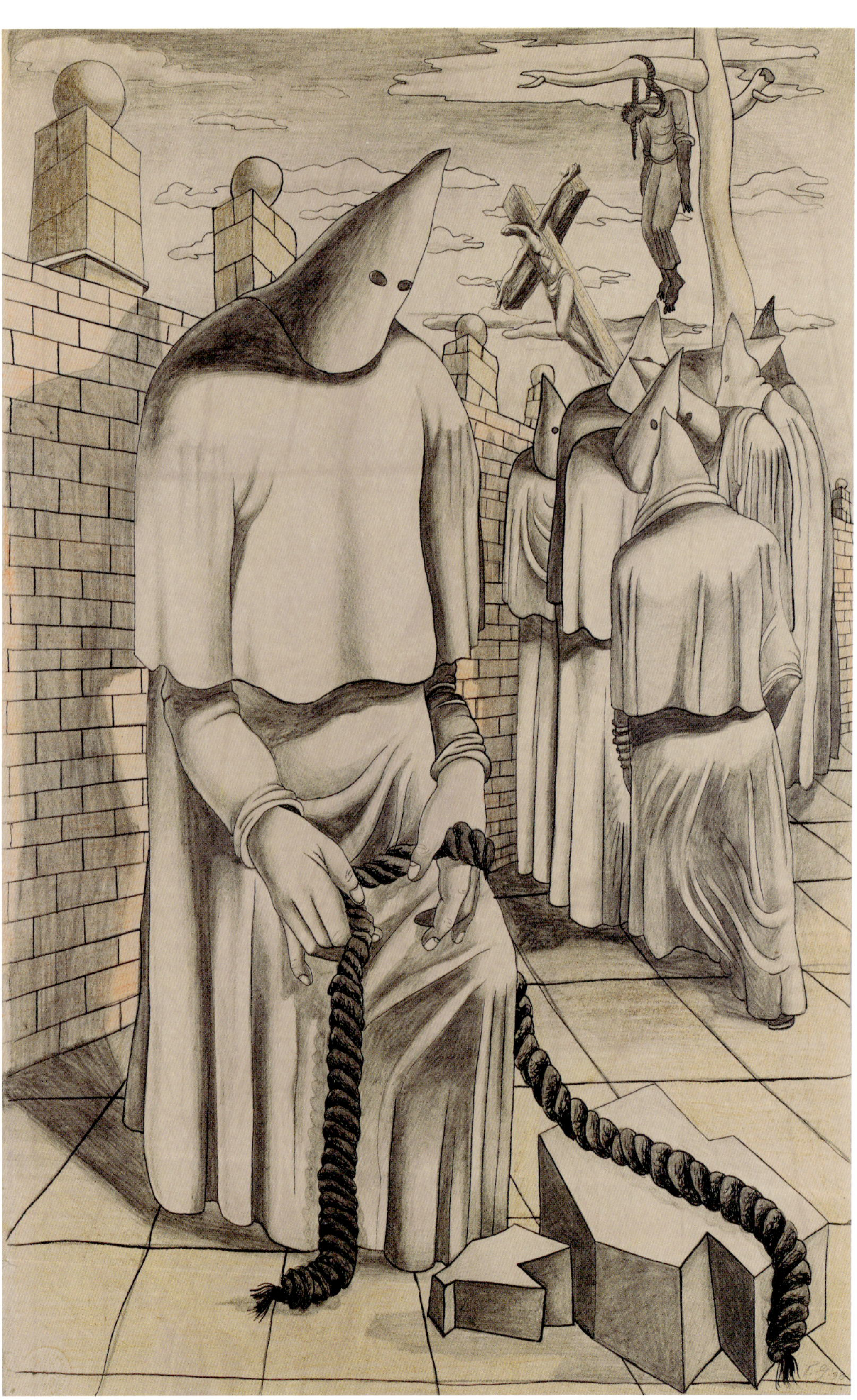

"[This is] a self-portrait developed in a darkroom by me in 1993. I was 19 years old, and I knew there was something deeply rotten in the area of Texas I grew up in. Insidious behavior and thoughts can be concealed by Southern pleasantries, the pulpits of churches, and suburban attics. I didn't understand what white supremacy was in 1993, but I knew there was something invisible operating on my body. I could feel that much. My folks never sat me down to talk about it, but I was starting to piece something together from observing their relationships with white folks over the years. I was never called [the n-word] to my face (like my parents were), but you don't have to be. There's a zillion other ways to be called that. I was beginning to get that, too. I was naive then and running on pure intuition. My need to express some growing unease came out in my pencil, brush, or camera whether I wanted it to or not. I didn't know what the art world was or what galleries were in 1993, so these images were just for me. Now they're for you, too."
—Trenton Doyle Hancock, September 2020

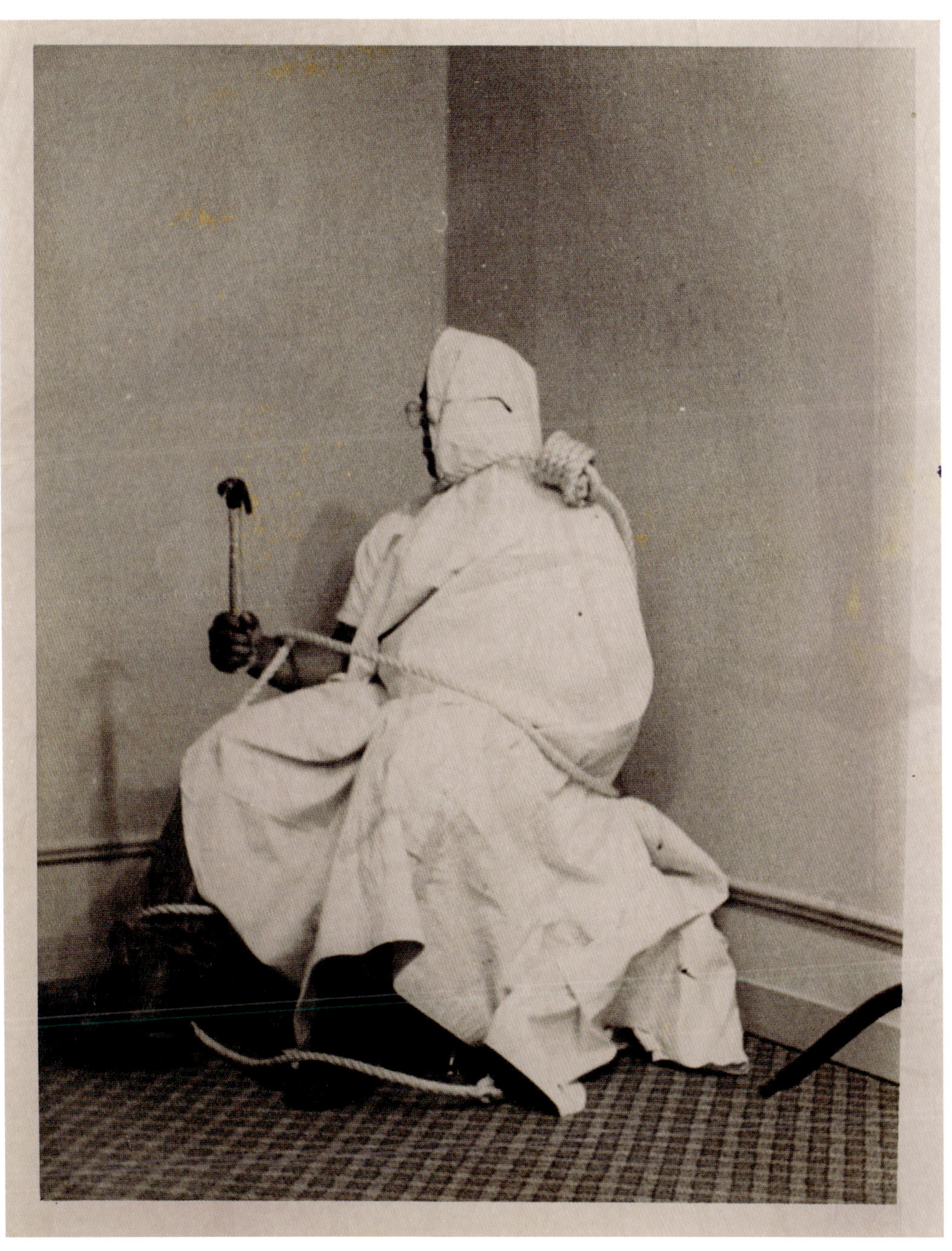

The hammer is rich in meaning in Hancock's universe, alternately a tool of oppression and resistance. "A hammer can be used to build, but also to destroy," Hancock has said. In that way, "it was a stand-in for Christianity. It's all in how you use it."

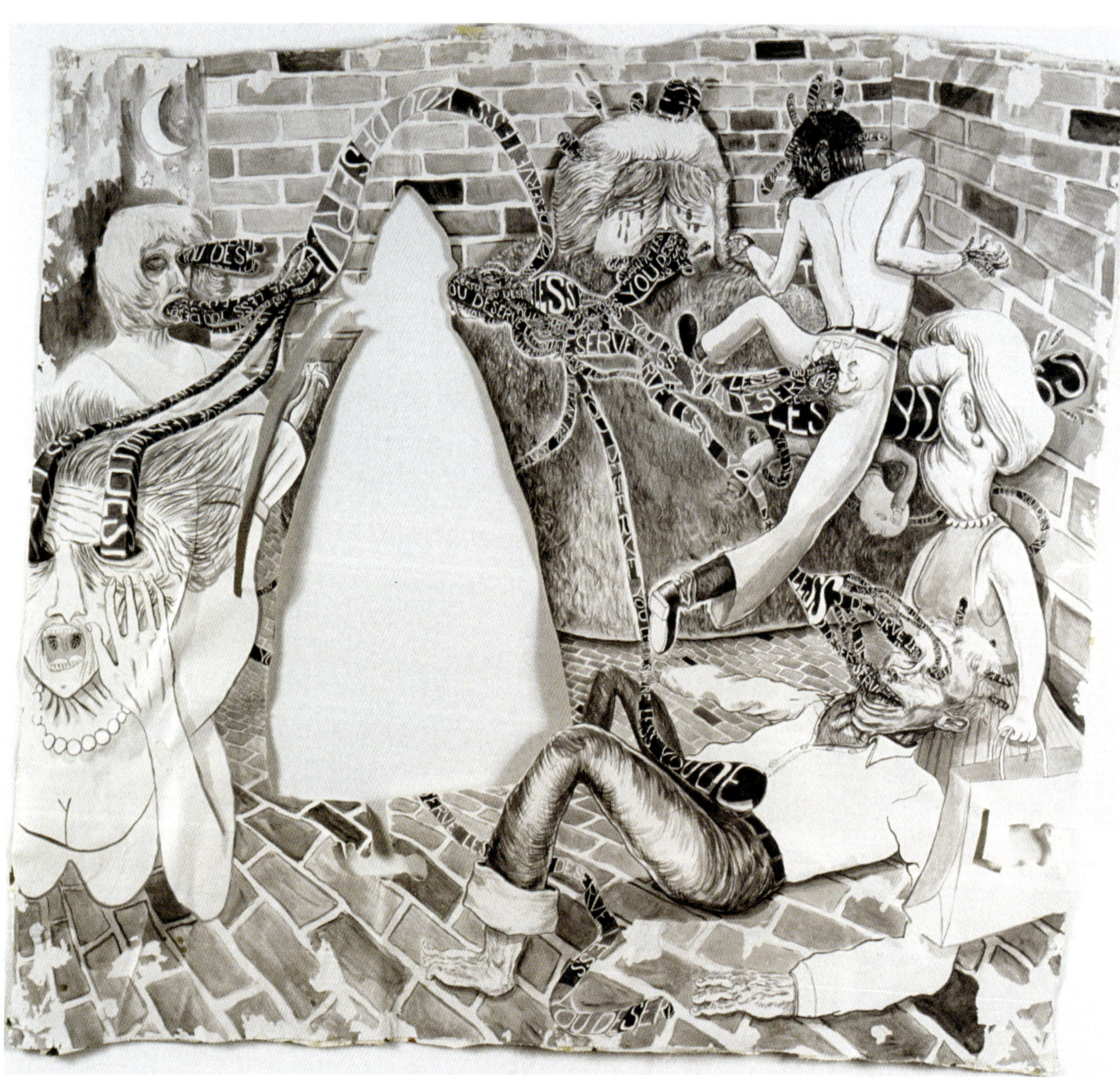

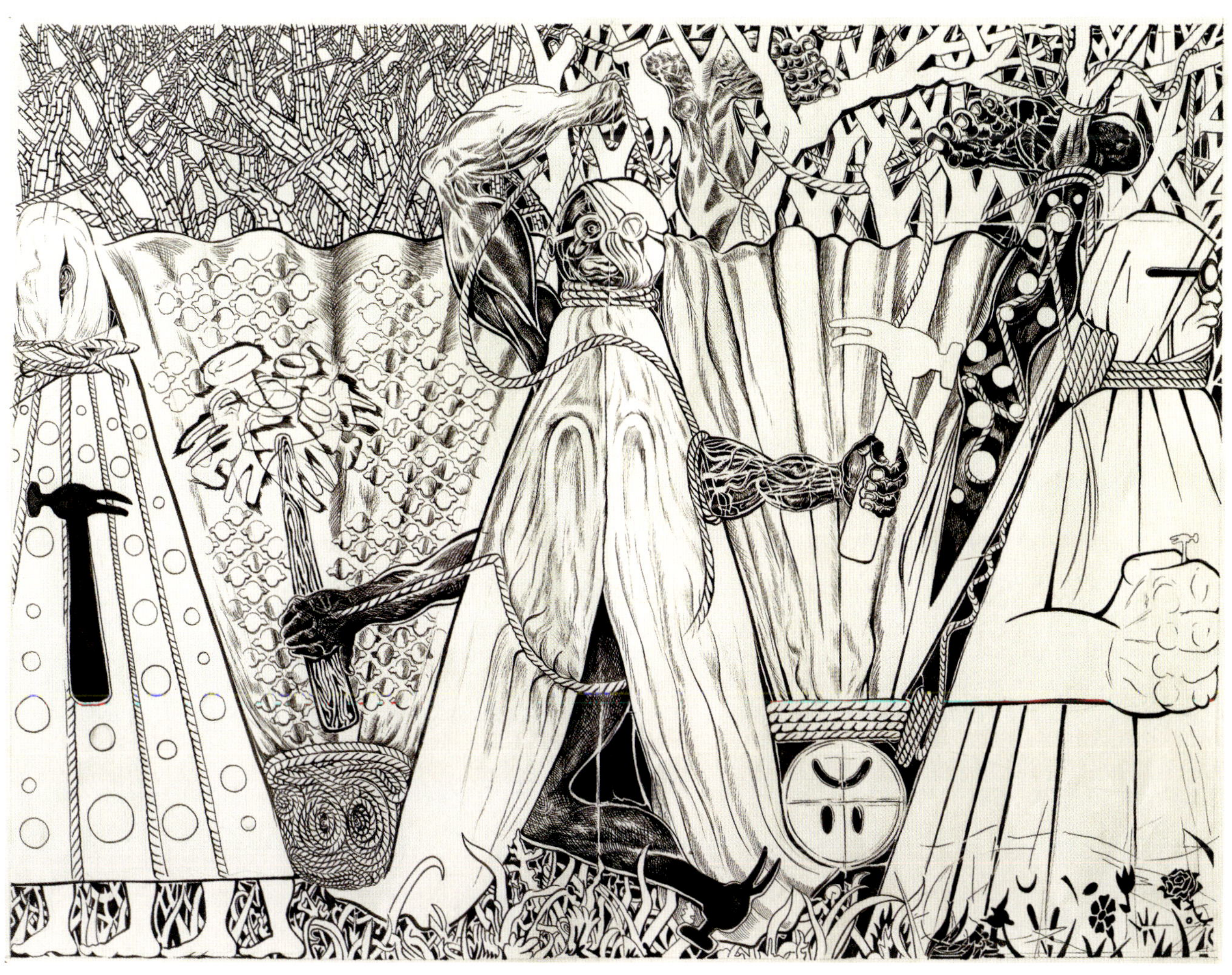

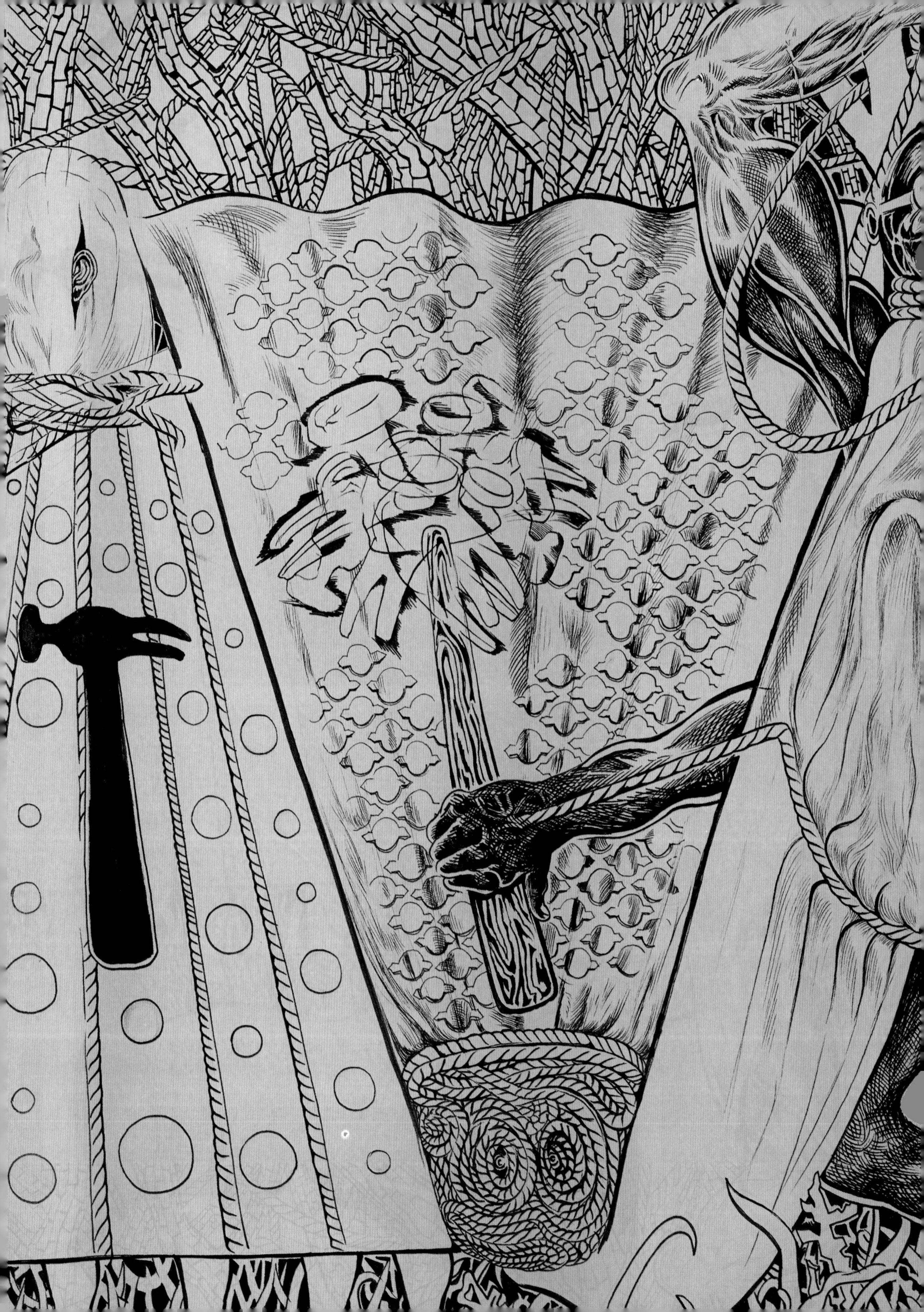

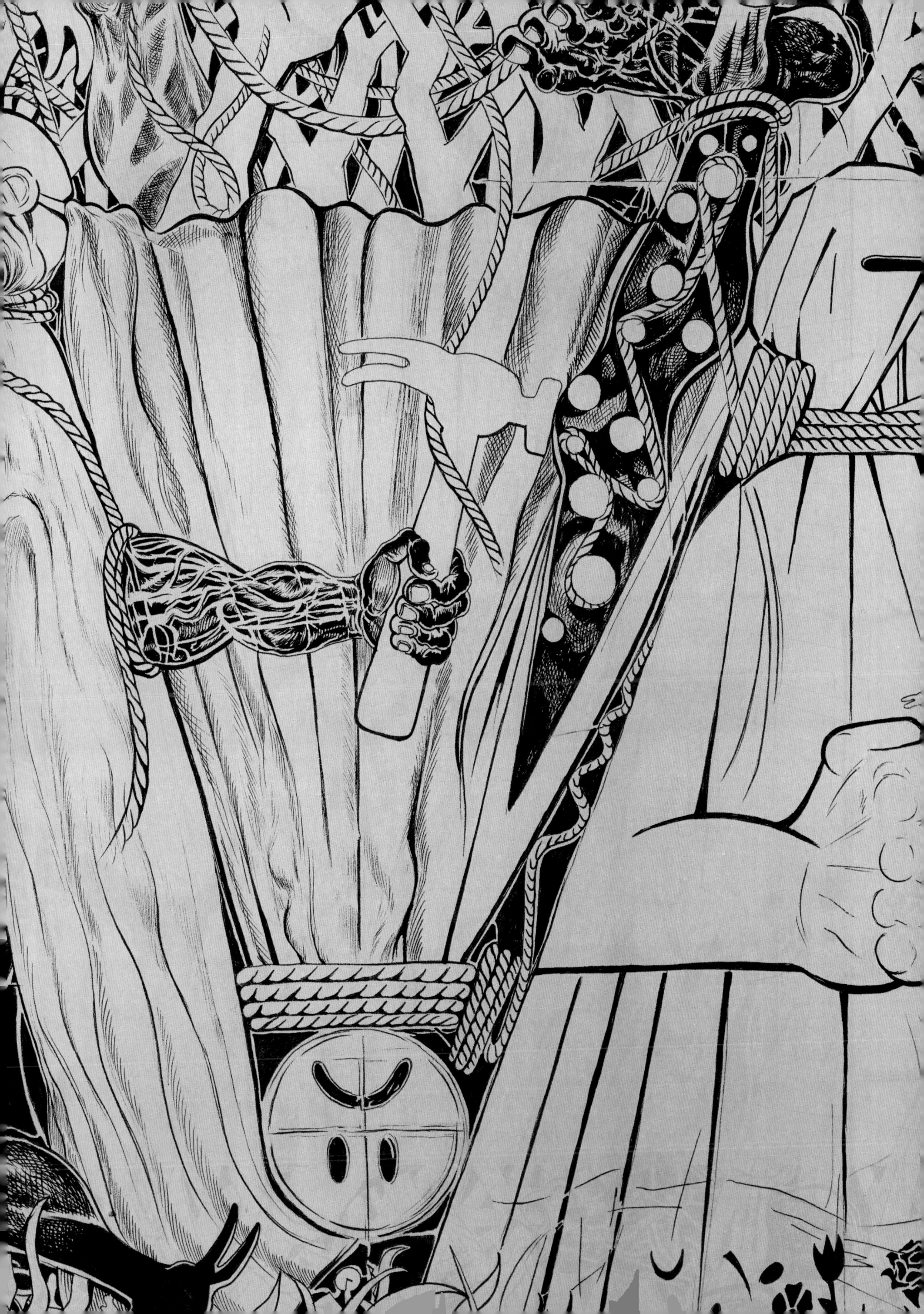

Trenton Doyle Hancock
Little Ploid Blue, 2013
Acrylic on canvas, 10 × 8 × 3 in.
(35.4 × 20.3 × 7.6 cm)
Private collection, London

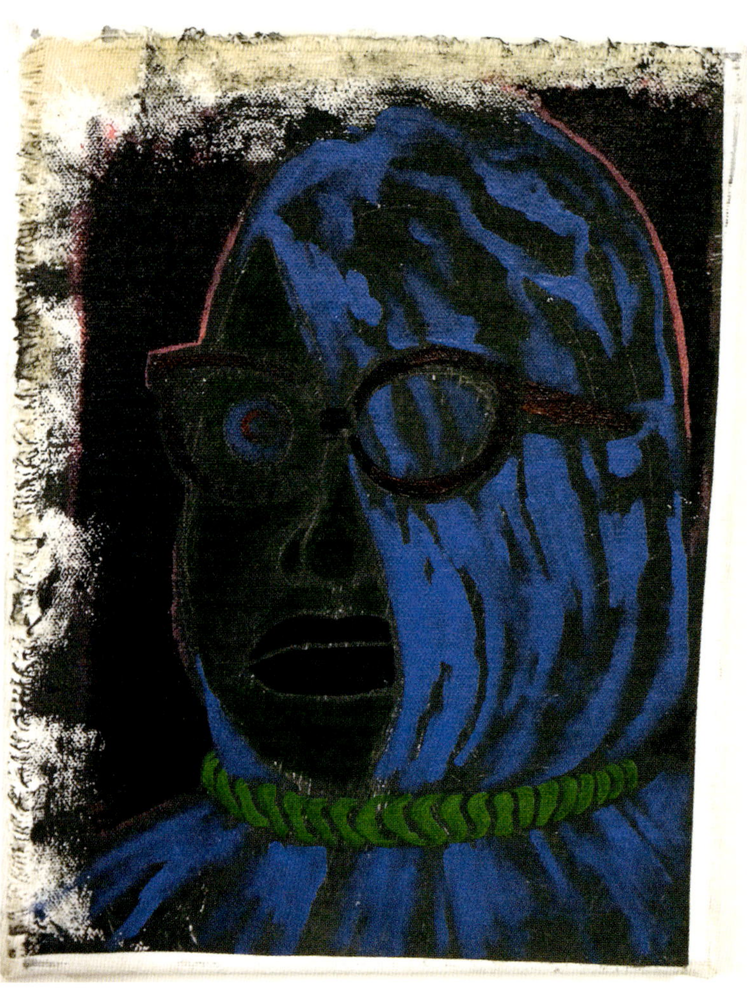

Trenton Doyle Hancock
I Know Just How You Feel, 2015
Acrylic and mixed media on canvas,
66 × 108 × 4¾ in.
(167.6 × 274.3 × 12.1 cm)
Private collection, London

Trenton Doyle Hancock
Referee, 2014
Acrylic and mixed media on canvas,
66 × 108 × 4¼ in.
(167.6 × 274.3 × 10.8 cm)
Nazarian / Curcio Gallery, Los Angeles

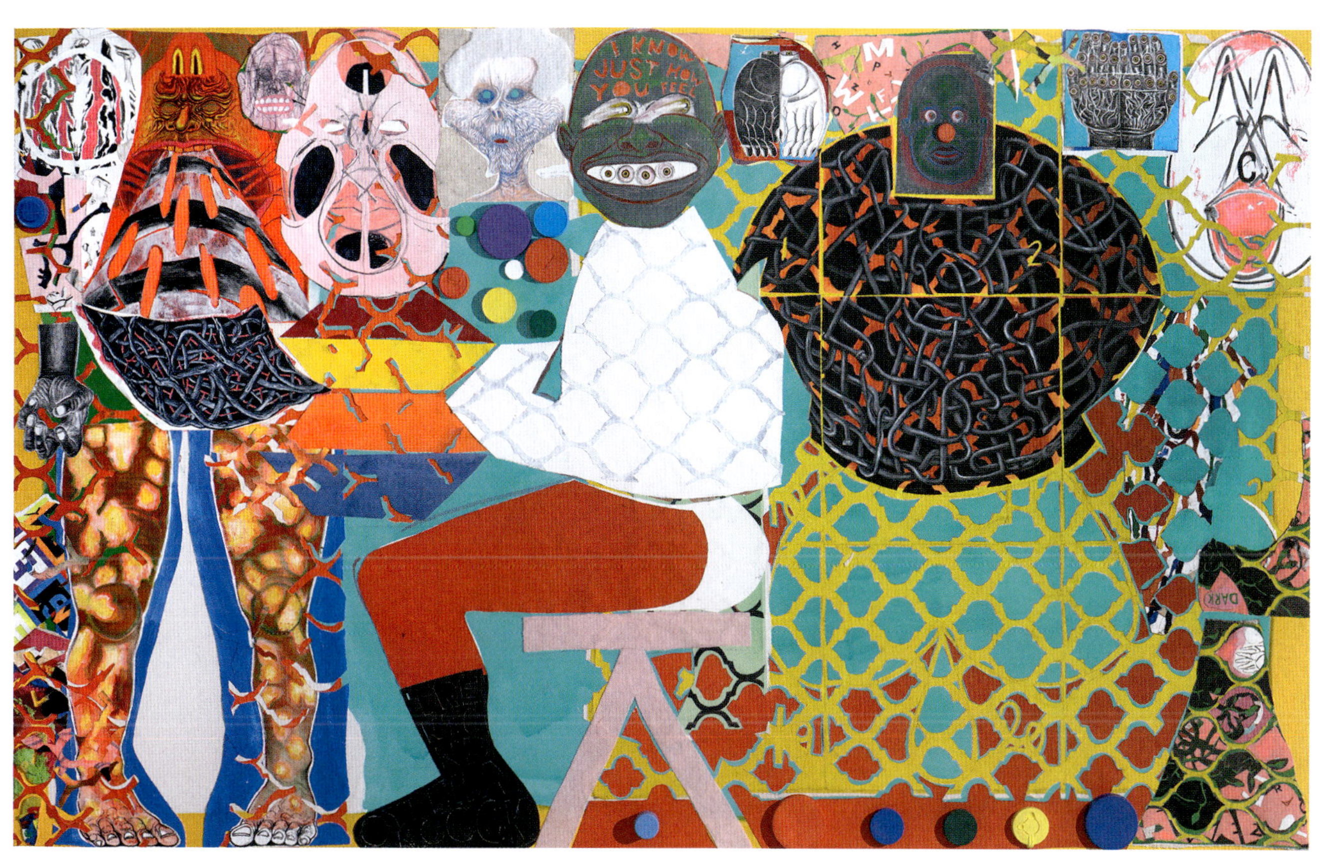

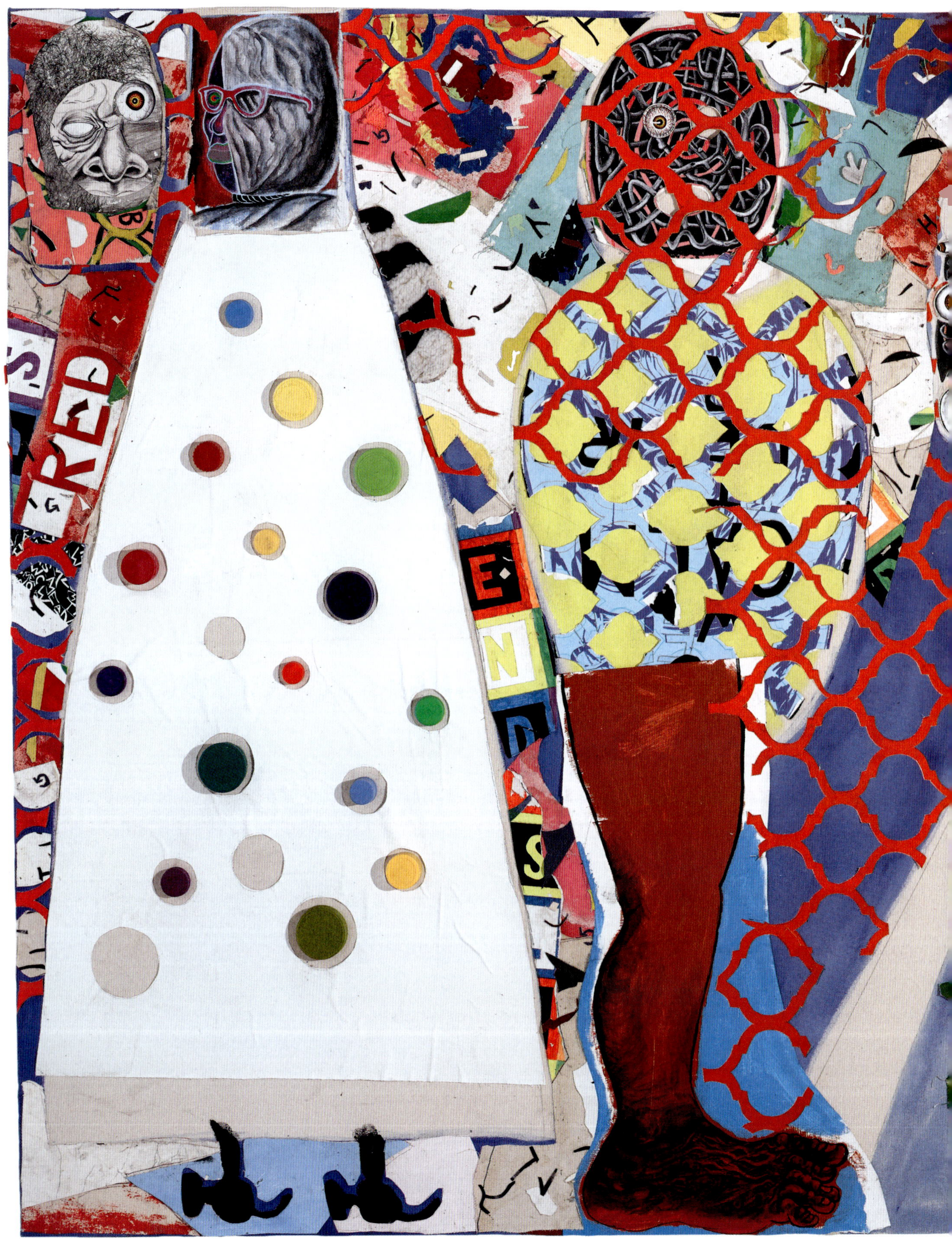

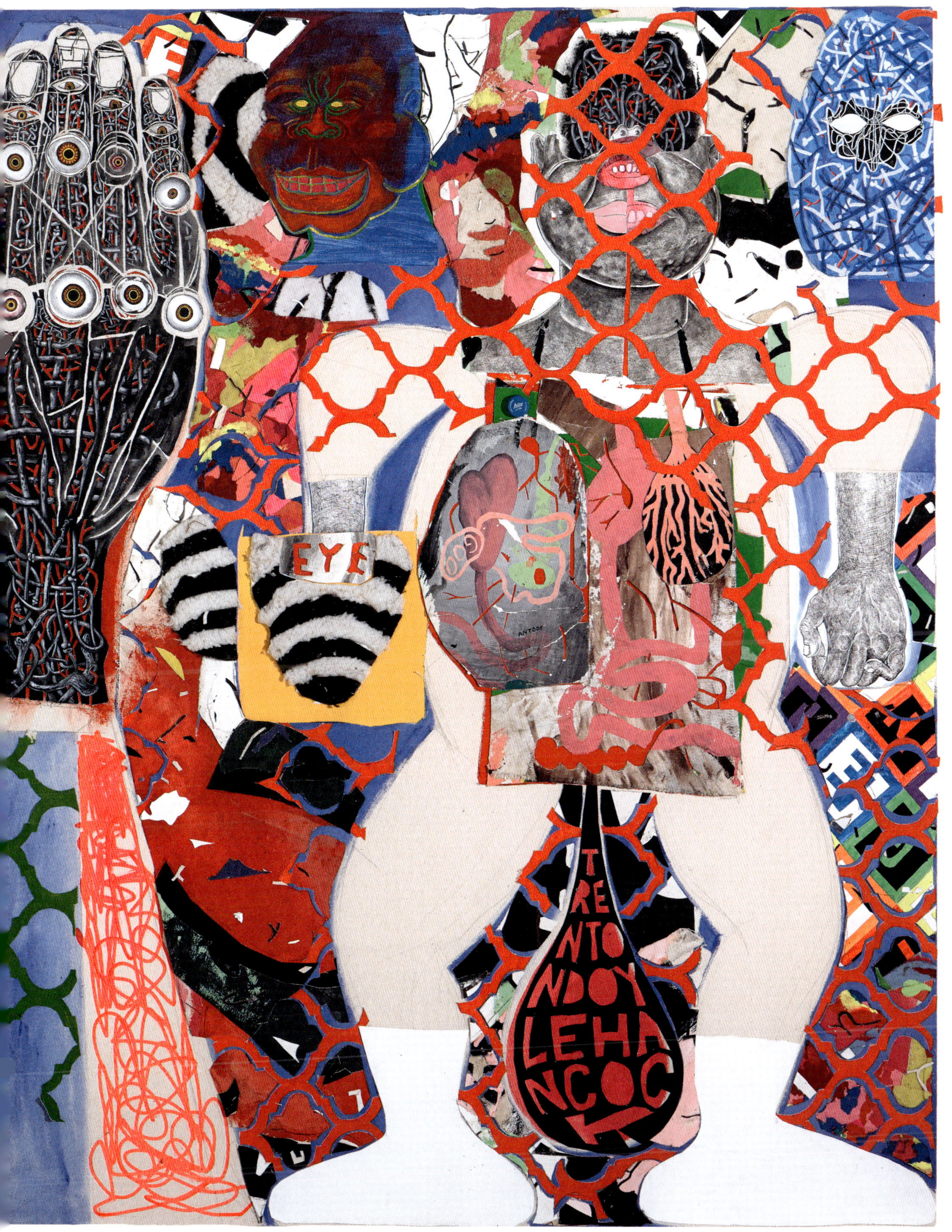

EYE
TRENTONDOYLEHANCOCK

Trenton Doyle Hancock
*I Want to Be at the Meeting After
the Separation*, 2014
Acrylic and mixed media on canvas,
90 × 108 × 3¼ in. (228.6 × 274.3 × 8.2 cm)
Collection of Hedy Fischer and
Randy Shull, Asheville, North Carolina

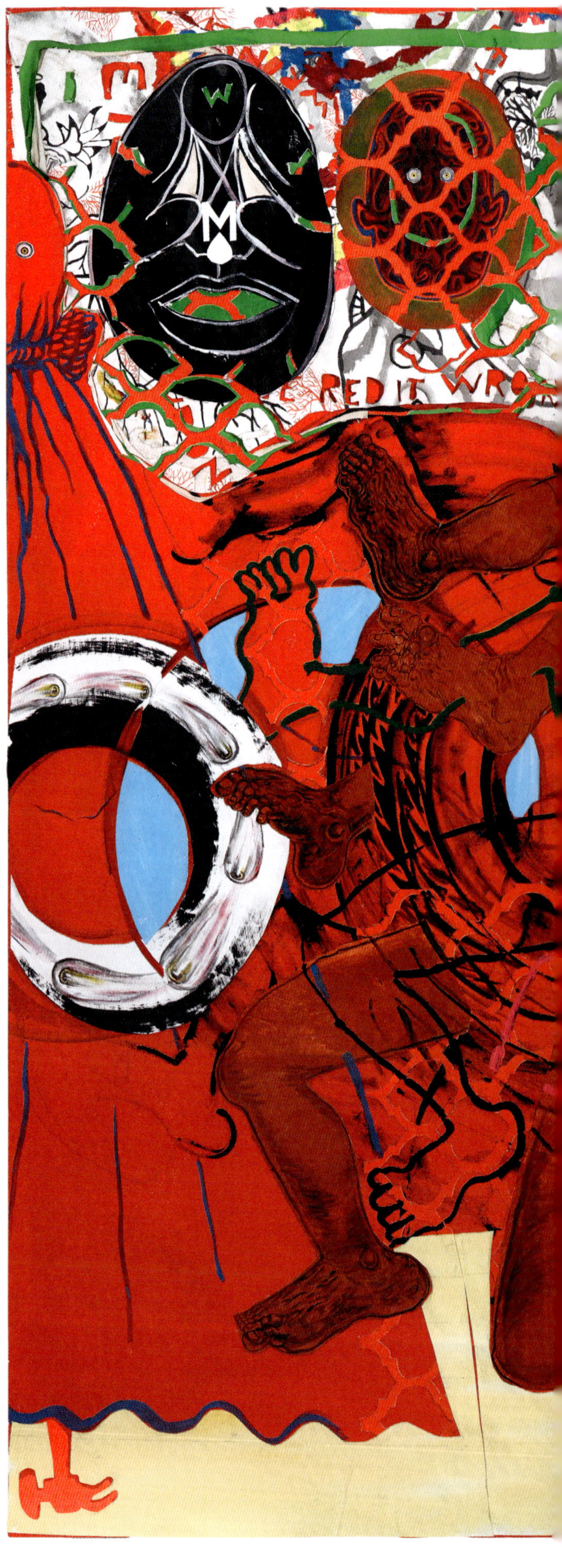

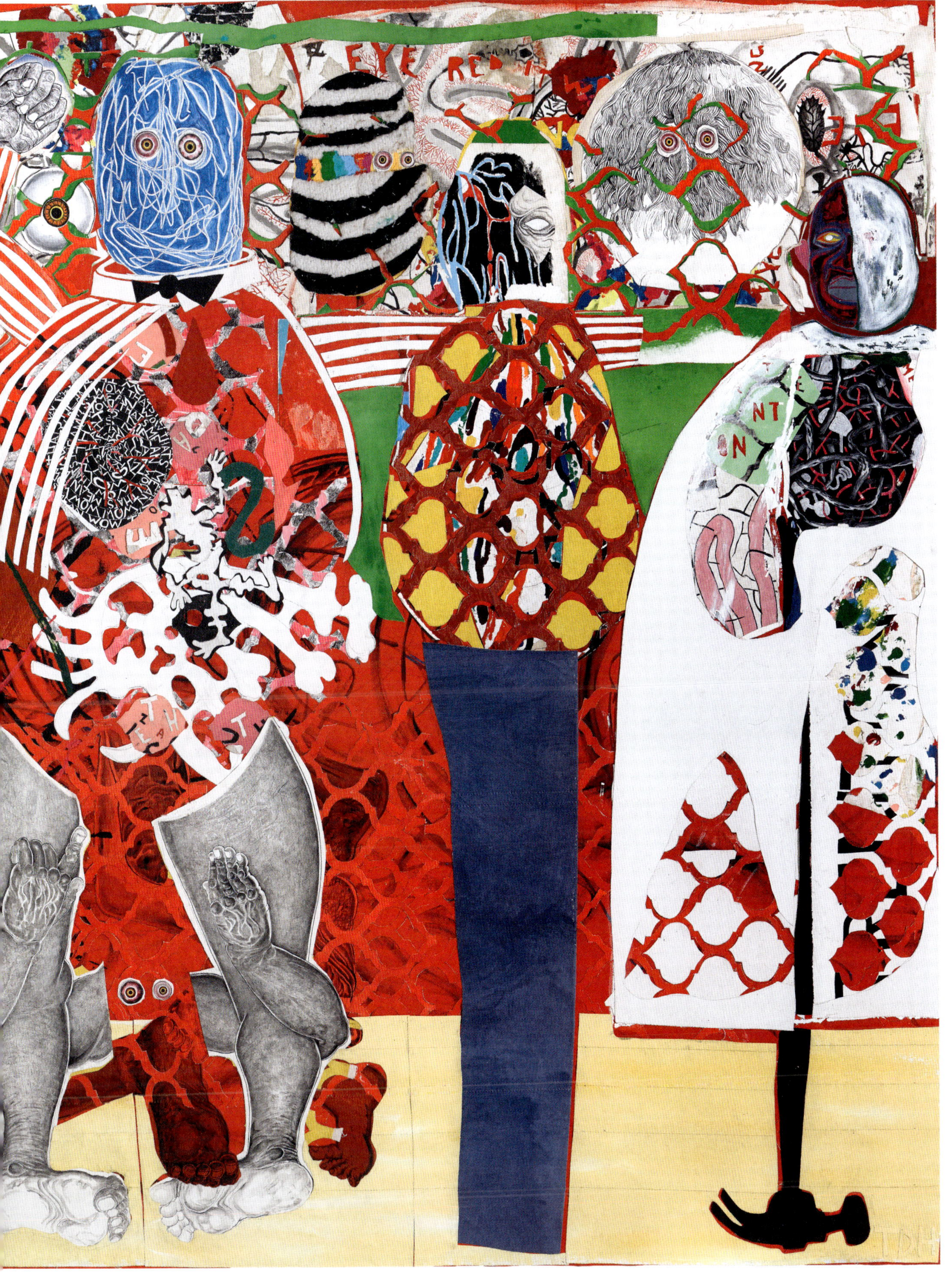

Thirty years after his first encounters with Guston's work, Hancock continues to make new discoveries. Since beginning work on the present exhibition, he has retroactively conceived of Loid as the reembodiment of the lynching victim in Guston's *Drawing for Conspirators*, a figure with whom Hancock also self-identifies, and whose spirit now lives on in Hancock's bold new visions.

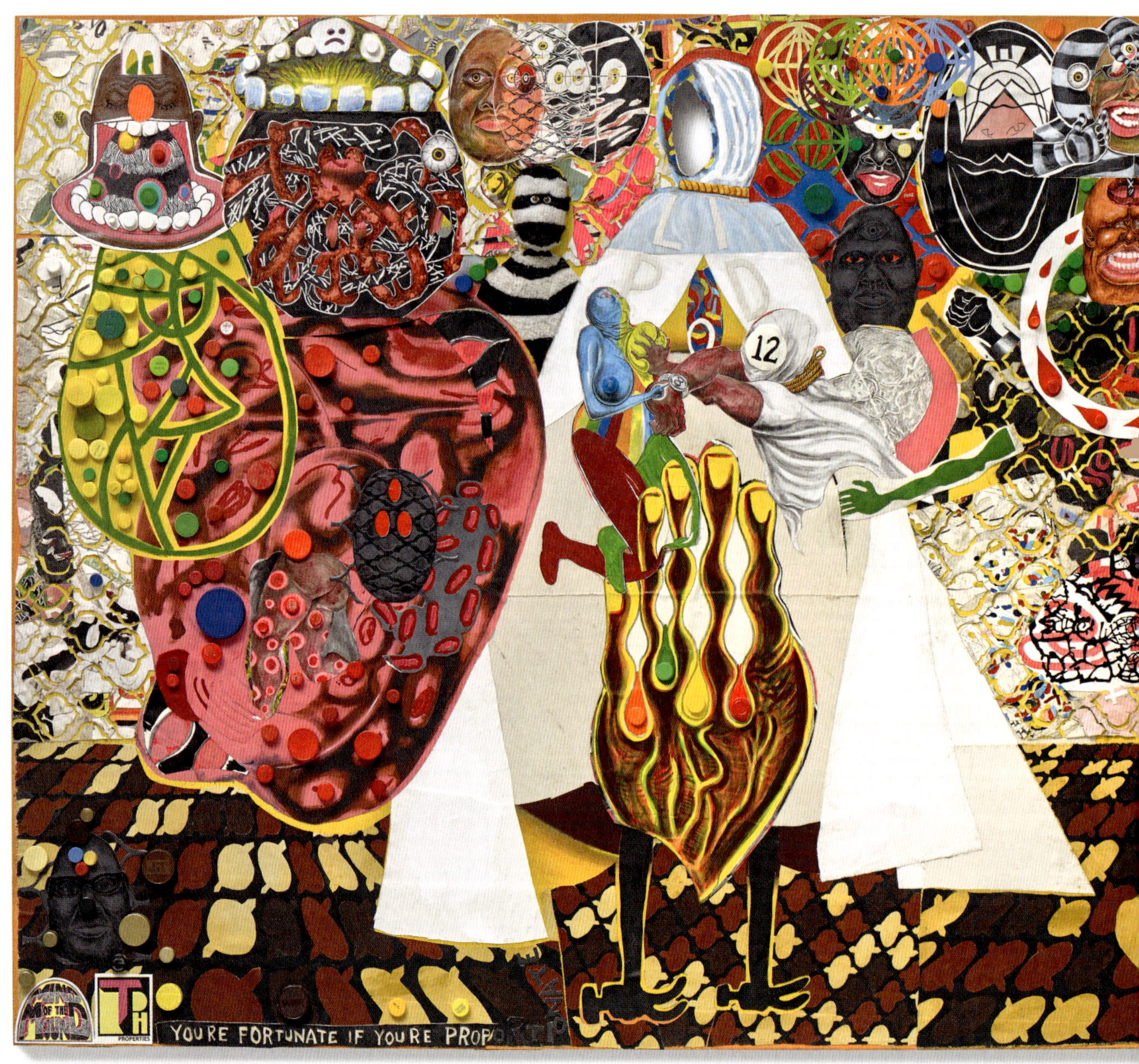

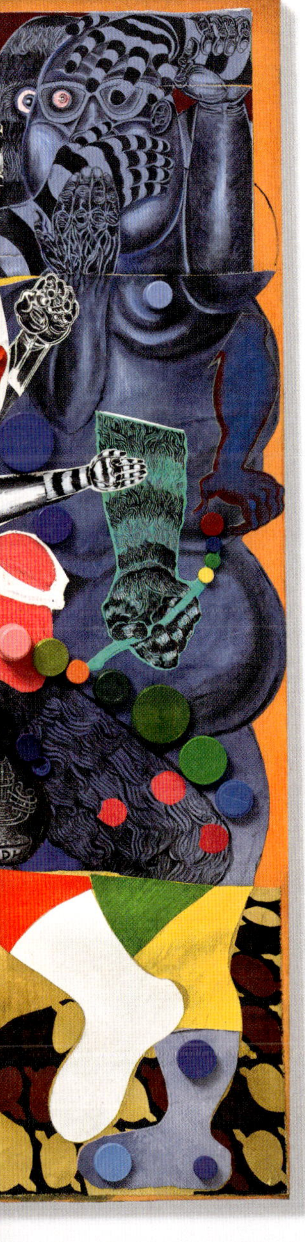

N

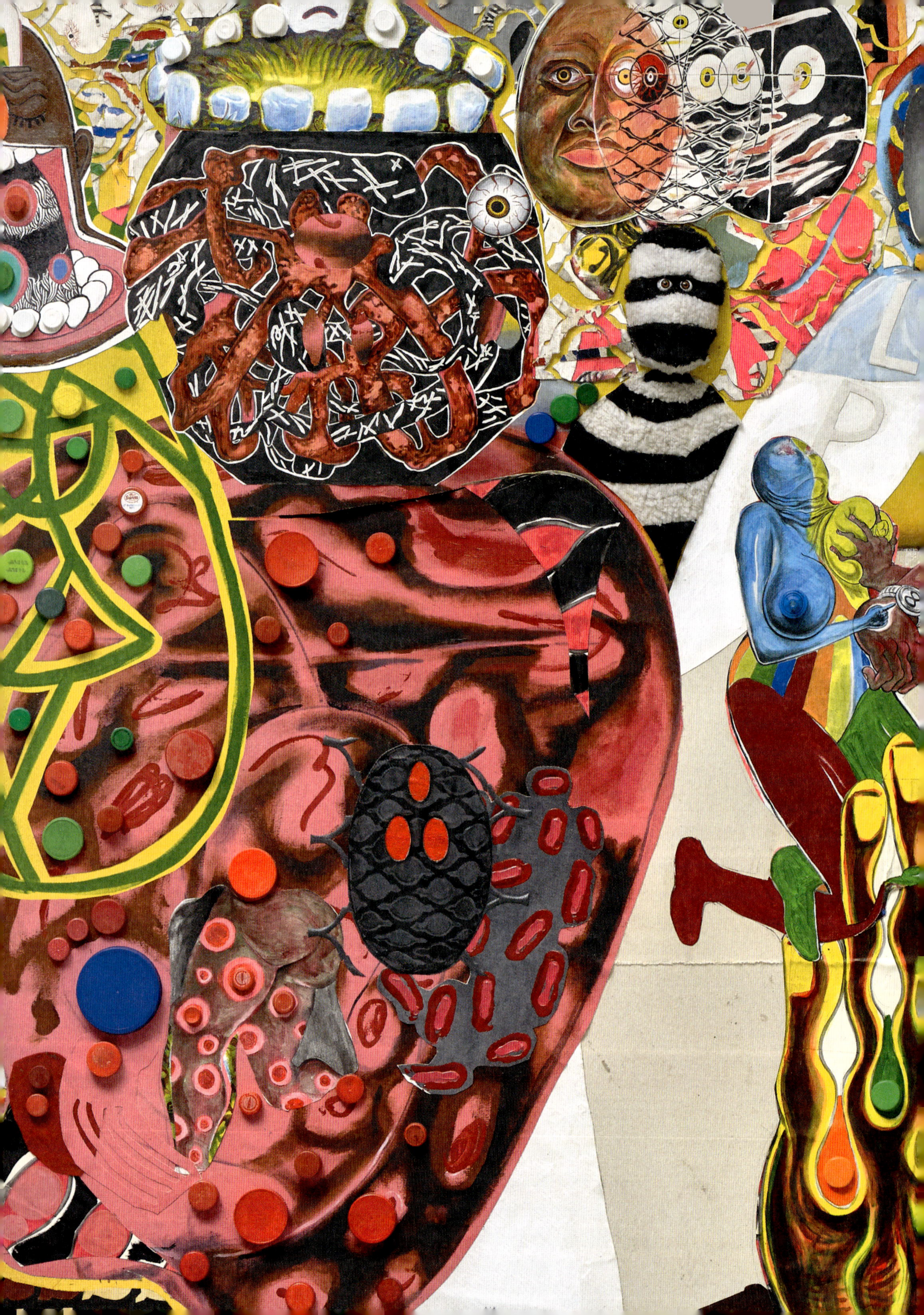

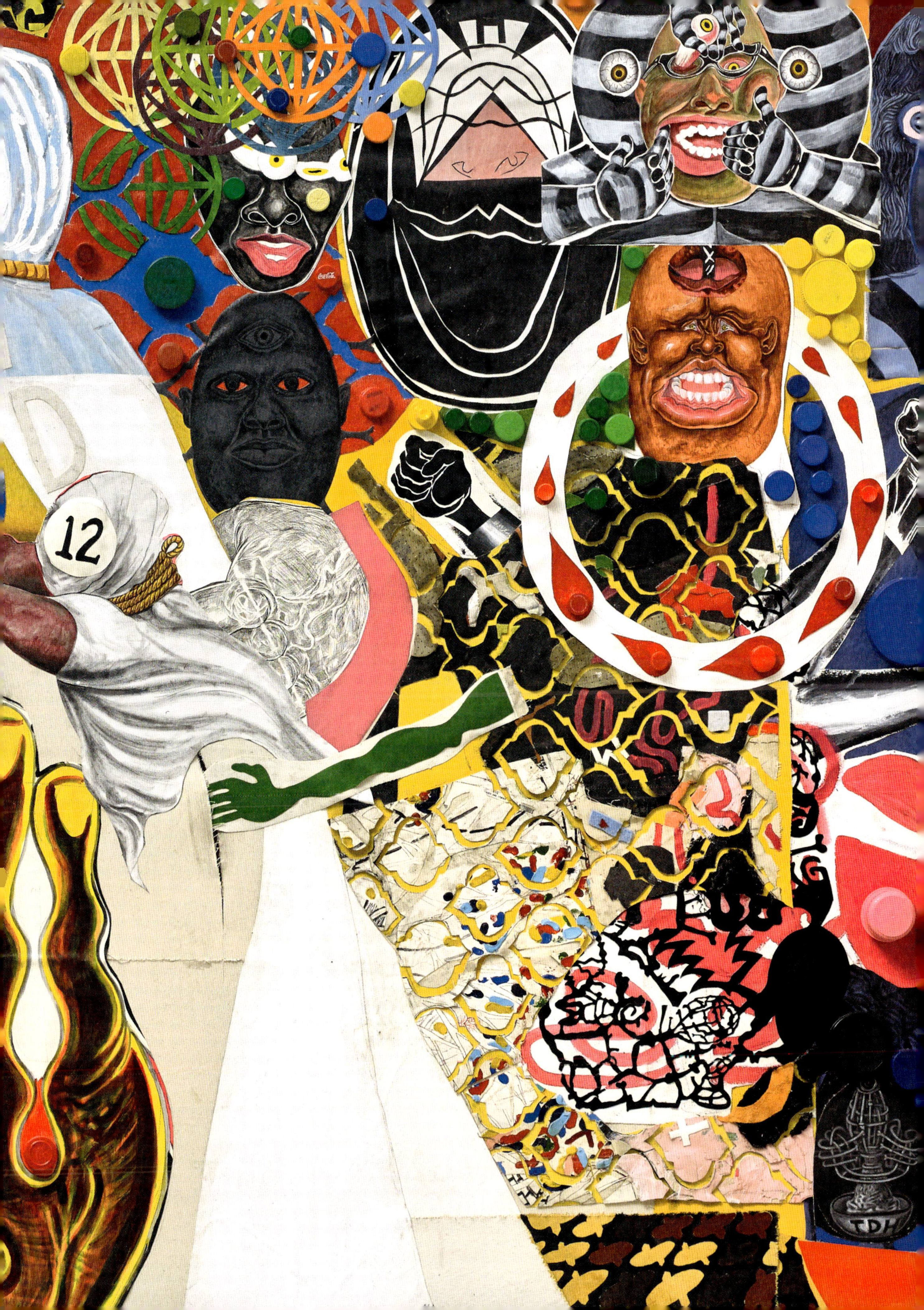

Speaking in 1978, Guston explained, "I perceive myself as being behind the hood. In the new series of 'hoods' my attempt was really not to illustrate, to do pictures of the Ku Klux Klan, as I had done earlier," but rather to consider "what would it be like to be evil? To plan, to plot."

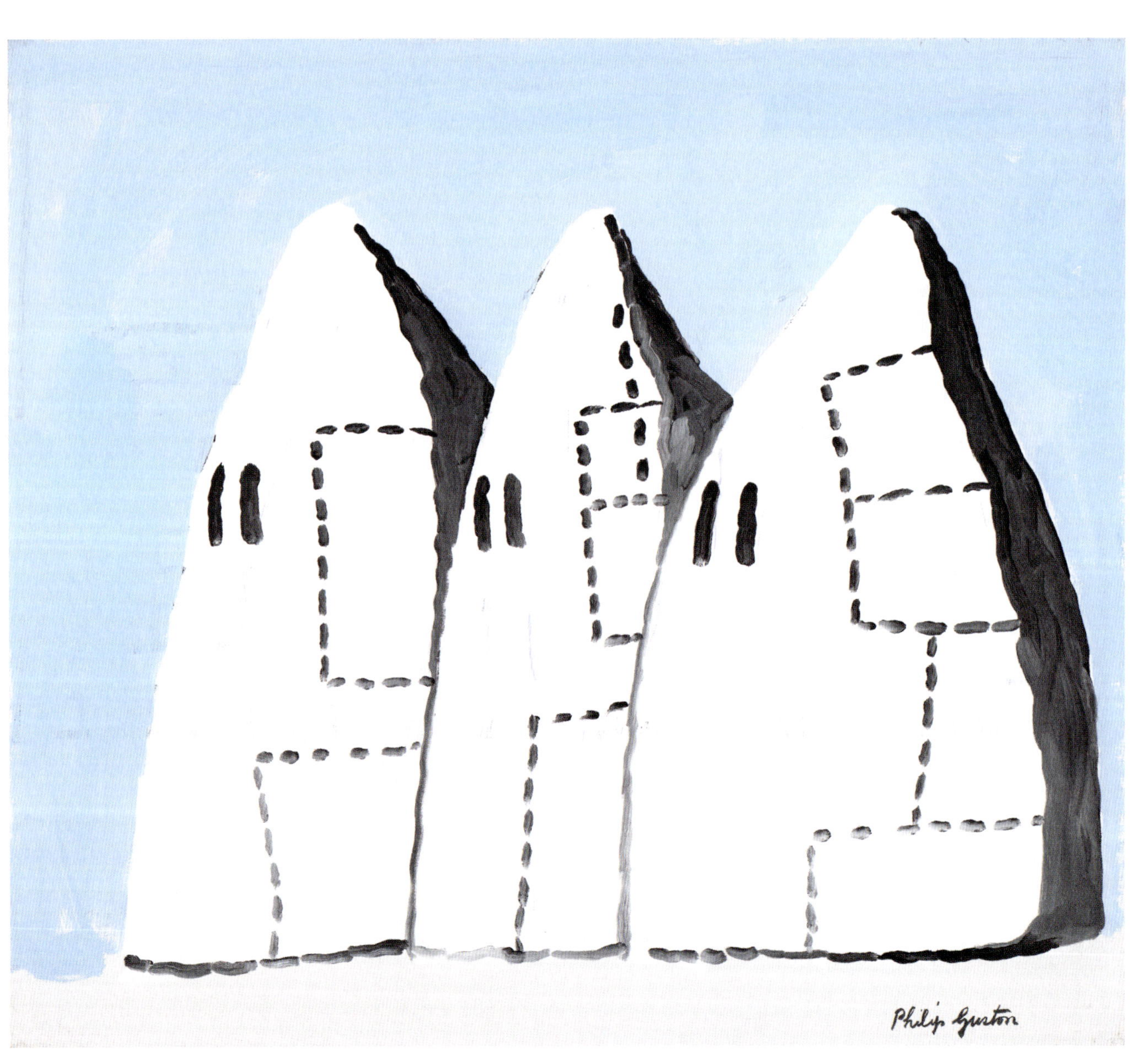

Philip Guston
The Studio, 1969
Oil on canvas, 48 × 42 in.
(121.9 × 106.7 cm)
Metropolitan Museum of Art,
New York, promised gift
of Musa Guston Mayer

"*The Studio* is the quintessential Guston image. There are several indicators of the passage of time: the daylight and the clock are obvious ones, but there is also the painter's brush, which rides counterclockwise down the left side of the canvas, pressing against time. The viewer becomes a collaborator in this scene, as the eye naturally wants to help the Klan Painter finish his mark making. The clunky vertical and horizontal lines are echoed throughout the work, creating a loose grid of quadrants, like a clock."

—Trenton Doyle Hancock, March 2024

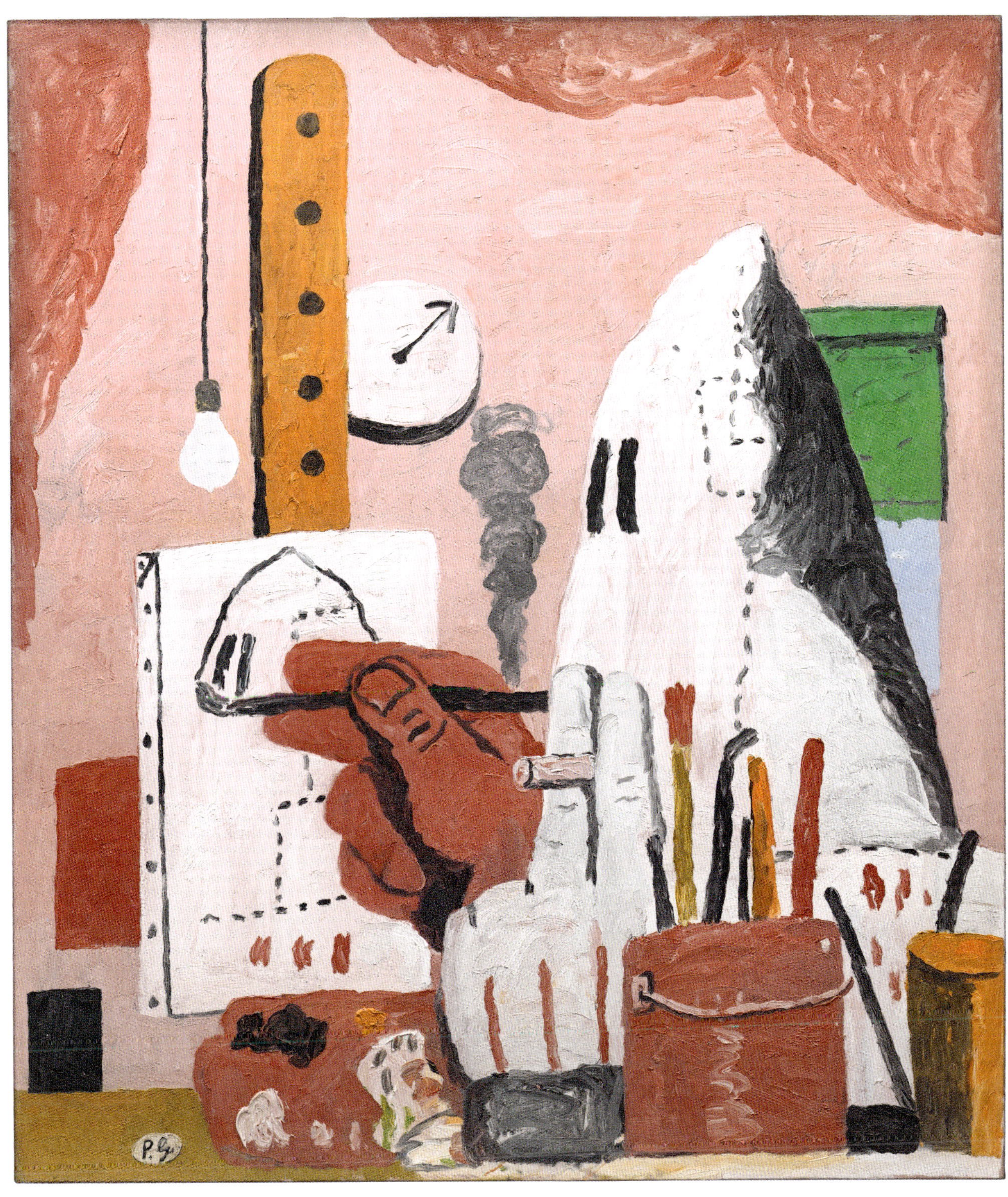

Philip Guston
Riding Around, 1969
Oil on canvas, 54 × 79 in.
(137.2 × 200.7 cm)
Metropolitan Museum
of Art, New York,
promised gift of Musa
Guston Mayer

"*Riding Around* at first suggests that the getaway car is moving at a leisurely pace. However, the edges of the painting contradict how the car is moving, if it moves at all. The red buildings bite the back of the car, locking it in place, while the front of the car is wedged against the canvas's right edge, effectively preventing our protagonists' escape. The clouds act as thought bubbles, encasing empty thoughts."
—Trenton Doyle Hancock, March 2024

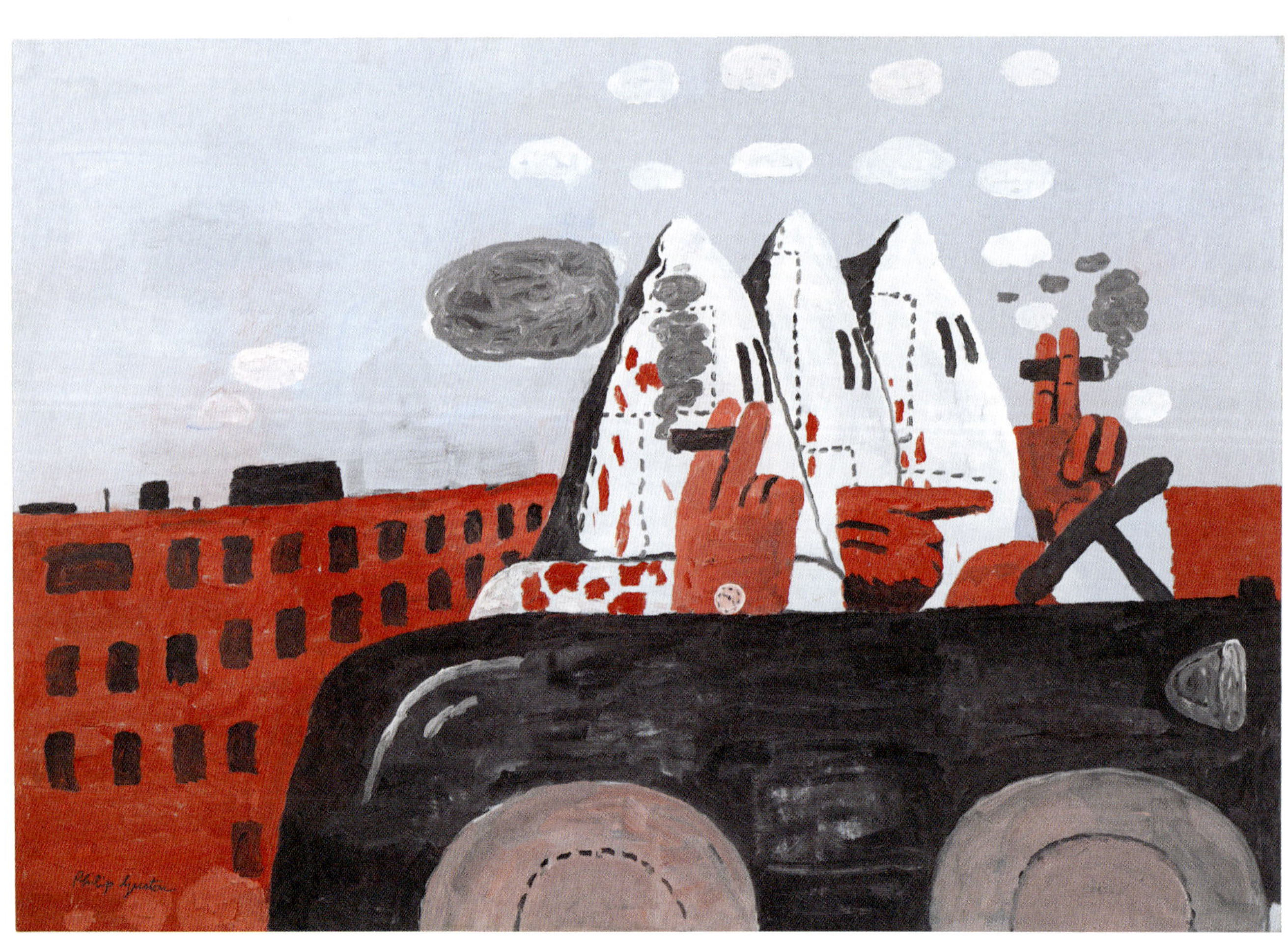

Philip Guston
Scared Stiff, 1970
Oil on canvas, 57 × 81 in.
(144.8 × 205.7 cm)
Private collection

"Watching true-crime documentaries has taught me that you can't predict how blood will splatter during a crime scene. *Scared Stiff* goes hilariously against those rules by having the Klansman's hood covered in equally spaced bloodstains."

—Trenton Doyle Hancock, March 2024

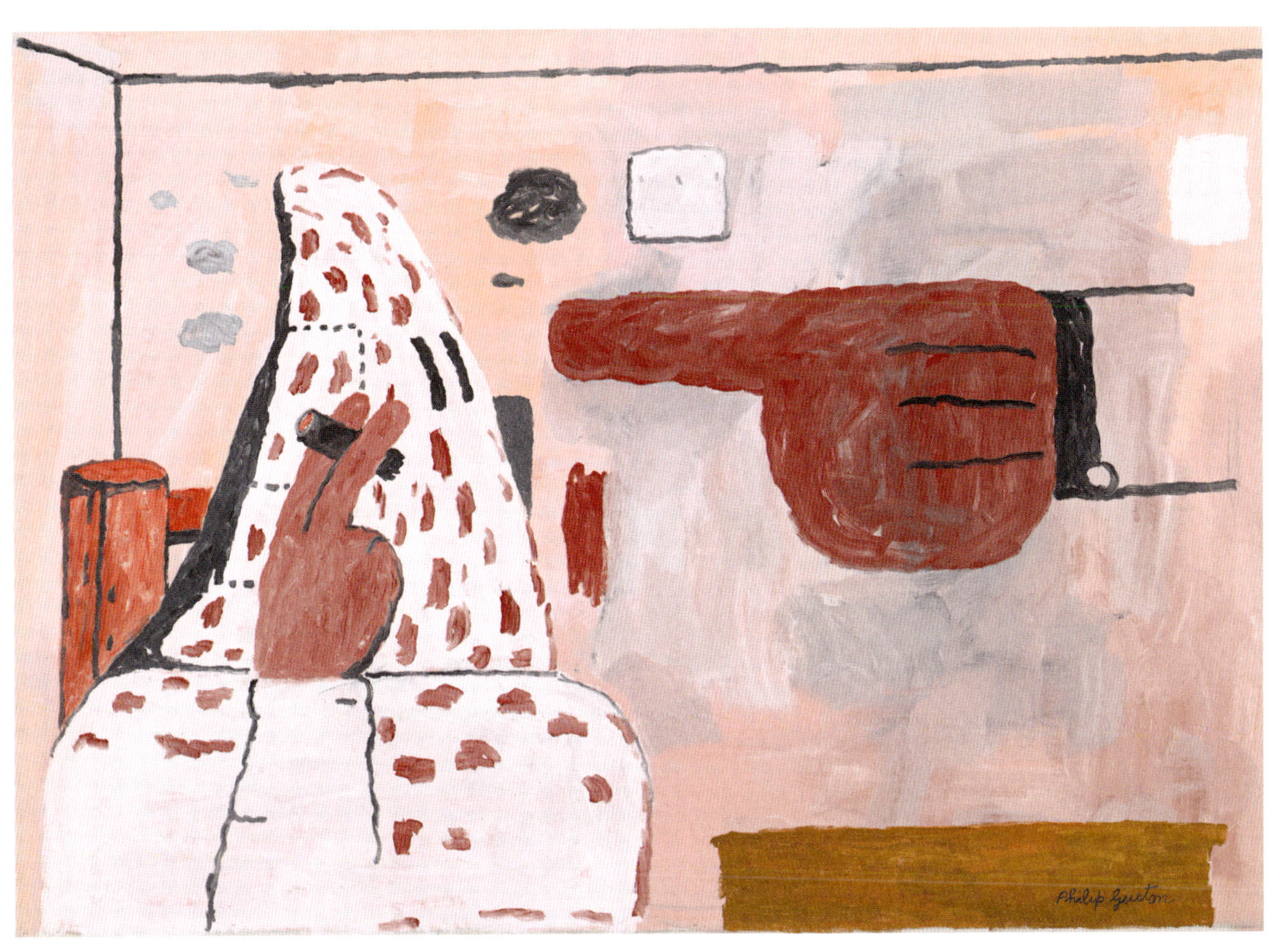

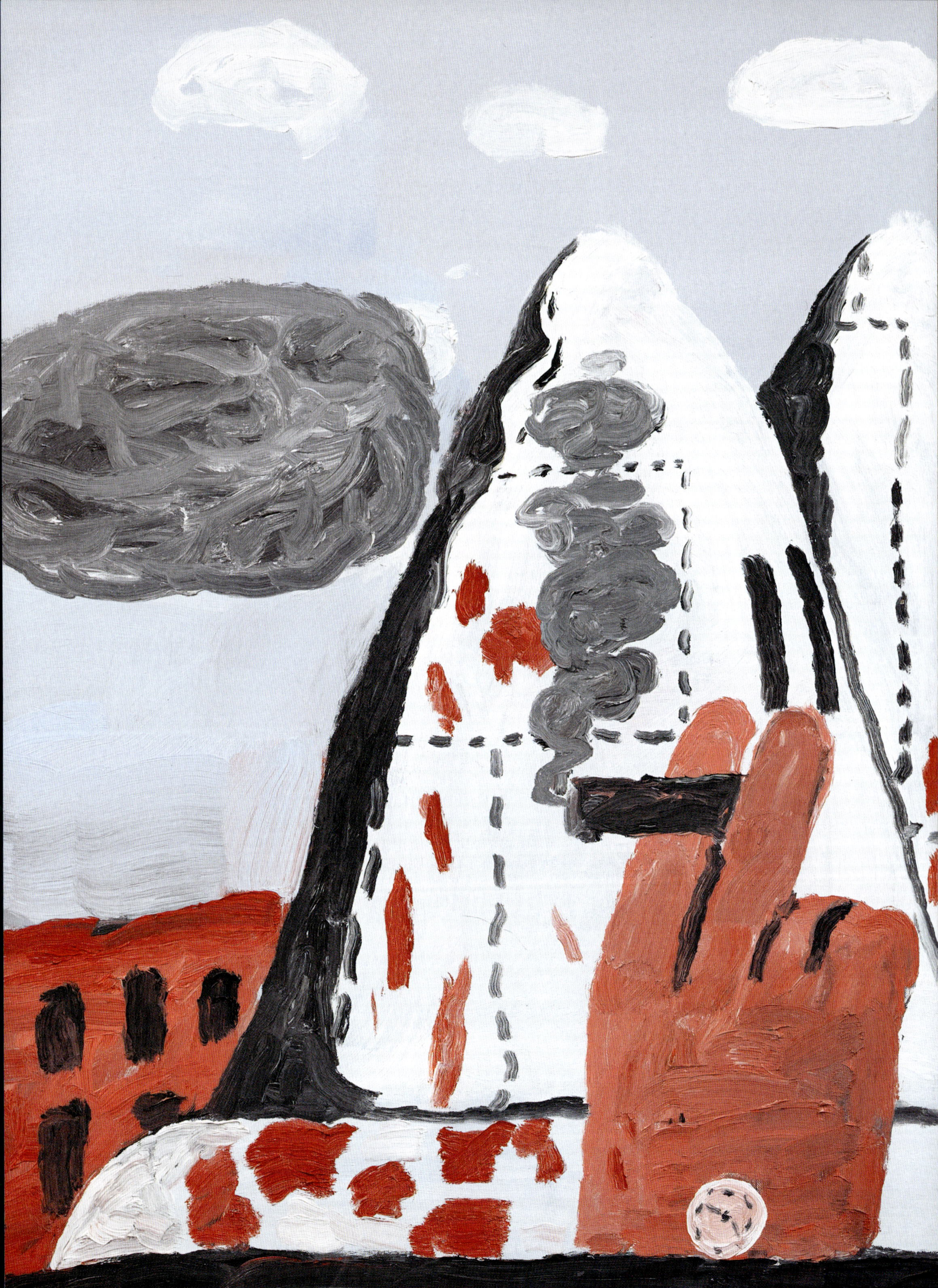

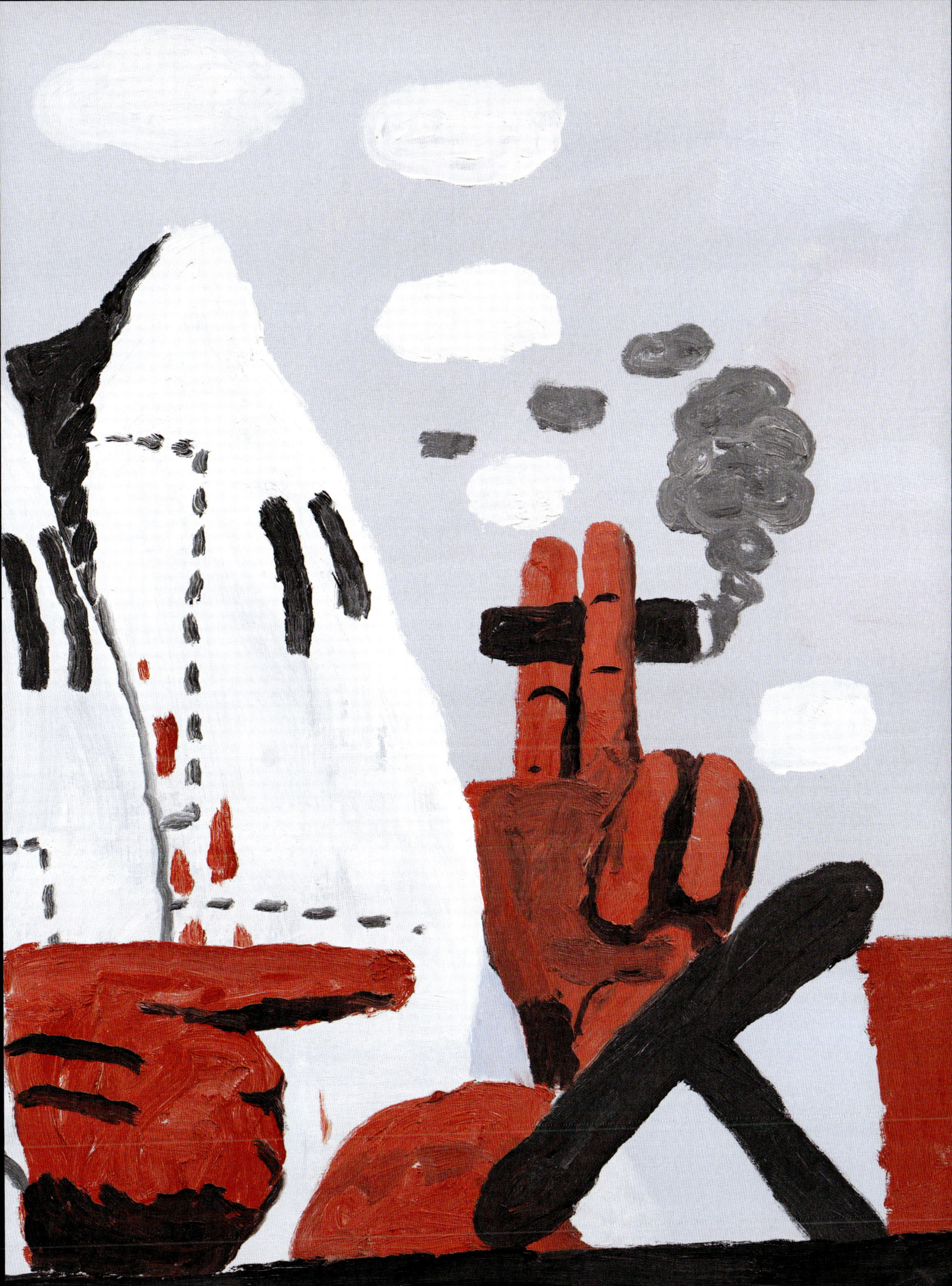

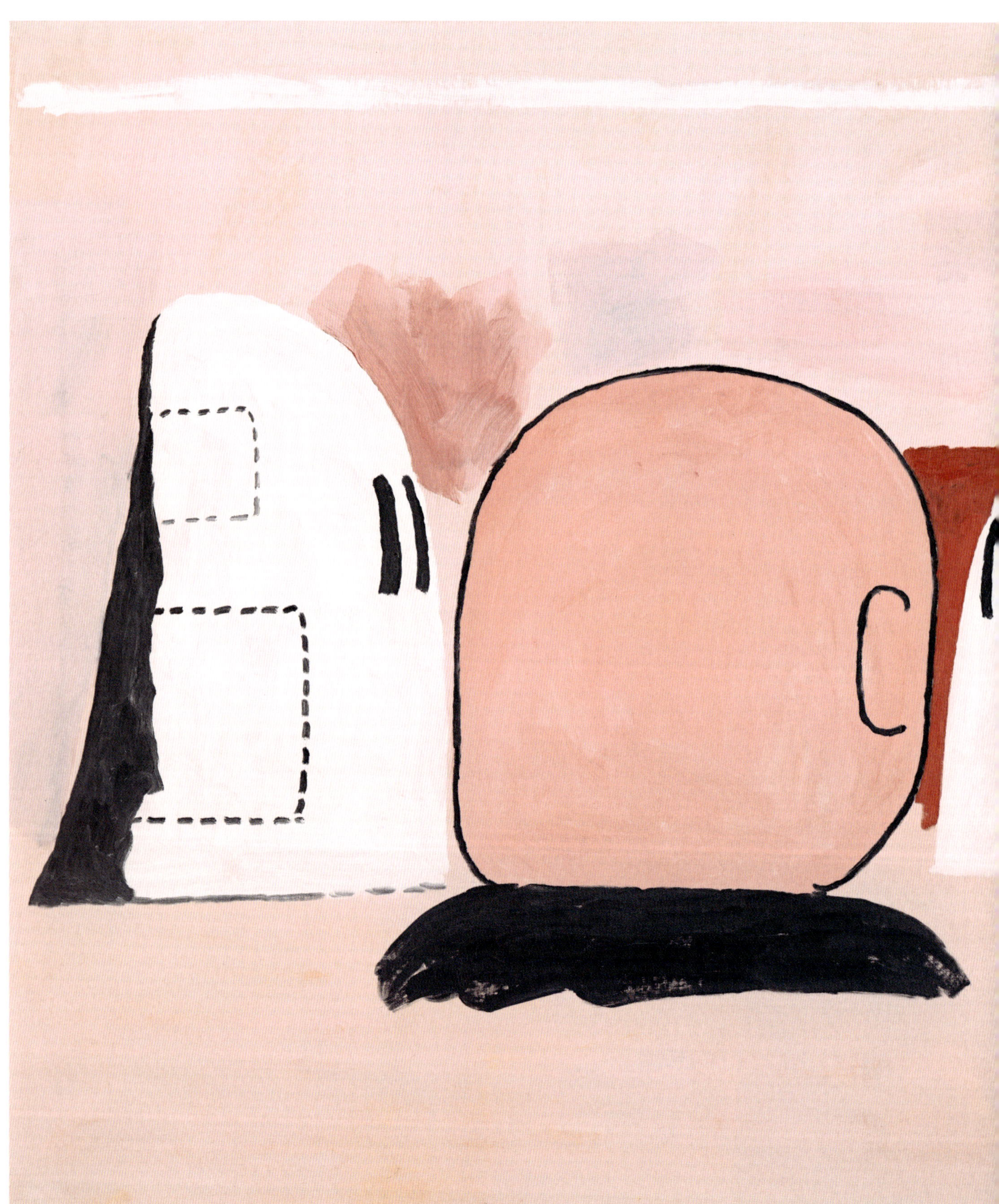

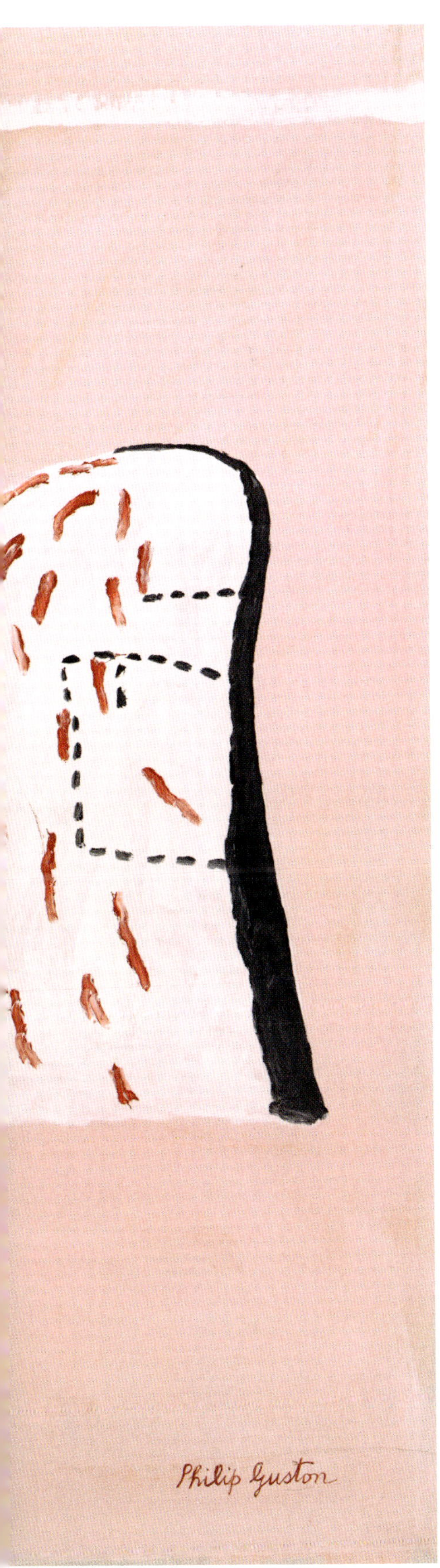

Philip Guston
Sheriff, 1970
Oil on canvas, 66 × 80 in.
(167.6 × 203.2 cm)
Private collection

"There's something about this sheriff. His head is so meaty and vulnerable. But there's also a chimera. All three of those heads make a new creature, where the hoods become butterfly wings. For me, this picture doesn't rest completely on something nefarious happening between the Klansmen and cops, [in part because of] the softness of the color palette and the whimsy of Guston's line. There's the language of Krazy Kat in those eyes, and Charlie Brown, of course. Those cartoons revolve around pathetic characters, so there's something within the linework itself that culturally we understand as a kind of failure. If these paintings were just about the nightmare, we wouldn't still be looking at them. In *Sheriff,* they might have just killed somebody, or they're planning to kill somebody, but it's also the butterfly. There's an exit. There's a way out."

—Trenton Doyle Hancock, August 2023

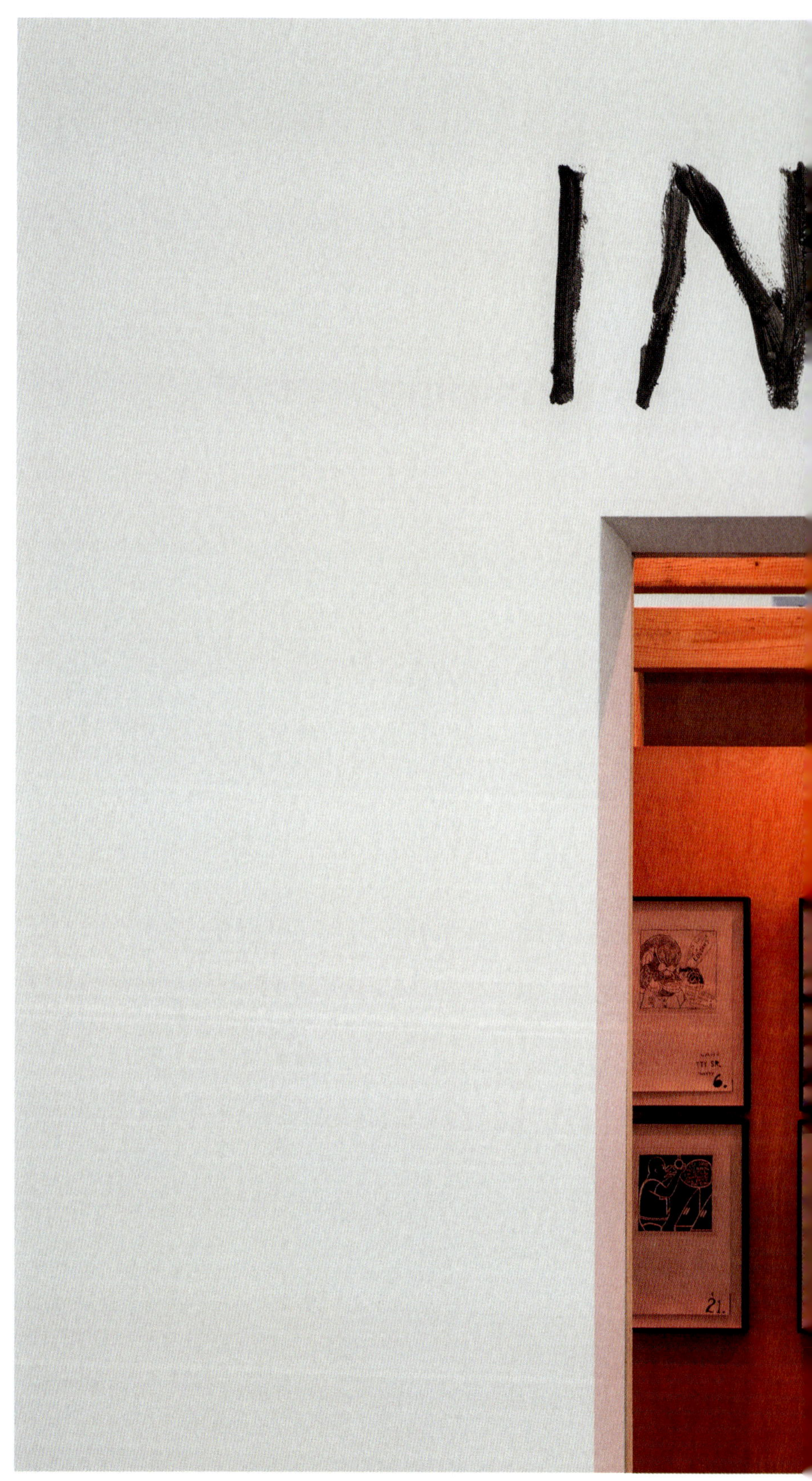

Installation view of Trenton Doyle
Hancock's *Epidemic! Presents: Step and
Screw!*, 2014, at the Menil Collection,
Houston, 2019

PAGES 68–97
Trenton Doyle Hancock
Epidemic! Presents: Step and Screw!, 2014
Ink and acrylic on paper and mat board
with excised lettering and gesso, 30 sheets,
each 19 × 12 in. (48.3 × 30.5 cm)
Menil Collection, Houston

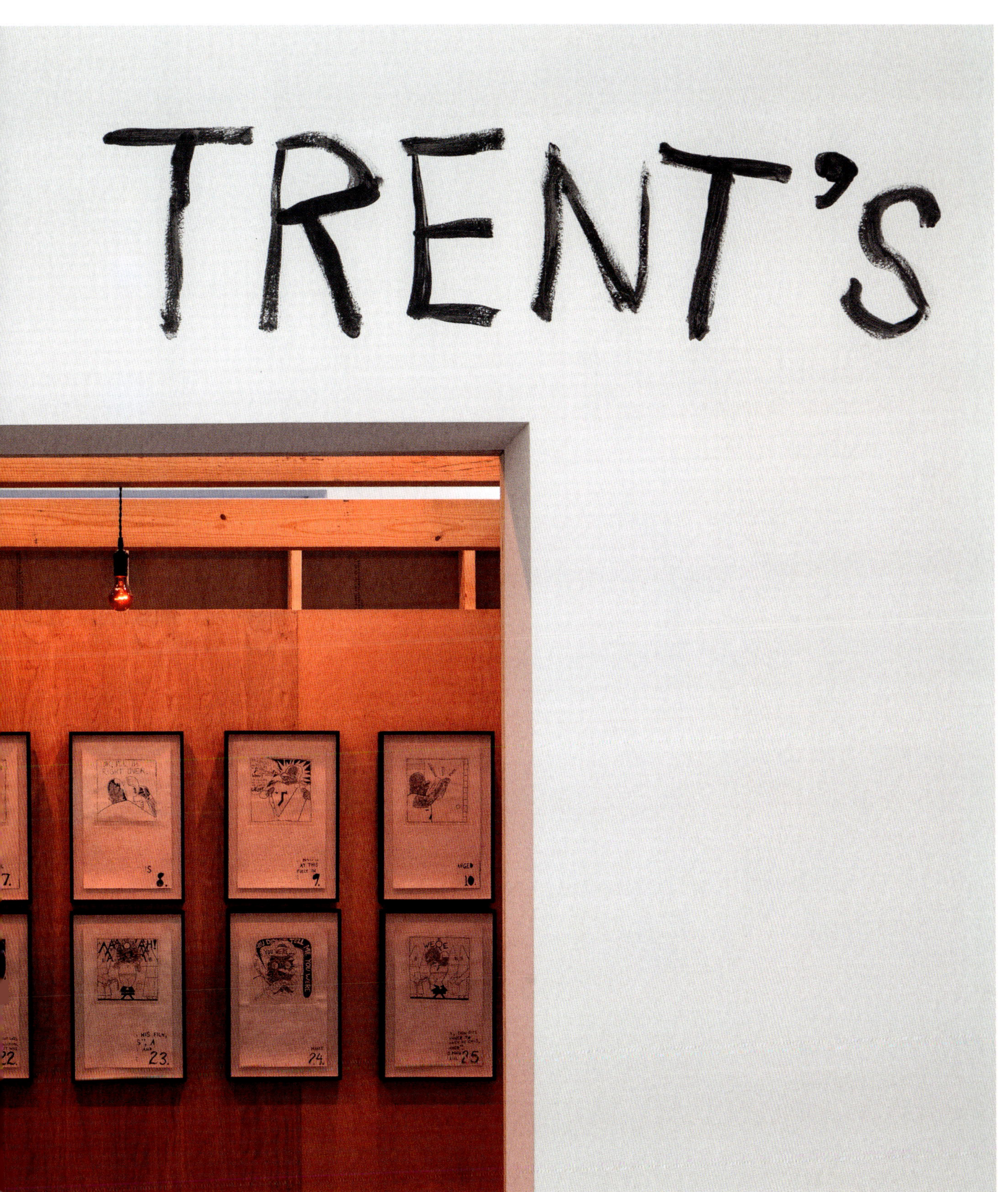

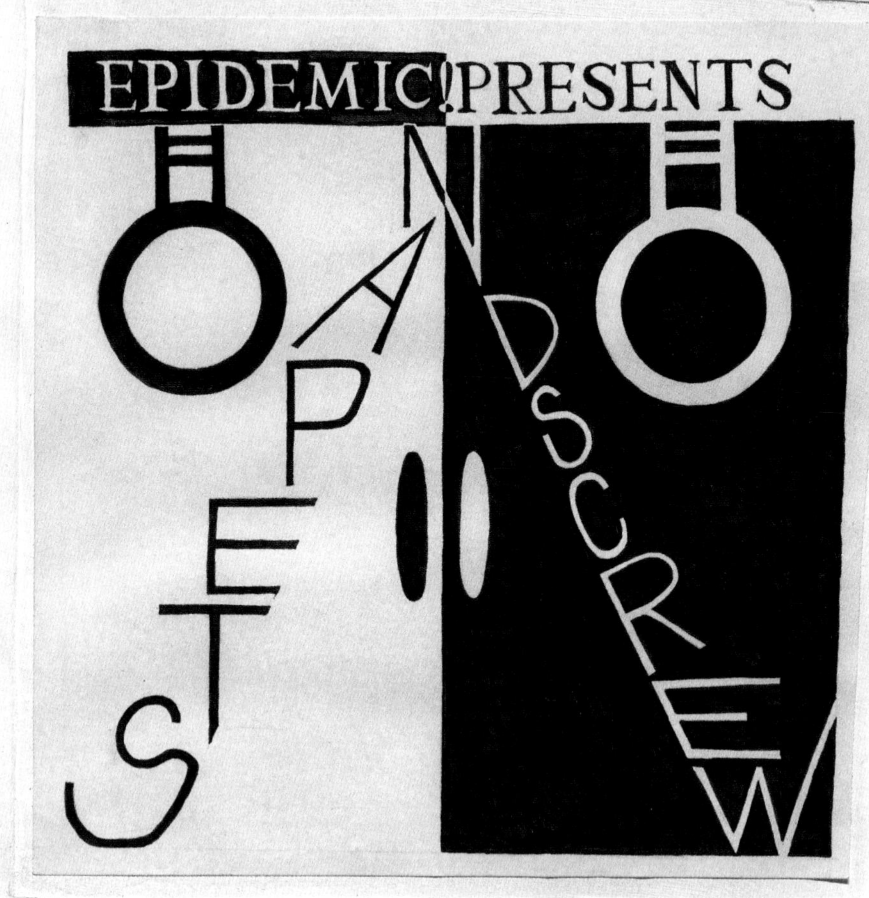

1878
AN EPIDEMIC OF YELLOW
FEVER CLAIMS THE PARENTS
AND SIBLING OF EX-SLAVE AND
ABOLITIONIST, IDA B. WELLS

1.

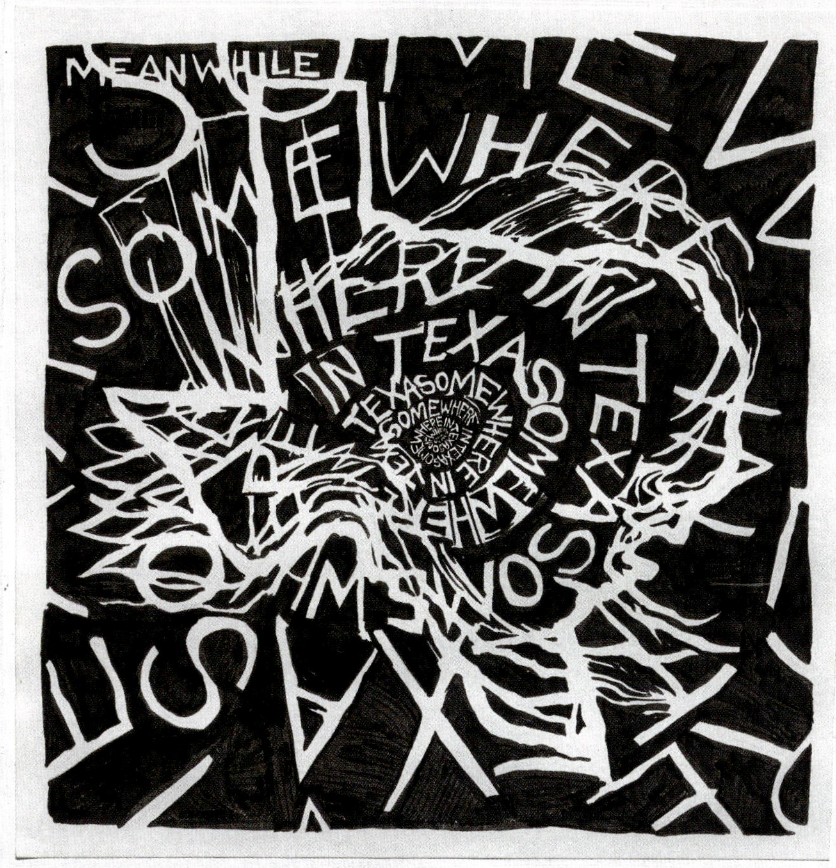

1883

FANNIE BUTLER, THE AUNT OF
IDA B. WELLS CONVINCES HER
TO MOVE TO MEMPHIS, TENNESSEE
TO PURSUE A TEACHING JOB

2.

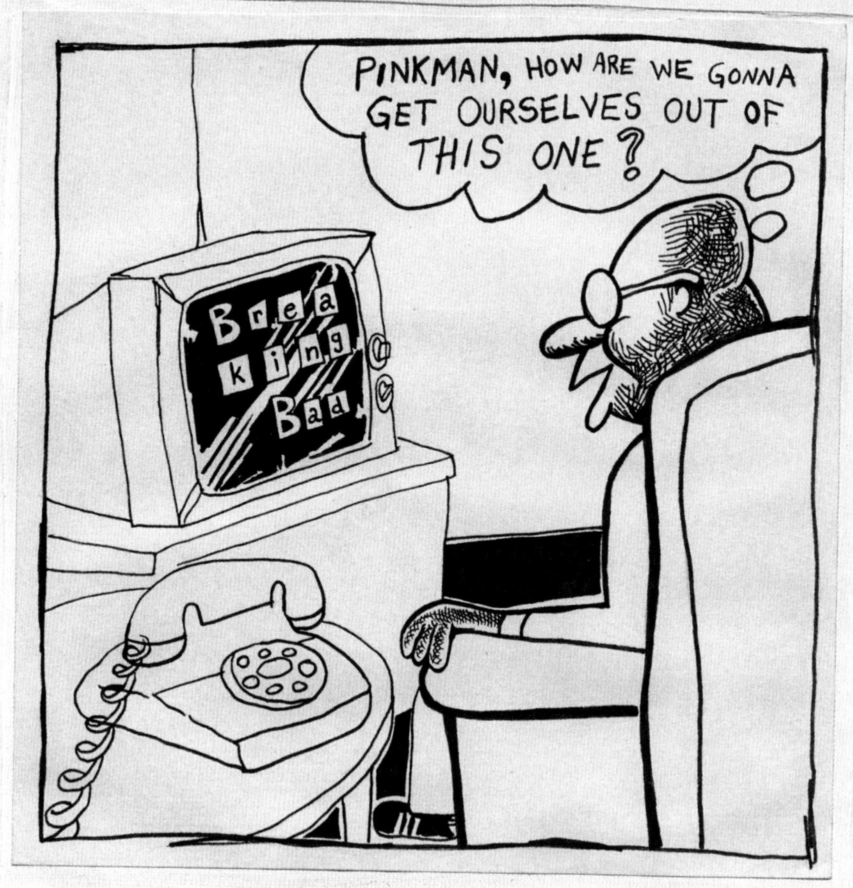

MARCH 1892

THE LYNCHING OF 3 INNOCENT BLACK MEN IN MEMPHIS PROMPTS IDA B. WELLS TO LAUNCH A CAMPAIGN AGAINST SUCH HATE CRIMES. WELLS ALSO PUBLISHES FINDINGS THAT CONSENSUAL RELATIONS BETWEEN BLACK MEN AND WHITE WOMEN WERE CONTINUALLY USED AS A REASON TO LYNCH BLACK MEN.

3.

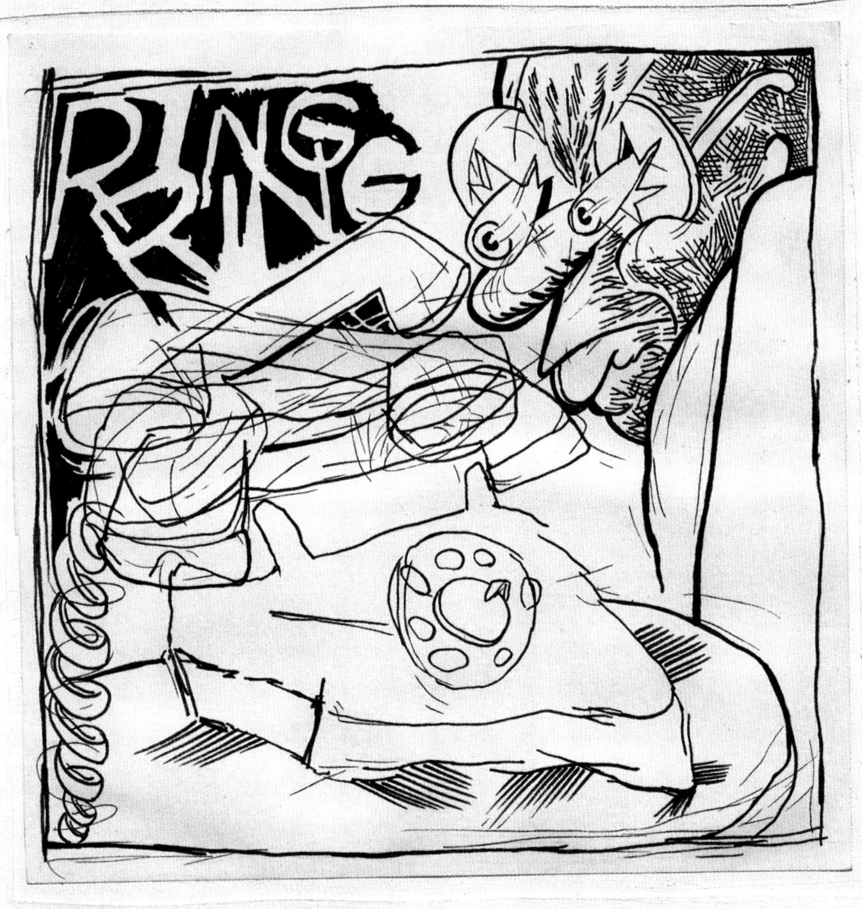

FEBRUARY 1, 1893
EX-SLAVE, HENRY SMITH IS
MUTILATED AND BURNED AT THE
STAKE BY THE KU KLUX KLAN.
THIS TOOK PLACE AT THE
PARIS, TEXAS FAIRGROUNDS WITH
AN AUDIENCE OF 10,000
ONLOOKERS

4.

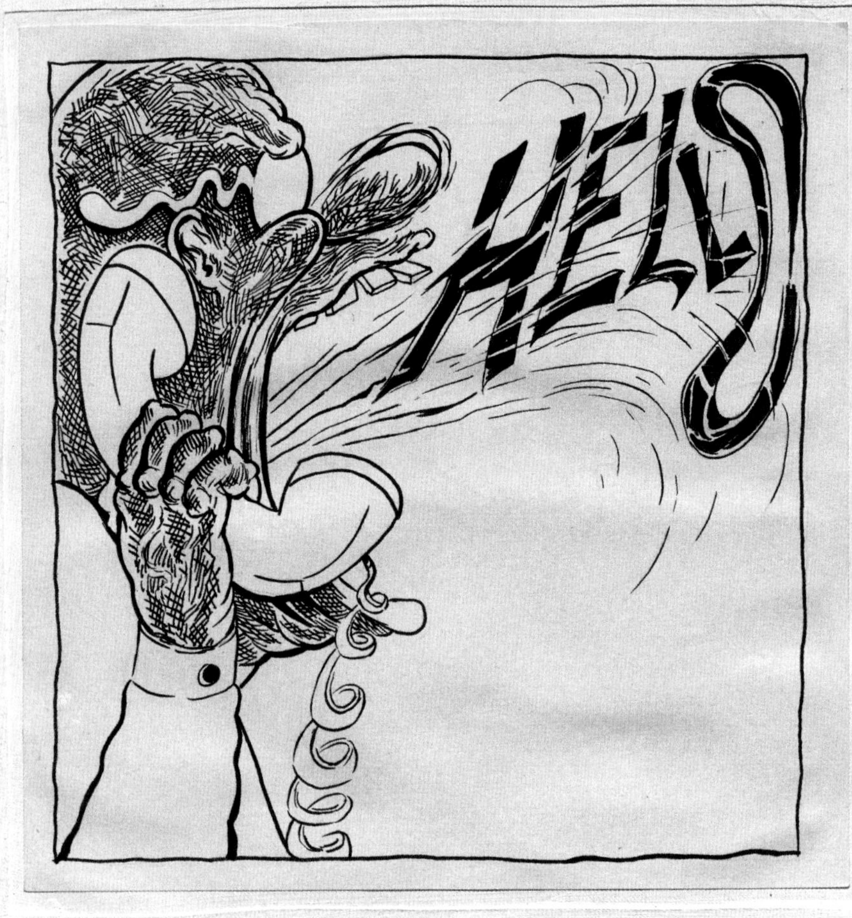

DECEMBER 13, 1895

A BOY NAMED HENRY ADLER BERLINER IS BORN IN WASHINGTON D.C. TO CORA ADLER AND INVENTOR EMILE BERLINER. THE CONSCIOUSNESS OF THE BEING KNOWN AS TORPEDOBOY IS TRANSFERRED TO THE NEWBORN.

5.

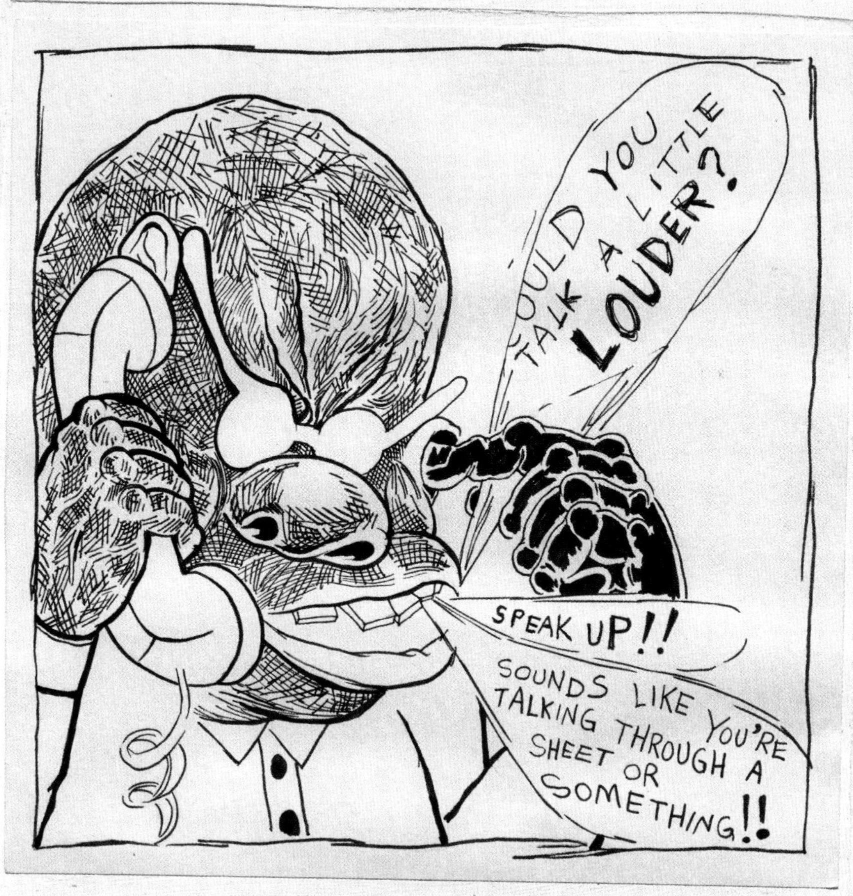

NOVEMBER 29, 1905

FANNIE MAE TWITTY IS BORN IN PARIS, TEXAS TO JOHNNY TWITTY SR. AND MAGNOLIA CARTER TWITTY

6.

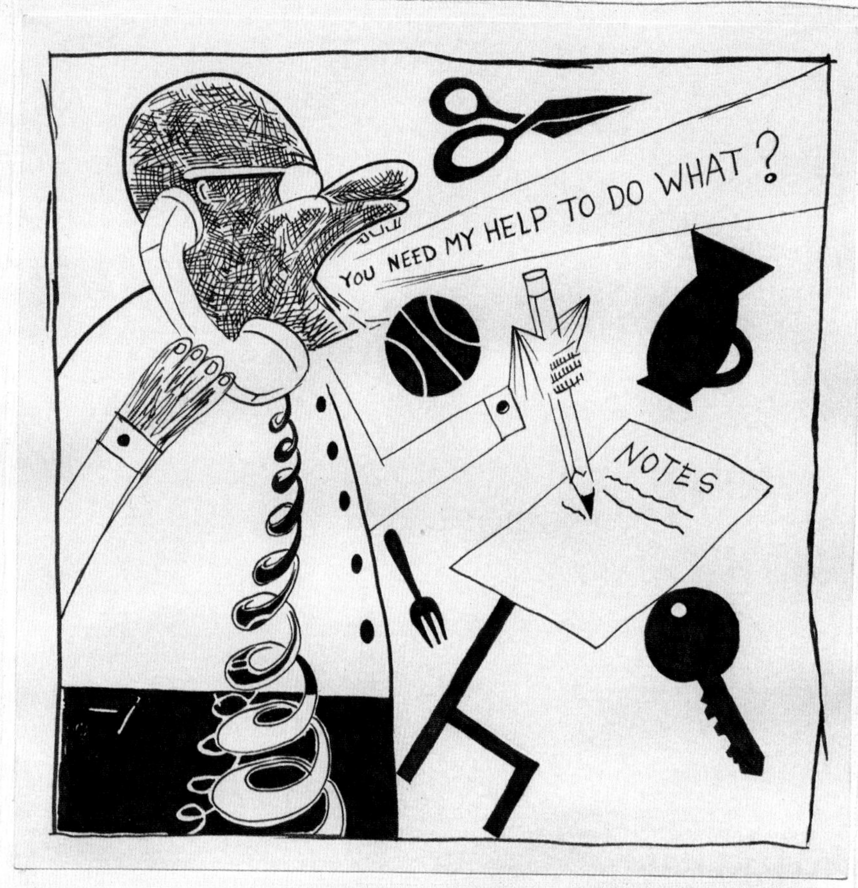

JUNE 27, 1913

A BOY NAMED

PHILIP GOLDSTEIN

IS BORN IN MONTREAL

CANADA TO LOUIS AND

RACHEL GOLDSTEIN

7.

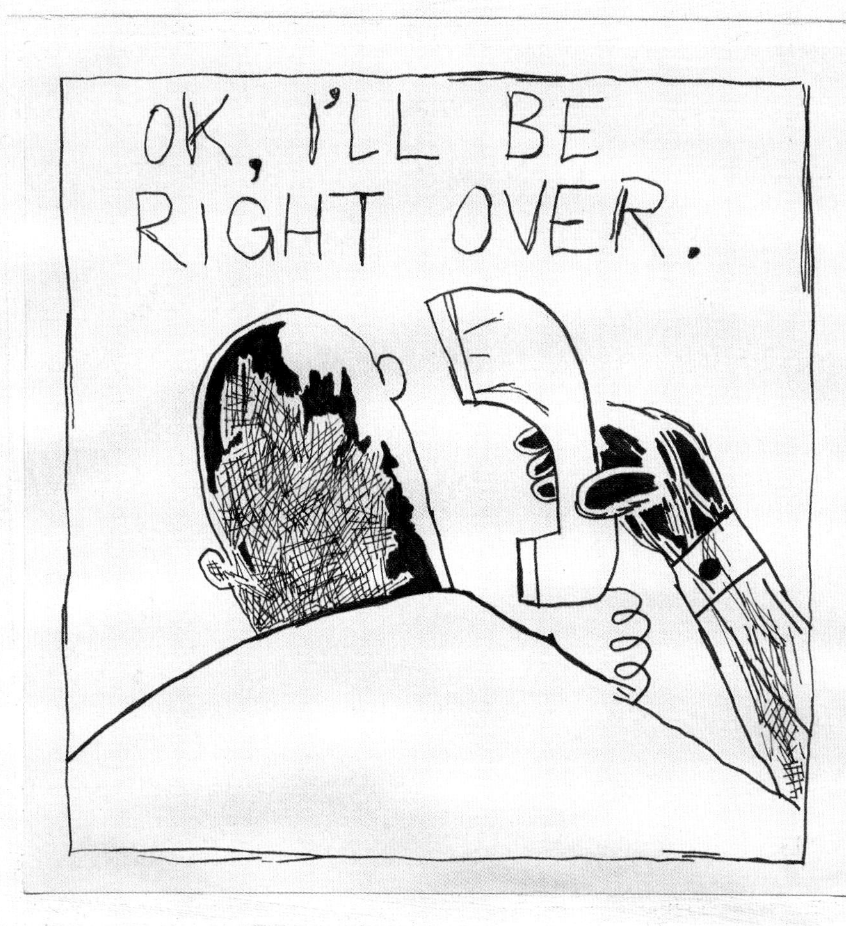

MARCH 21, 1916

PARIS, TEXAS IS

DESTROYED BY

A MYSTERIOUS

FIRE

8.

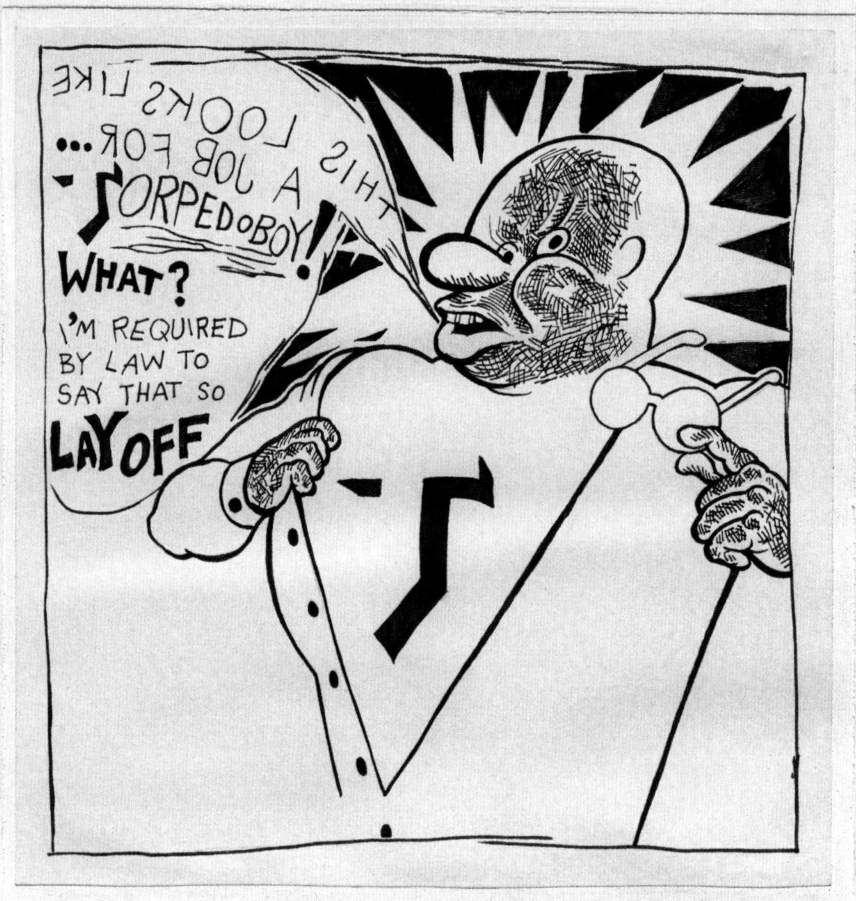

JUNE 16, 1922

HENRY ADLER BERLINER DEBUTED HIS HELICOPTER PROTOTYPE TO THE U.S. NAVY'S BUREAU OF AERONAUTICS. AT THIS TIME, BERLINER BECAME FULLY IN TOUGH WITH HIS POWERS AS TORPEDOBOY

9.

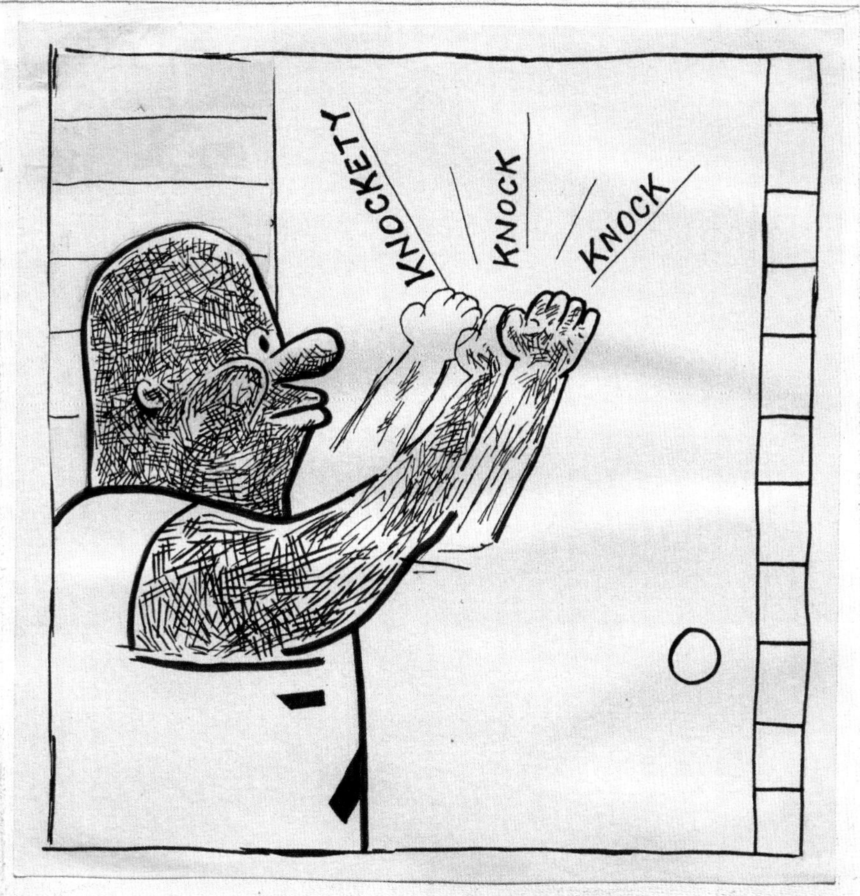

1723

10 YEAR OLD PHILIP GOLDSTEIN DISCOVERS THAT HIS FATHER HAD HANGED HIMSELF IN THE FAMILY SHED.

10.

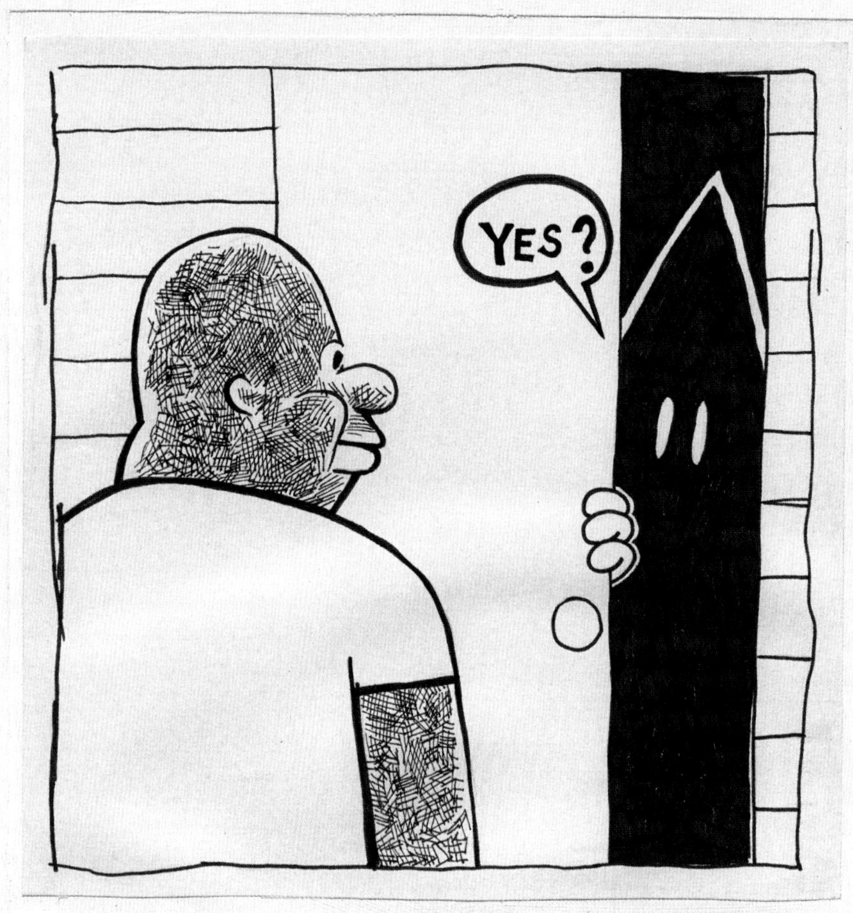

1735

PHILIP GOLDSTEIN
CHANGES HIS NAME TO
PHILIP GUSTON

11.

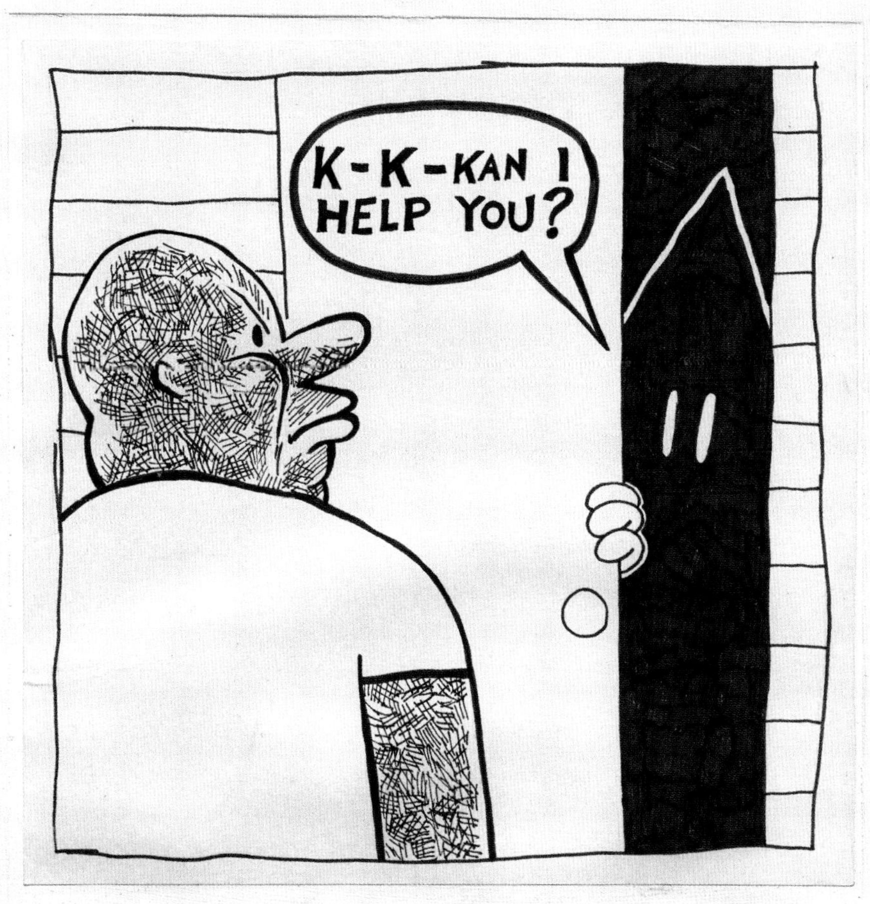

FEBRUARY 12, 1949

A BOY NAMED BRUCE
GENE HANCOCK IS BORN
IN OKLAHOMA CITY,
OKLAHOMA, TO
IDA JEAN WELLS

12.

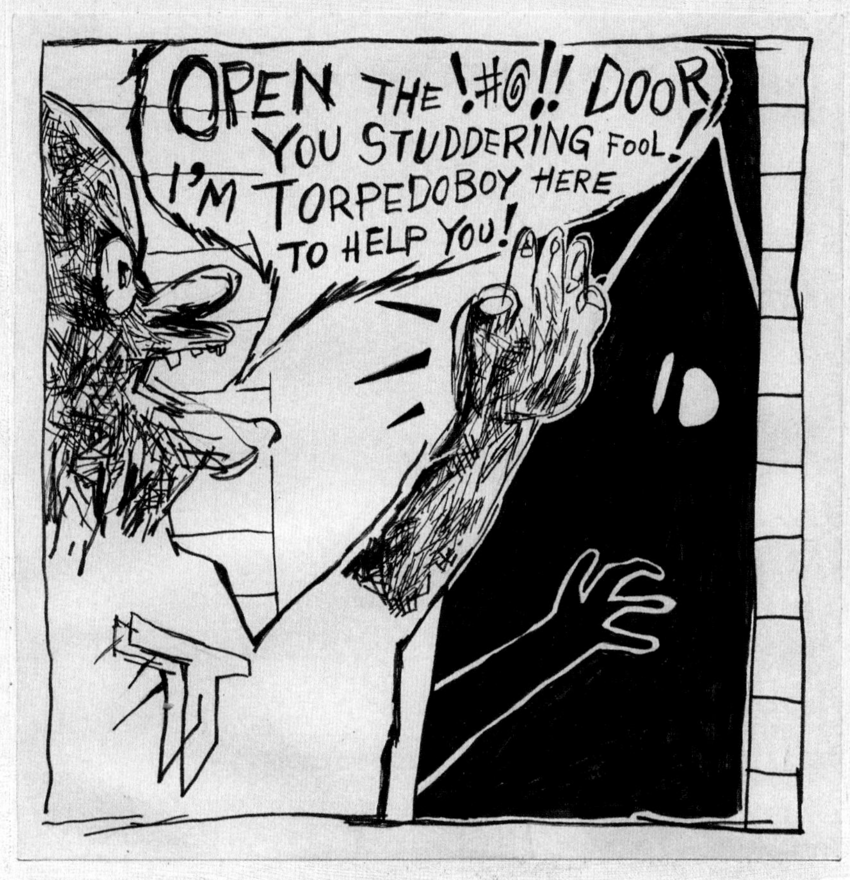

AUGUST 21, 1947
A GIRL NAMED
CAROLYN JOYCE TWITTY
IS BORN IN PARIS, TEXAS
TO SCHOOL TEACHER,
ALMA TWITTY AND
HOMER TWITTY

13.

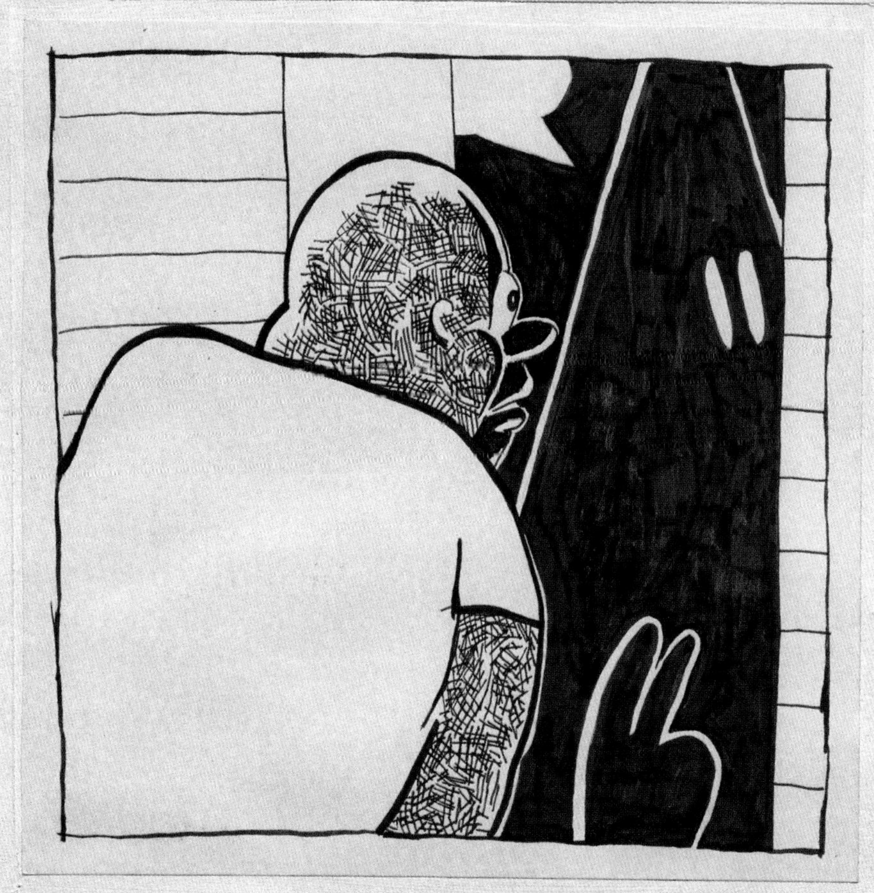

MAY 1, 1970

HENRY ADLER BERLINER DIES,
THE BEING KNOWN AS
TORPEDOBOY LEAVES BERLINER'S
BODY AND HIBERNATES FOR EXACTLY 4
YEARS UNTIL HE TRANSFERS TO
A NEW HOST

14.

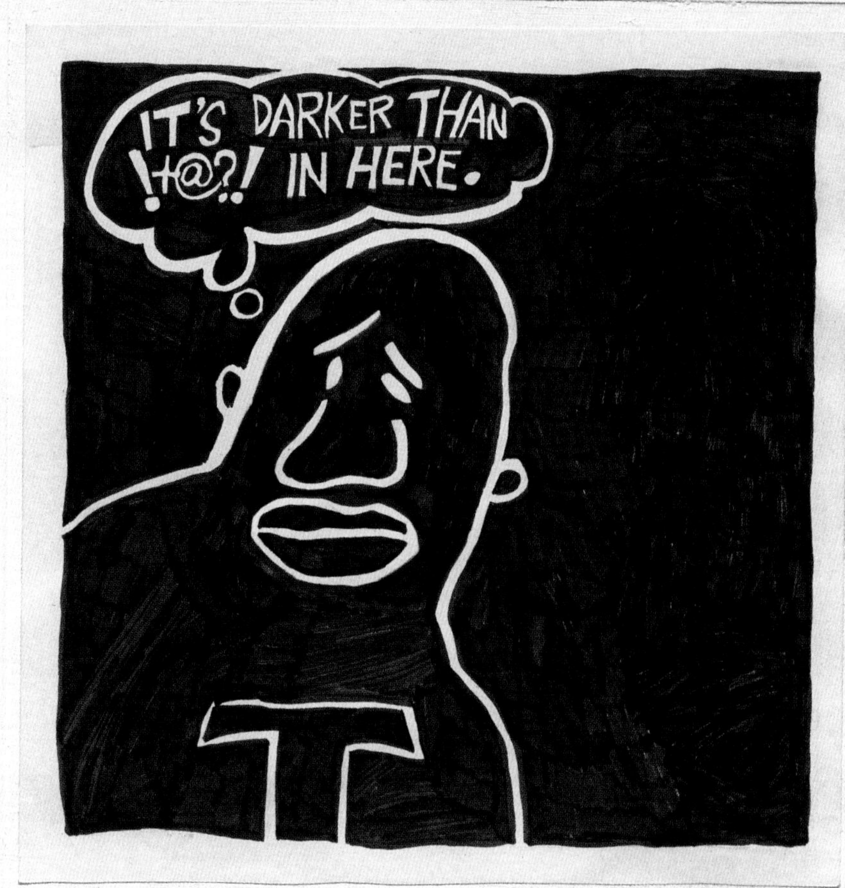

OCTOBER 17, 1970
PHILIP GUSTON EXHIBITS
HIS KLANSMEN PAINTINGS
FOR THE FIRST TIME AT
MARLBOROUGH GALLERY
IN NEW YORK CITY

15.

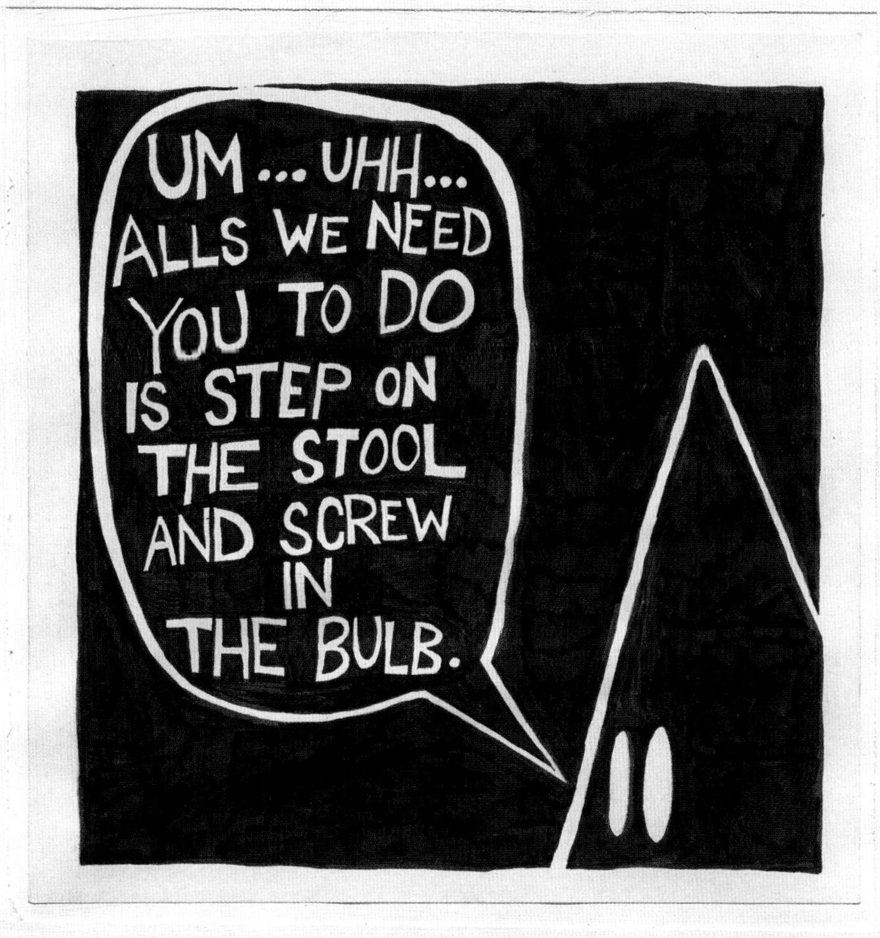

MAY 1, 1974

A BOY NAMED TRENTON DOYLE HANCOCK IS BORN IN OKLAHOMA CITY, OKLAHOMA TO SCHOOLTEACHER CAROLYN JOYCE TWITTY HANCOCK AND BRUCE GENE HANCOCK

16.

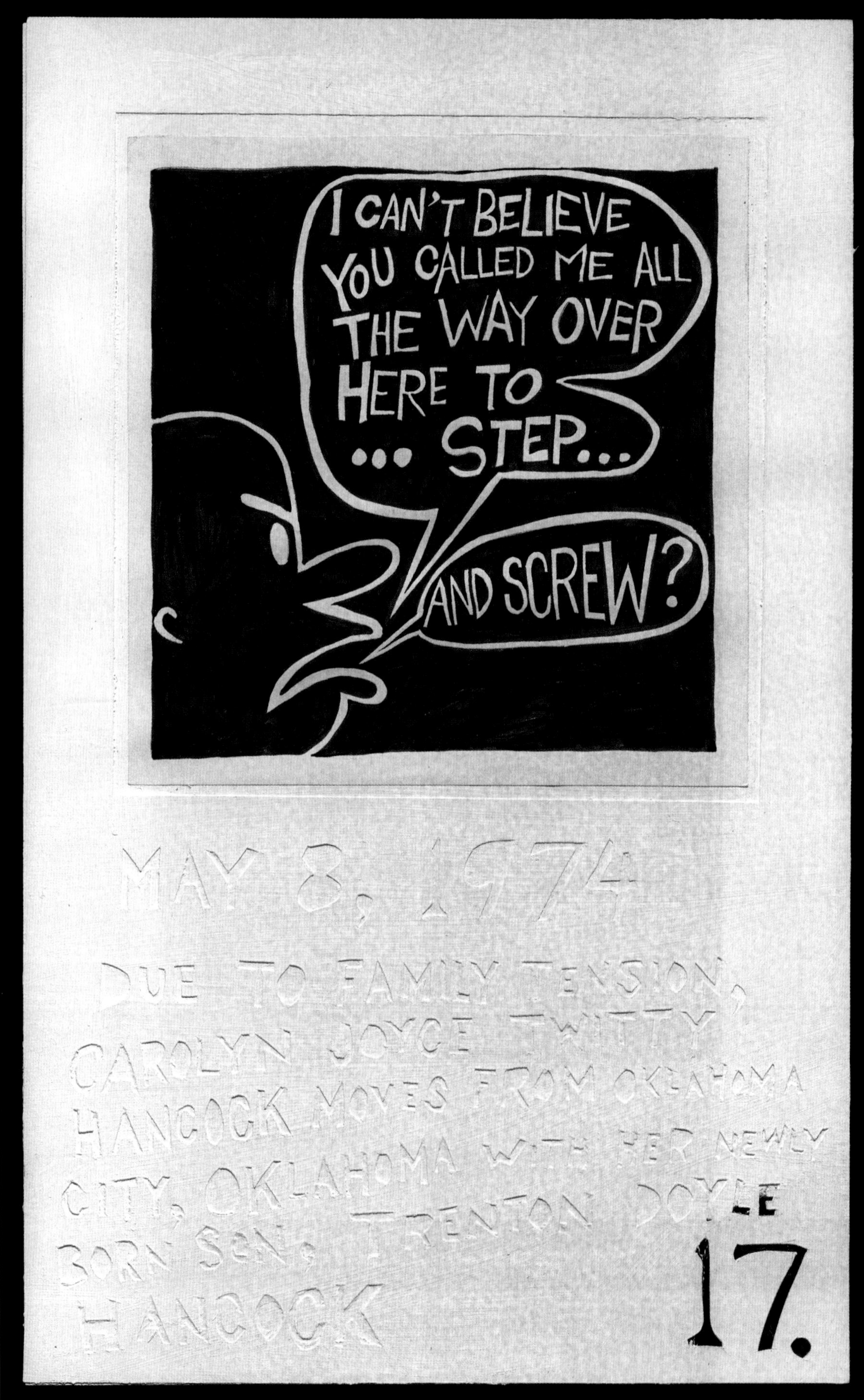

MAY 8, 1974

DUE TO FAMILY TENSION, CAROLYN JOYCE TWITTY HANCOCK MOVES FROM OKLAHOMA CITY, OKLAHOMA WITH HER NEWLY BORN SON, TRENTON DOYLE HANCOCK

17.

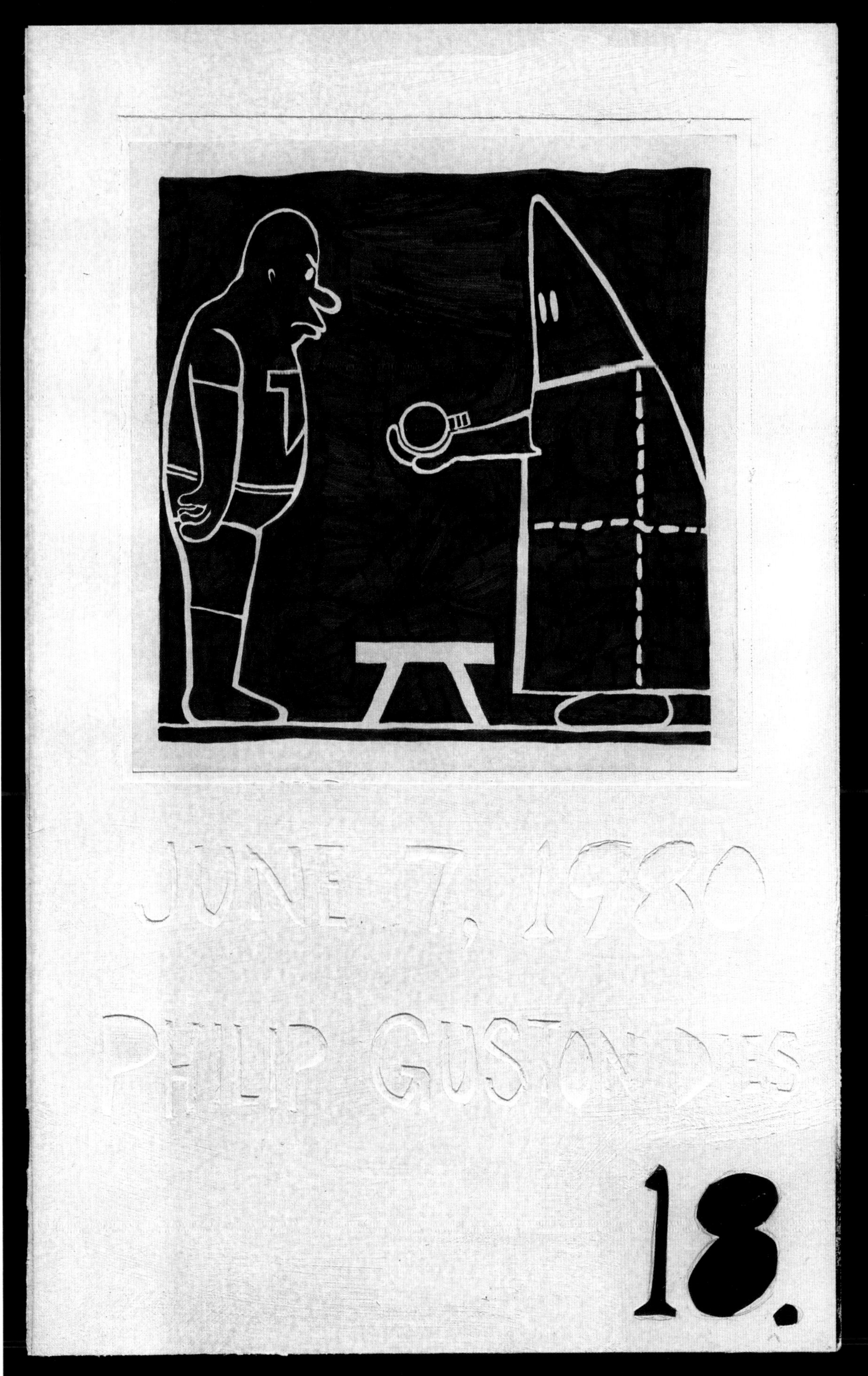

JUNE 7, 1980
PHILIP GUSTON DIES
18.

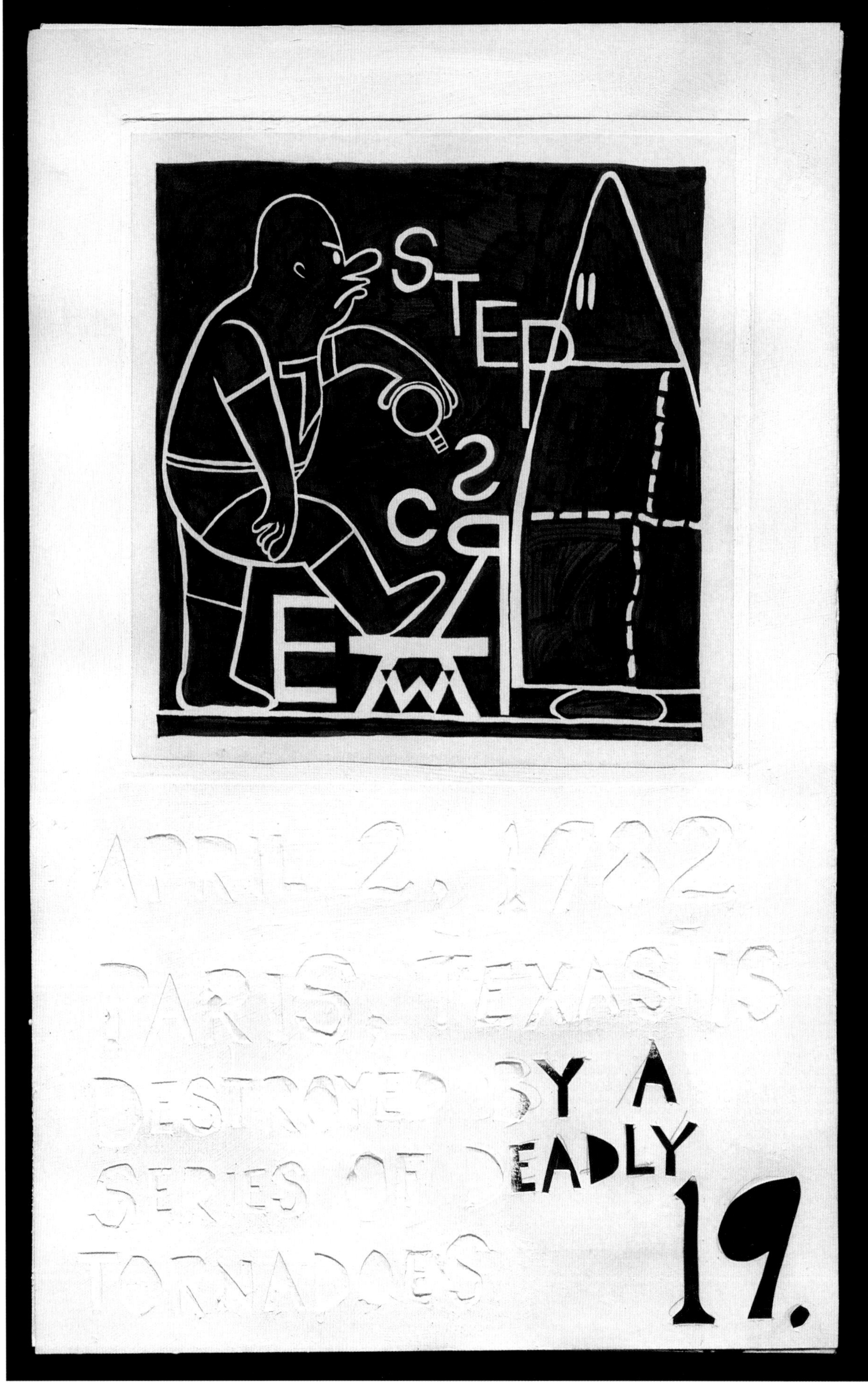

APRIL 2, 1982
PARIS, TEXAS IS
DESTROYED BY A
SERIES OF DEADLY
TORNADOES
19.

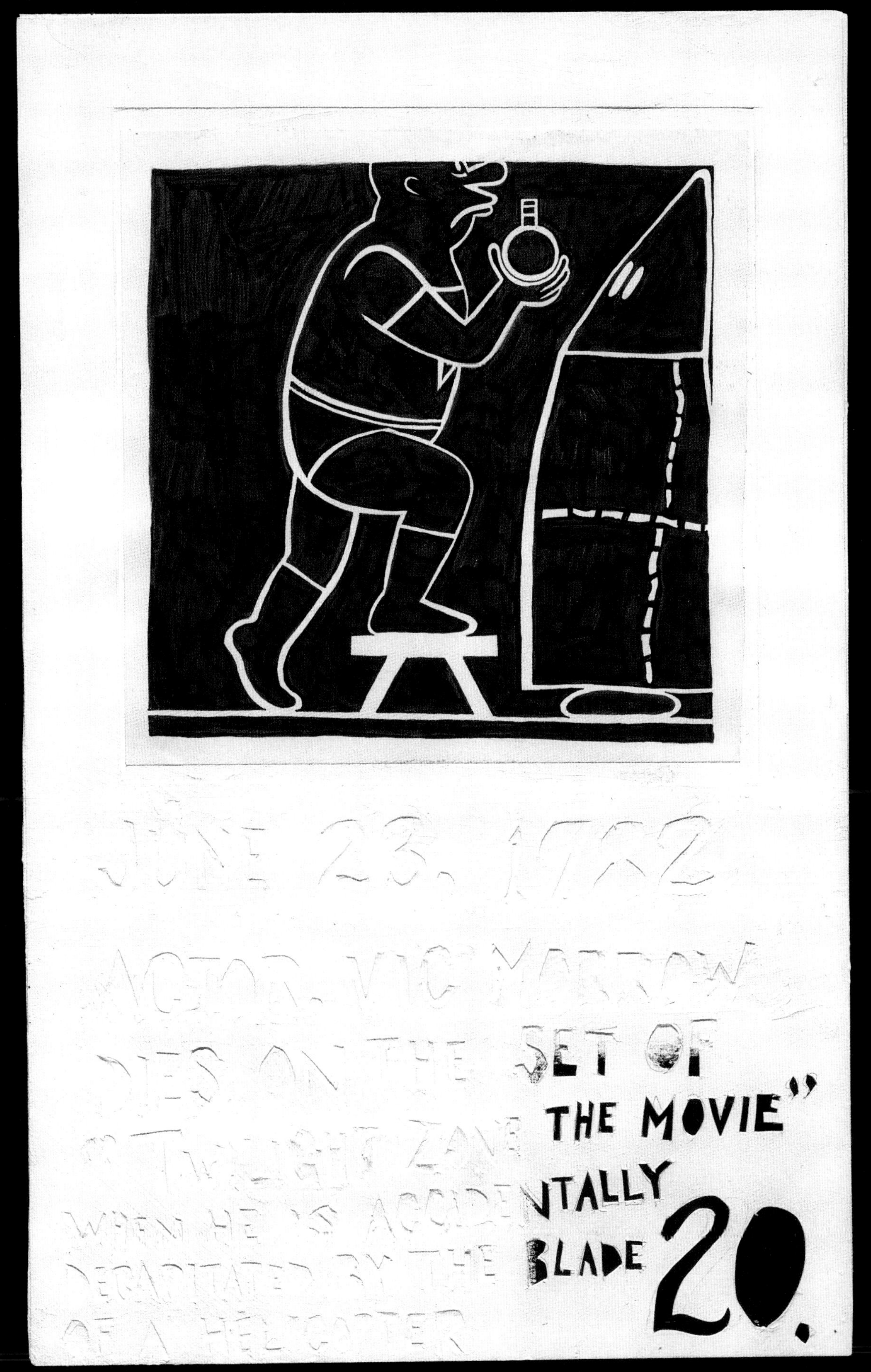

JUNE 23, 1982
ACTOR VIC MORROW
DIES ON THE SET OF
"TWILIGHT ZONE THE MOVIE"
WHEN HE IS ACCIDENTALLY
DECAPITATED BY THE BLADE
OF A HELICOPTER
20.

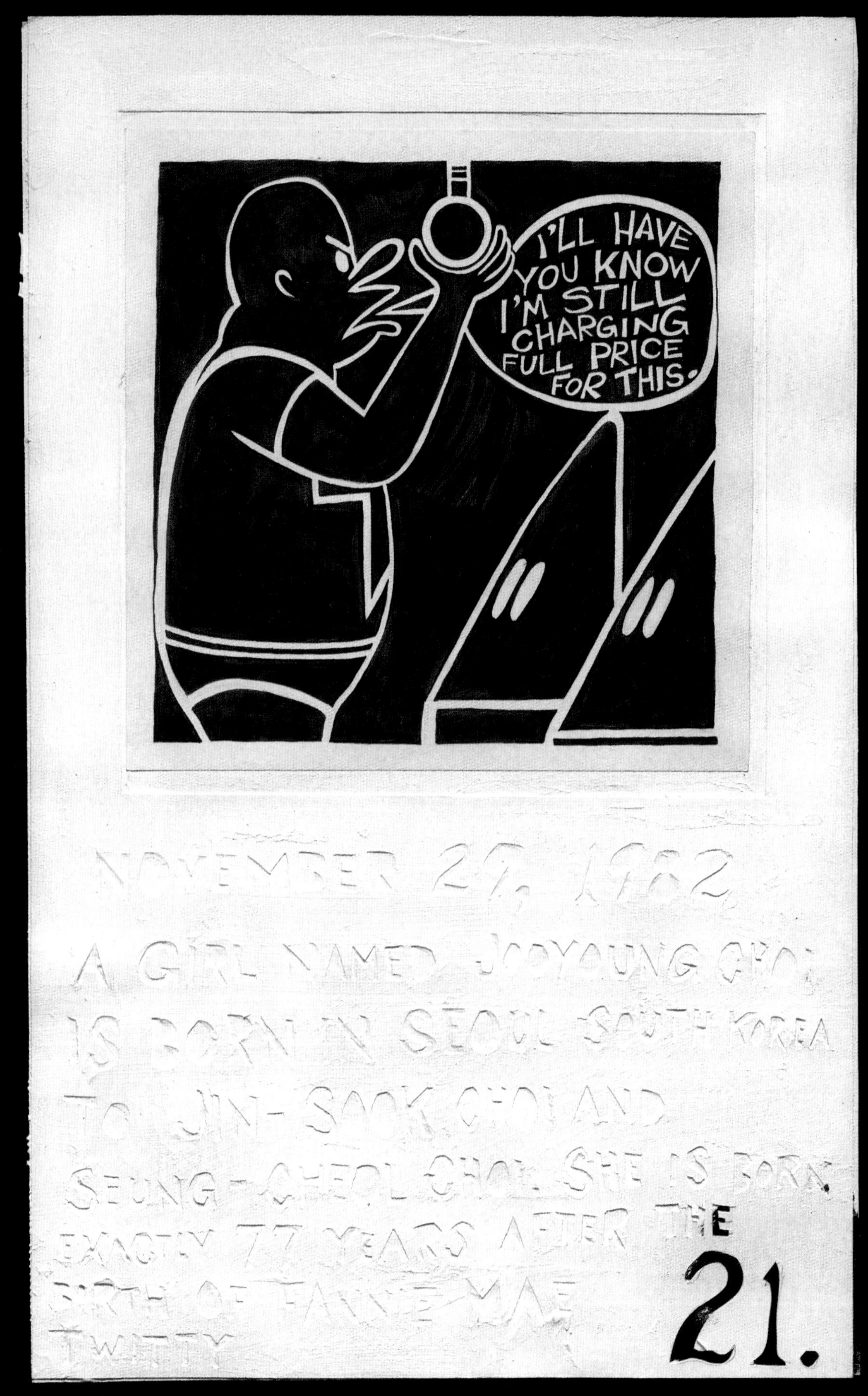

NOVEMBER 29, 1962
A GIRL NAMED JOOYOUNG CHOI
IS BORN IN SEOUL SOUTH KOREA
TO JIN-SOOK CHOI AND
SEUNG-CHEOL CHOI. SHE IS BORN
EXACTLY 77 YEARS AFTER THE
BIRTH OF FANNIE MAE
TWENTY

THE
21.

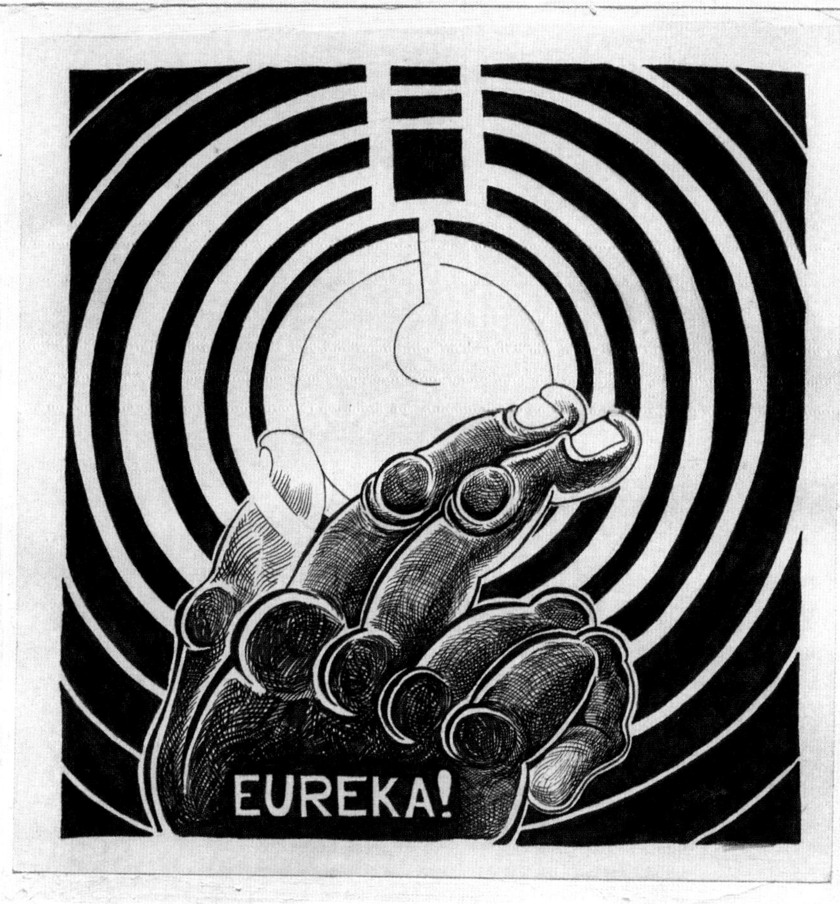

FALL 1984

10 YEAR OLD TRENTON DOYLE HANCOCK DISCOVERS HIS ALTER EGO TO BE TORPEDOBOY WHO MANIFESTS IN THE BAY'S WRITINGS AND DRAWINGS. HE USES THE CHARACTER TO COPE WITH THE RECENT LOSS OF HIS AUNT FANNIE MAE TWITTY ROLLERSON, WHO TAUGHT HIM HOW TO DRAW. IT WAS HIS FIRST PERSONAL EXPERIENCE WITH DEATH. HANCOCK KNEW HER AS AUNT FAN FAN. 22.

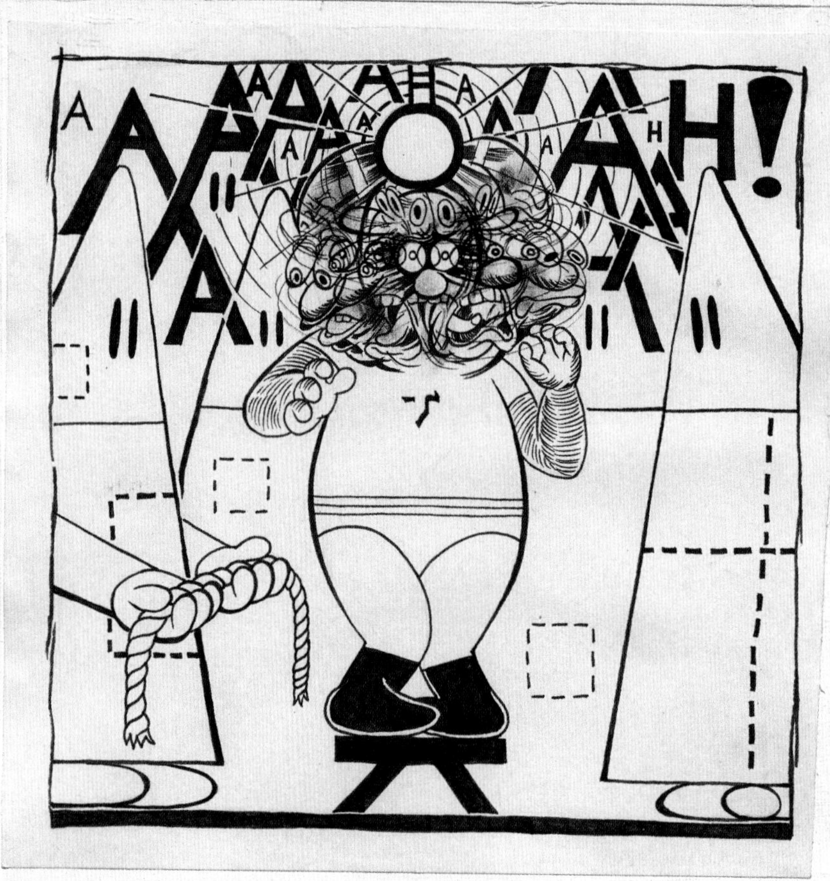

NOVEMBER 2, 1984.
GERMAN DIRECTOR, WIM
WENDERS OPENS HIS FILM,
"PARIS, TEXAS", A
STORY ABOUT A LASS AND
BURNING DESIRE.

23.

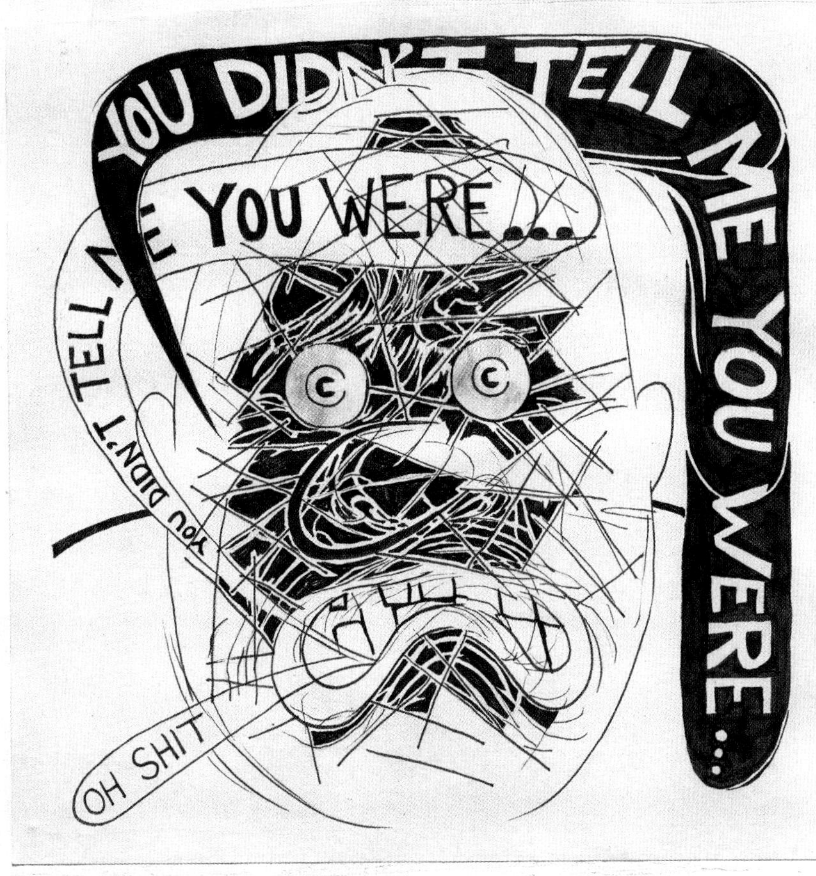

APRIL 30, 1972

ON THE SECOND DAY OF THE LA
RIOTS AND SEVERAL HOURS BEFORE
HIS 19TH BIRTHDAY TRENTON
DOYLE HANCOCK'S MOTHER FINDS
HIS PORNOGRAPHIC BOOKS UNDER A
STACK OF TOWELS. HIS MOTHER
A NOTE OF CONCERN THAT ALL OF
THE WOMEN IN THE BOOKS ARE
CAUCASIAN

MAKES

24.

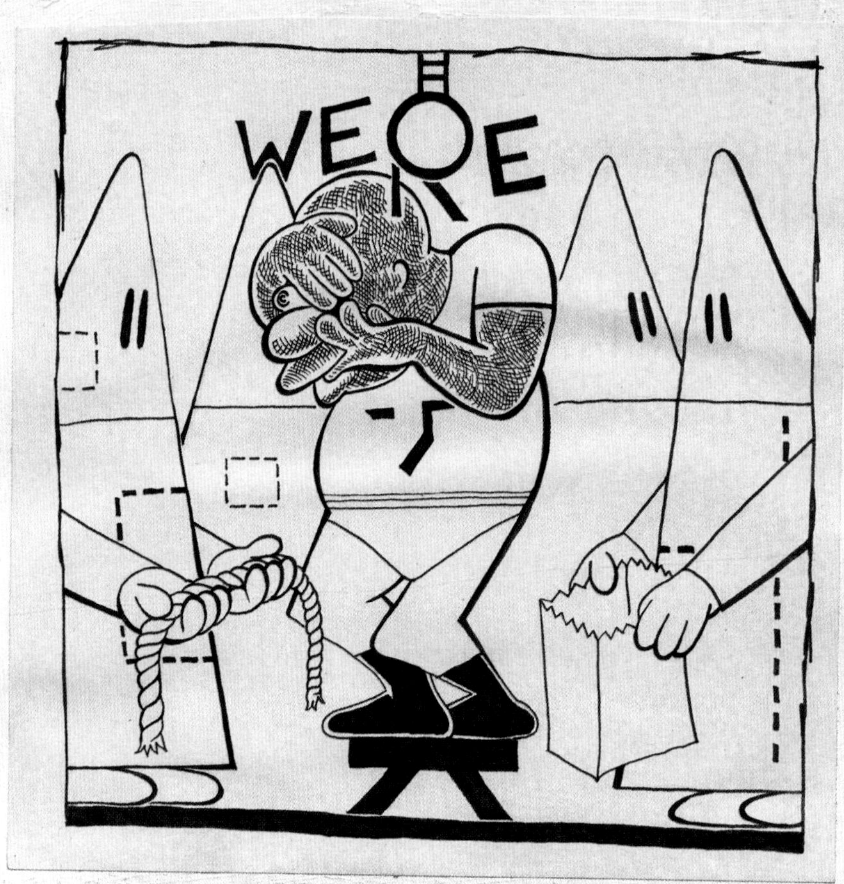

SPRING 1994

TRENTON DOYLE HANCOCK
COVERS HIMSELF IN A SHEET, TIES A
NOOSE AROUND HIS NECK, THEN SITS
IN A CHAIR HOLDING A HAMMER TO
CREATE A SURREAL PHOTO WHICH HE CALLS,
"PROPERTIES OF THE HAMMER".
HANCOCK FEELS THAT THIS PHOTO
HOUSED WITHIN IT THE MATERIAL
OF A TRUE GHOST

25.

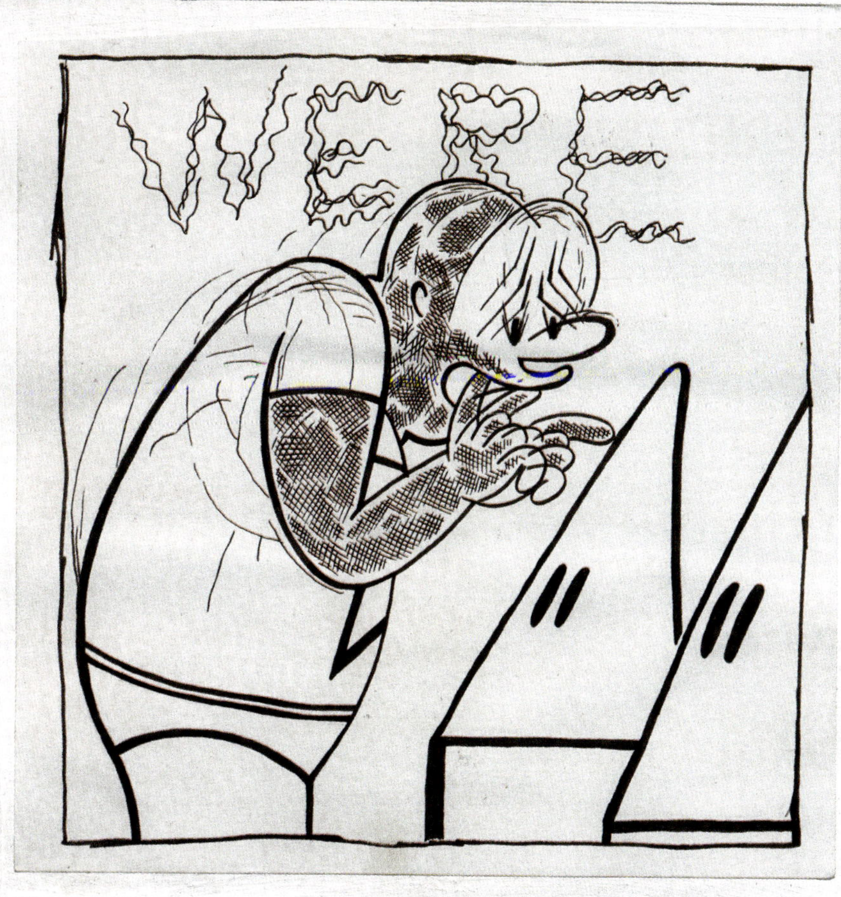

FALL 1995

TRENTON DOYLE HANCOCK LEARNS OF THE PAINTER, PHILIP GUSTON IN HIS SERIGRAPHY CLASS AT EAST TEXAS STATE UNIVERSITY. HE RESPONDS FAVORABLY TO GUSTON'S WHIMSICAL KLAN CHARACTERS 26.

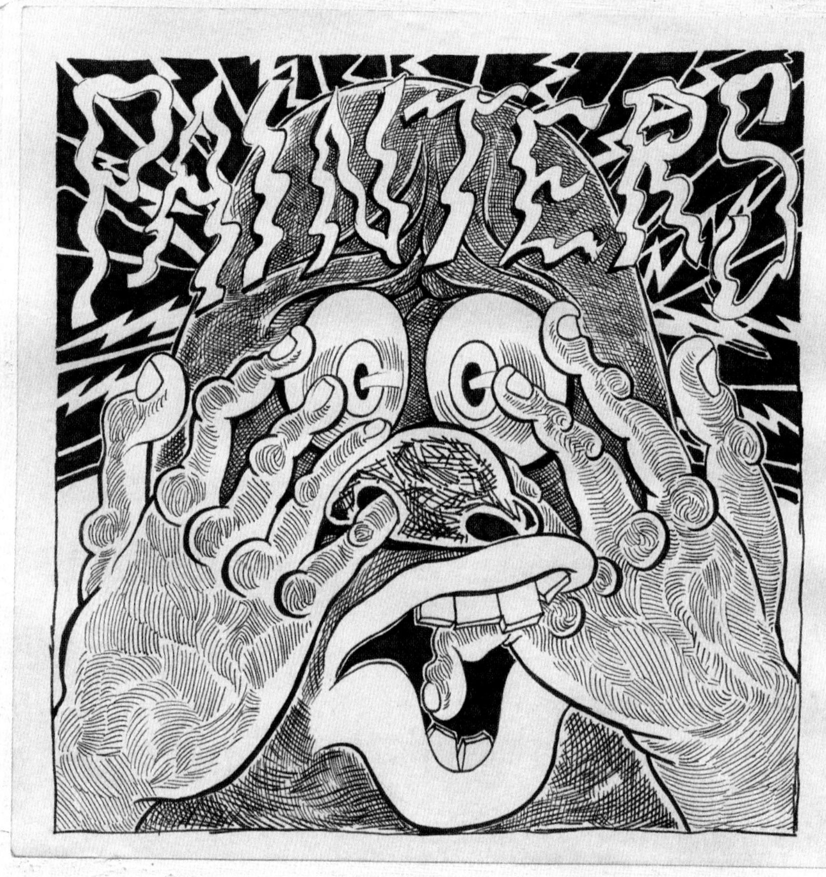

SPRING 1996

TRENTON DOYLE HANCOCK WRITES AND
ILLUSTRATES A STORY OF A BLACK MAN WHO
IS LYNCHED FOR TALKING TO A WHITE
WOMAN. HANCOCK NAMES THE YOUNG MAN,
LORD. THIS NAME IS ARRIVED AT BY
CROSSING OUT LETTERS IN THE WORDS
"LORD HELP ME." AND AROUND 1992 HE THEN
CHANGES THE TITLE OF HIS WEEKLY
COMIC STRIP TO "EPIDEMIC!"

27.

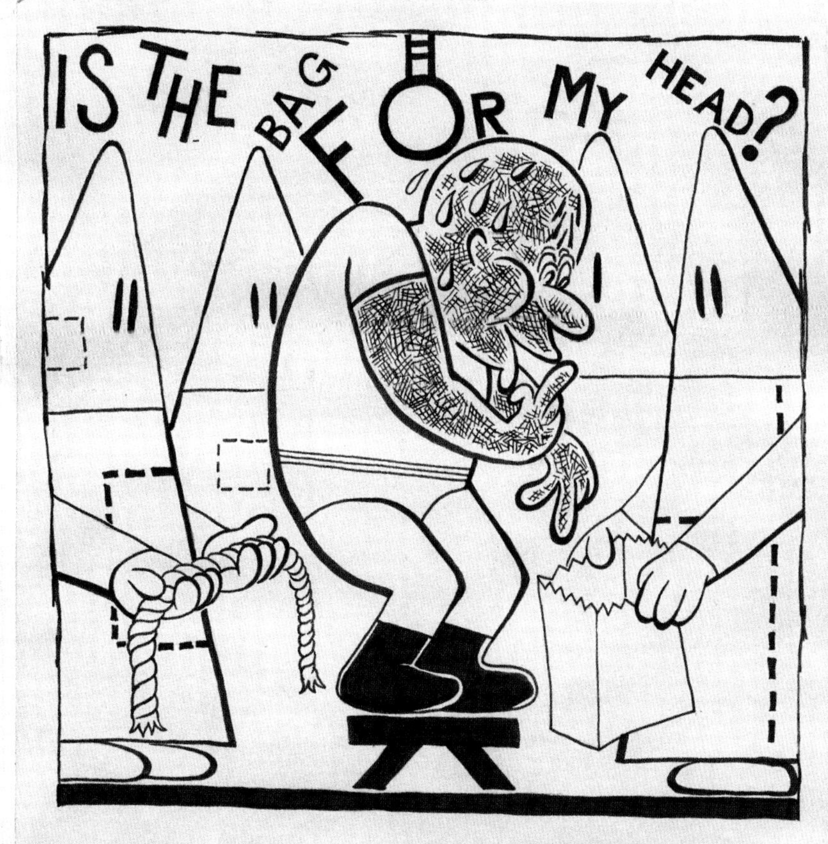

SPRING 1976 CONTINUED

AT EAST TEXAS STATE UNIVERSITY, STUDENT JOURNALIST VINCE LEIBOWITZ AND STUDENT CARTOONIST TREVOR DOYLE HANCOCK PRINT MATERIAL CRITICIZING CAMPUS FRATERNITIES IN THE SCHOOL NEWSPAPER. IN RESPONSE, A FRATERNITY THROWS AN "ANTI-LEIBOWITZ HANCOCK" NEWSPAPER BURNING PARTY.

28.

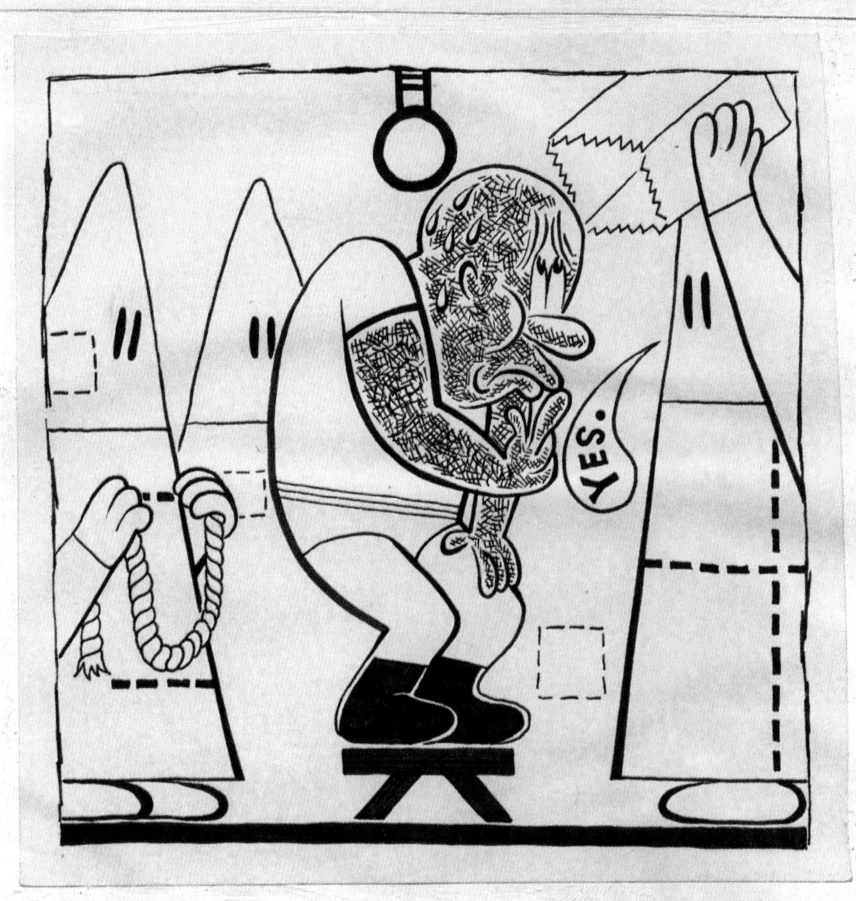

MAY 16, 2003
TRENTON DOYLE HANCOCK
GIVES A MUSEUM WALKING
TOUR FOR THE PHILIP GUSTON
RETROSPECTIVE AT THE
FORTWORTH MODERN
MUSEUM

29.

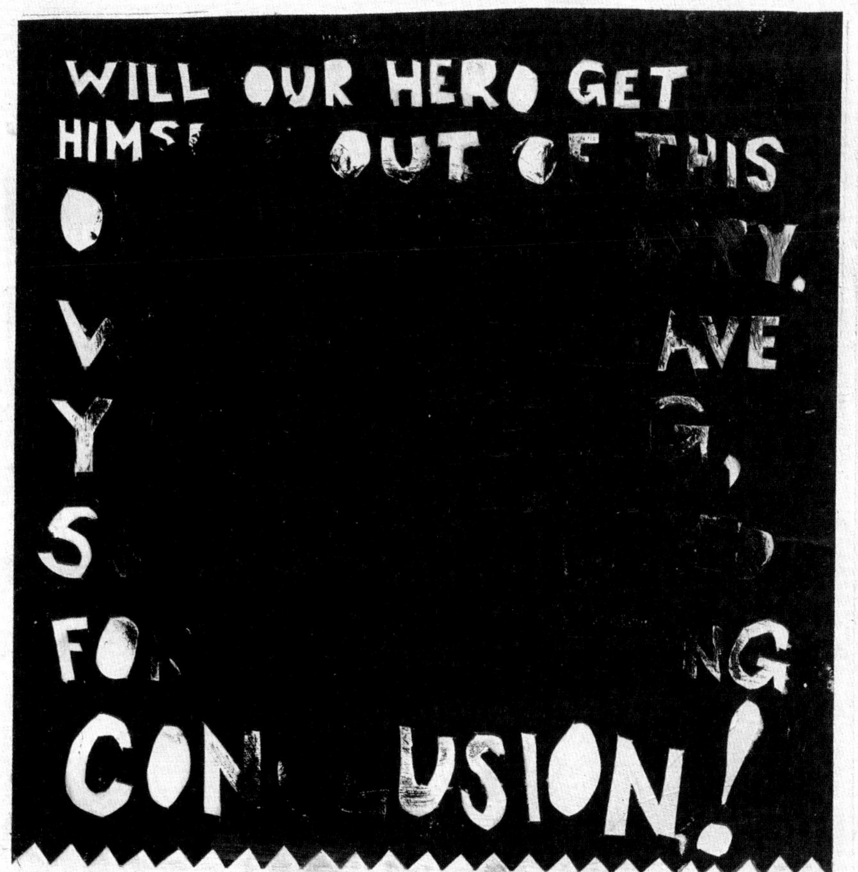

JULY 21, 2007

THE NEW BLACK PANTHERS AND THE KU KLUX KLAN HOLD OPPOSING RALLIES ON THE TOWN SQUARE OF PARIS, TEXAS. THE RALLIES ARE ORGANIZED DUE TO THE ACQUITTAL OF 2 WHITE MEN WHO WERE ACCUSED OF DRAGGING A BLACK MAN TO DEATH UNDER THEIR TRUCK 30.

PAGES 98–101
Trenton Doyle Hancock
Preparatory drawings for *Epidemic! Presents:*
Step and Screw!, Part Two, 2019
Ink on paper, 15 sheets, each
7 × 7 in. (17.8 × 17.8 cm);
title page: 12 × 11 in. (30.5 × 27.9 cm)
Collection of the artist

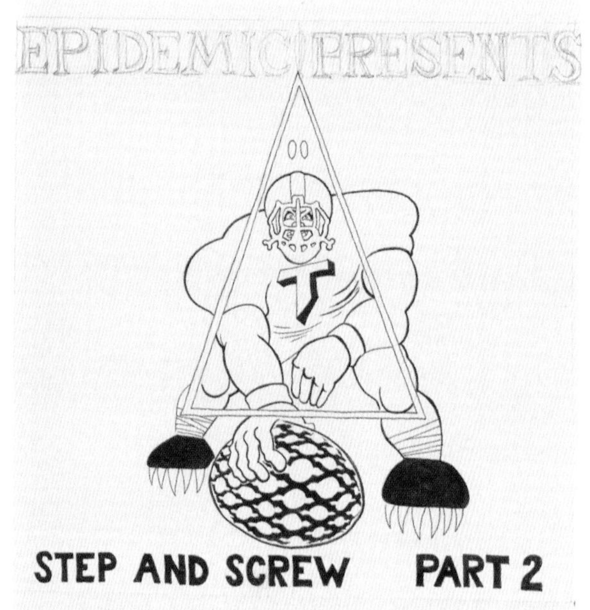

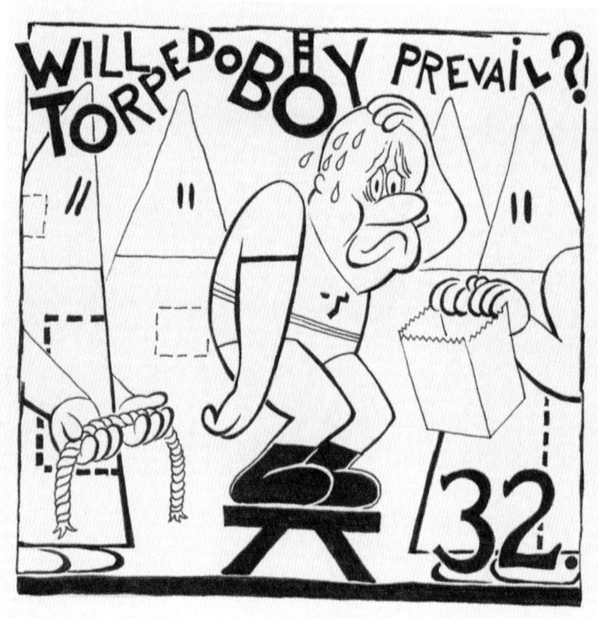

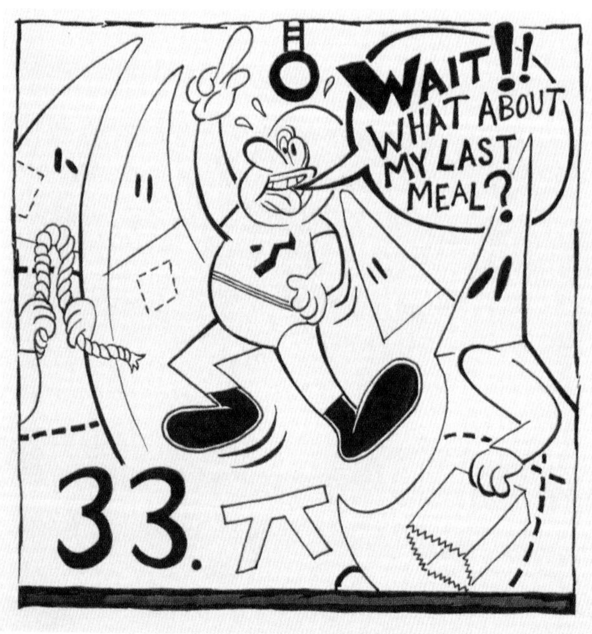

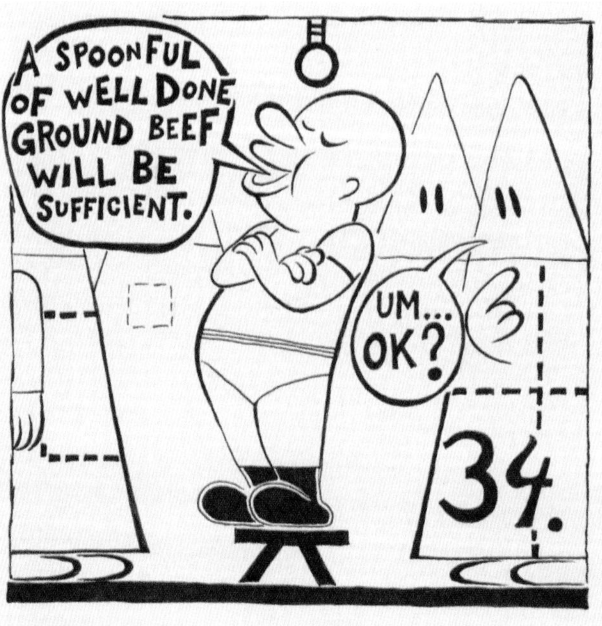

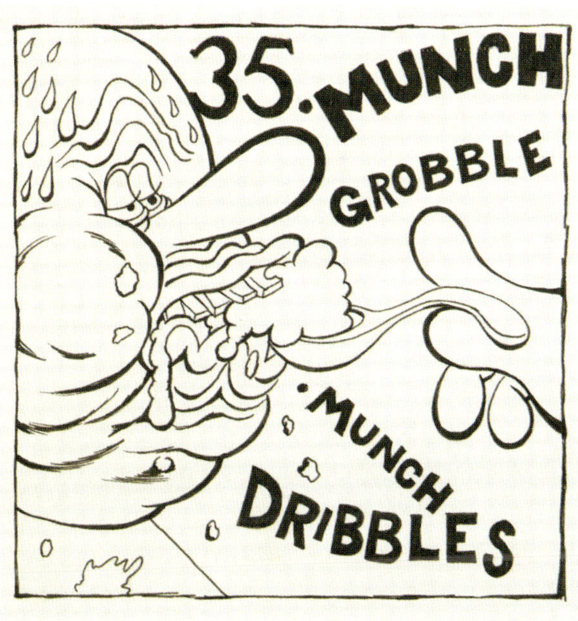

35. MUNCH
GROBBLE
·MUNCH
DRIBBLES

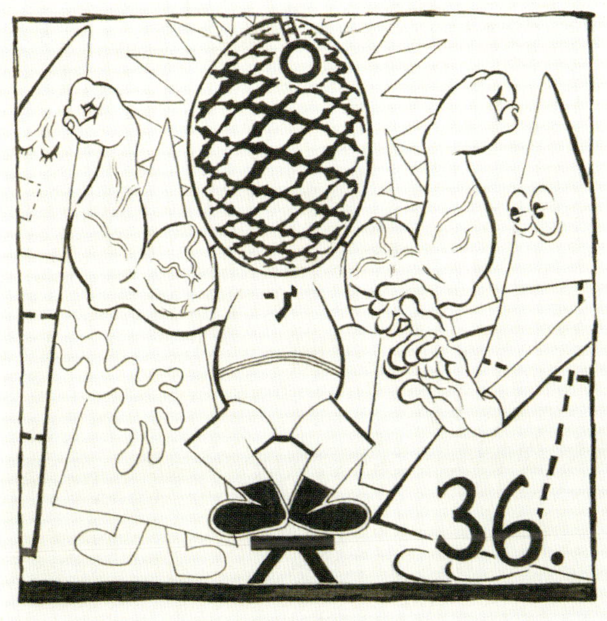

36.

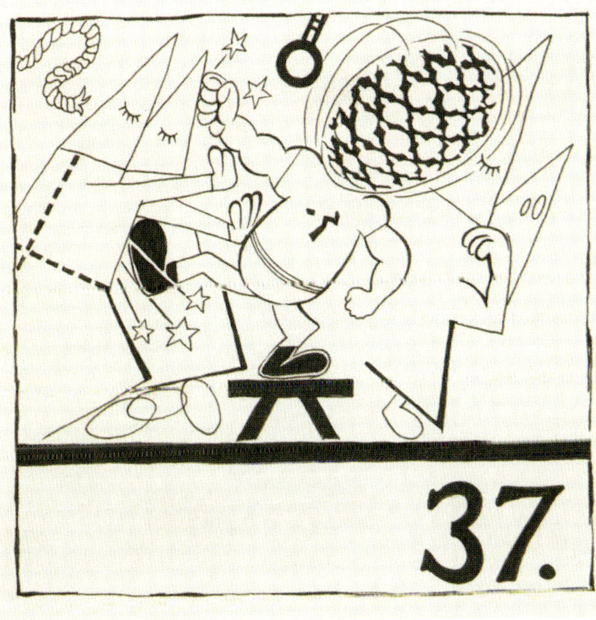

37.

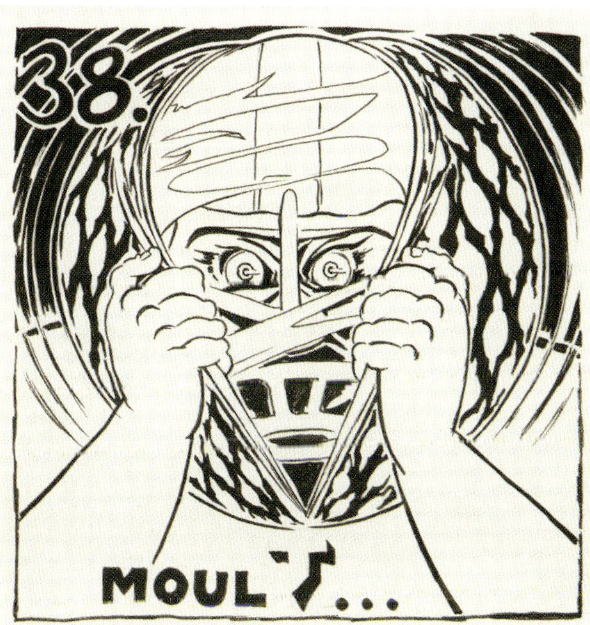

38.
MOUL'J...

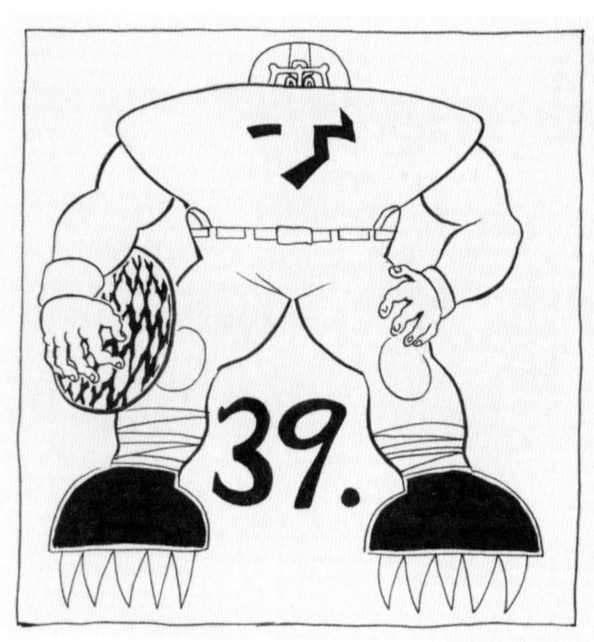

39.

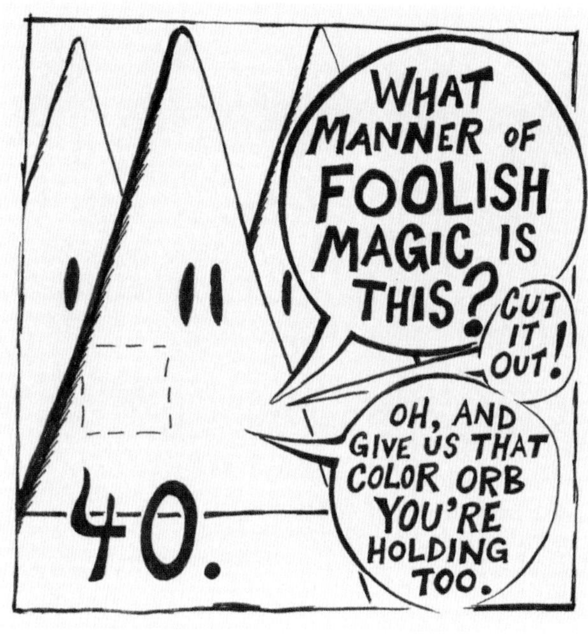

WHAT MANNER OF FOOLISH MAGIC IS THIS?
CUT IT OUT!
OH, AND GIVE US THAT COLOR ORB YOU'RE HOLDING TOO.
40.

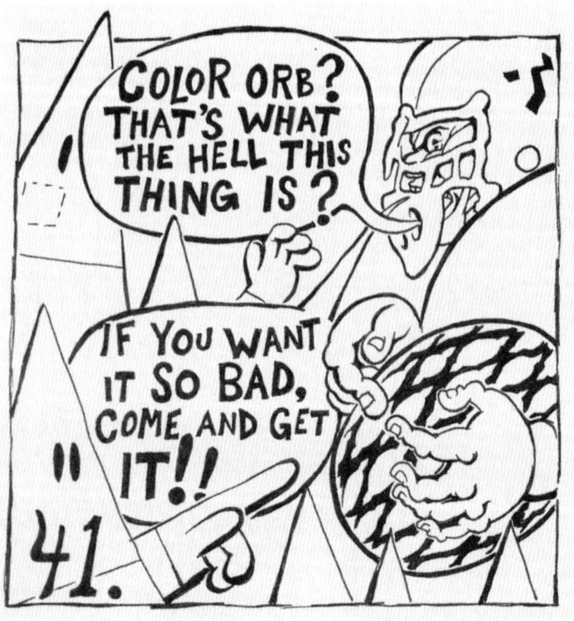

COLOR ORB? THAT'S WHAT THE HELL THIS THING IS?
IF YOU WANT IT SO BAD, COME AND GET IT!!
41.

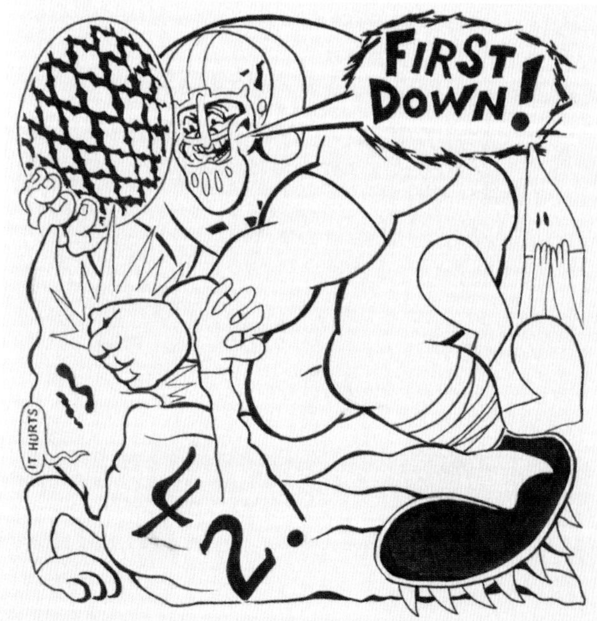

FIRST DOWN!
IT HURTS
42.

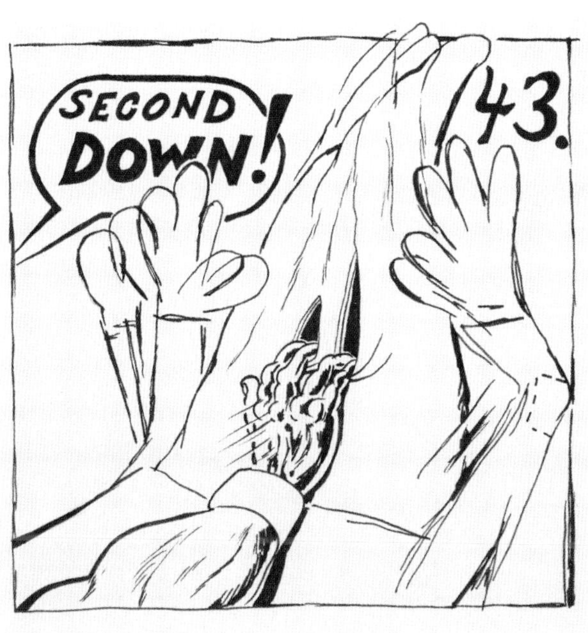

SECOND DOWN!
43.

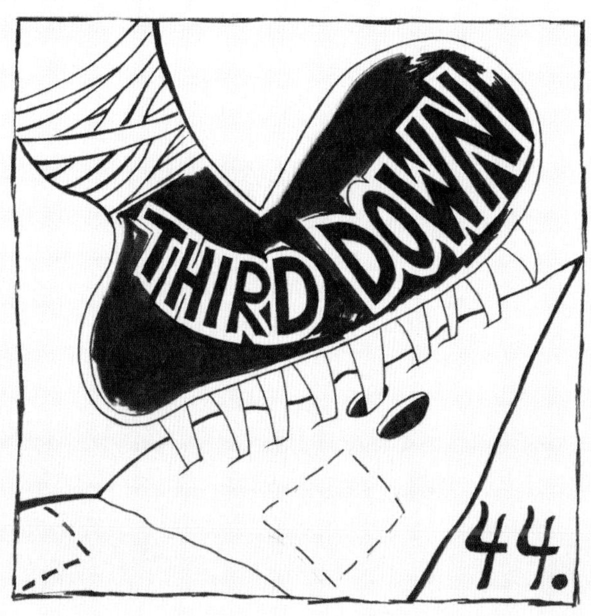

THIRD DOWN!
44.

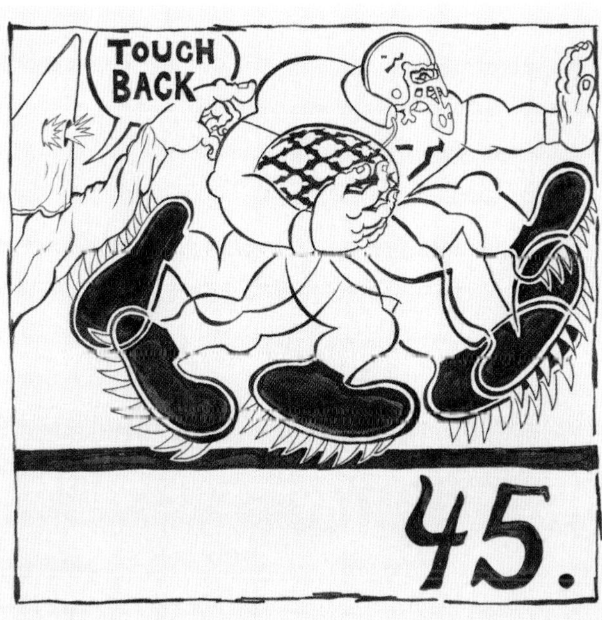

TOUCH BACK
45.

Trenton Doyle Hancock
Step and Screw #18-1, the Handoff, 2015
Mixed media on canvas,
60 × 60 in. (152.4 × 152.4 cm)
Collection of JKiZ, Lisbon, Portugal

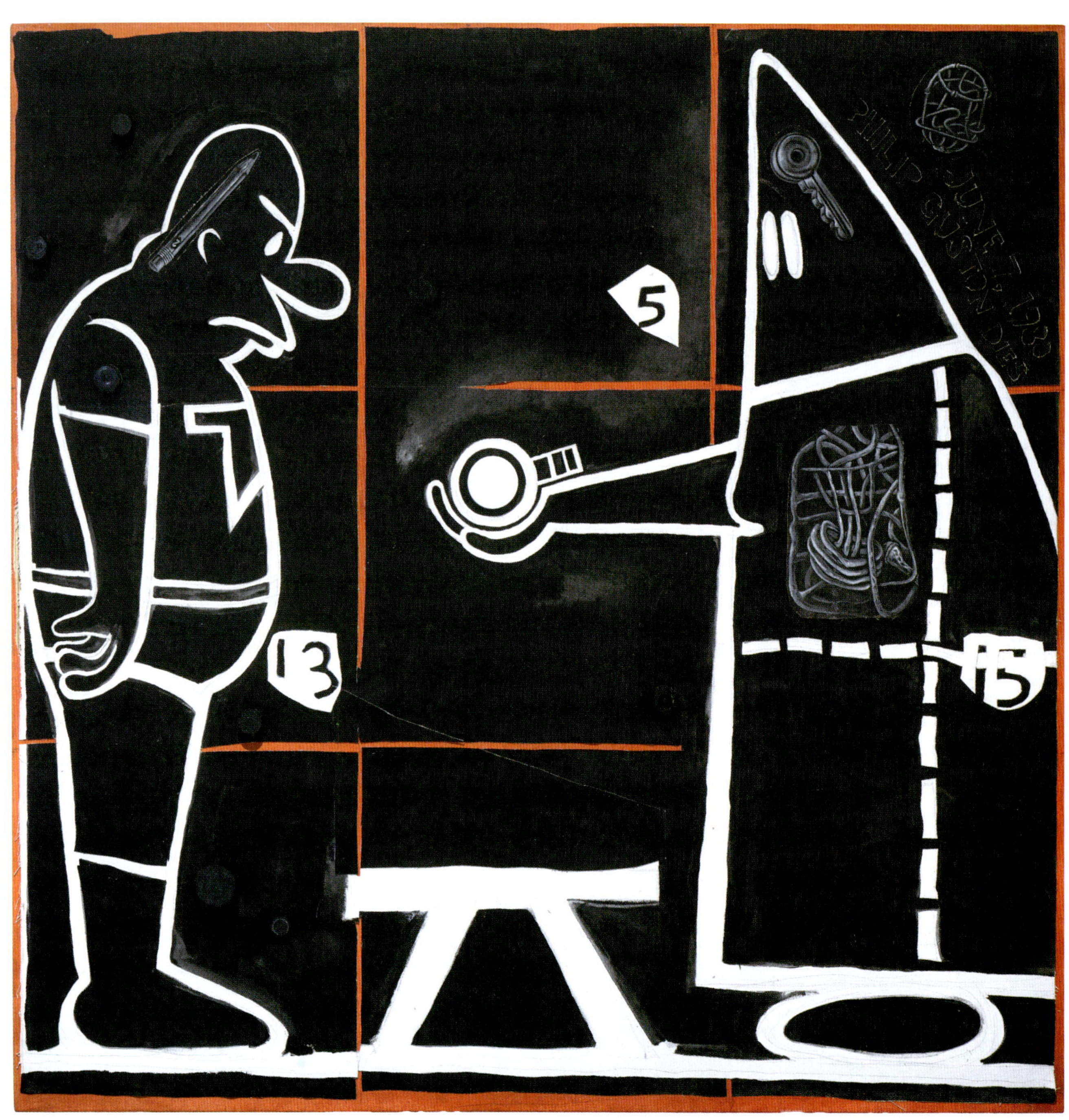

PHILIP GUSTON DIES JUNE 7 1980
5
13
15

Trenton Doyle Hancock
*Schlep and Screw, Knowledge Rental Pawn
Exchange Service*, 2017
Acrylic and mixed media on canvas,
60 × 60 × 6 in. (152.4 × 152.4 × 15.2 cm)
Collection of Hedy Fischer and
Randy Shull, Asheville, North Carolina

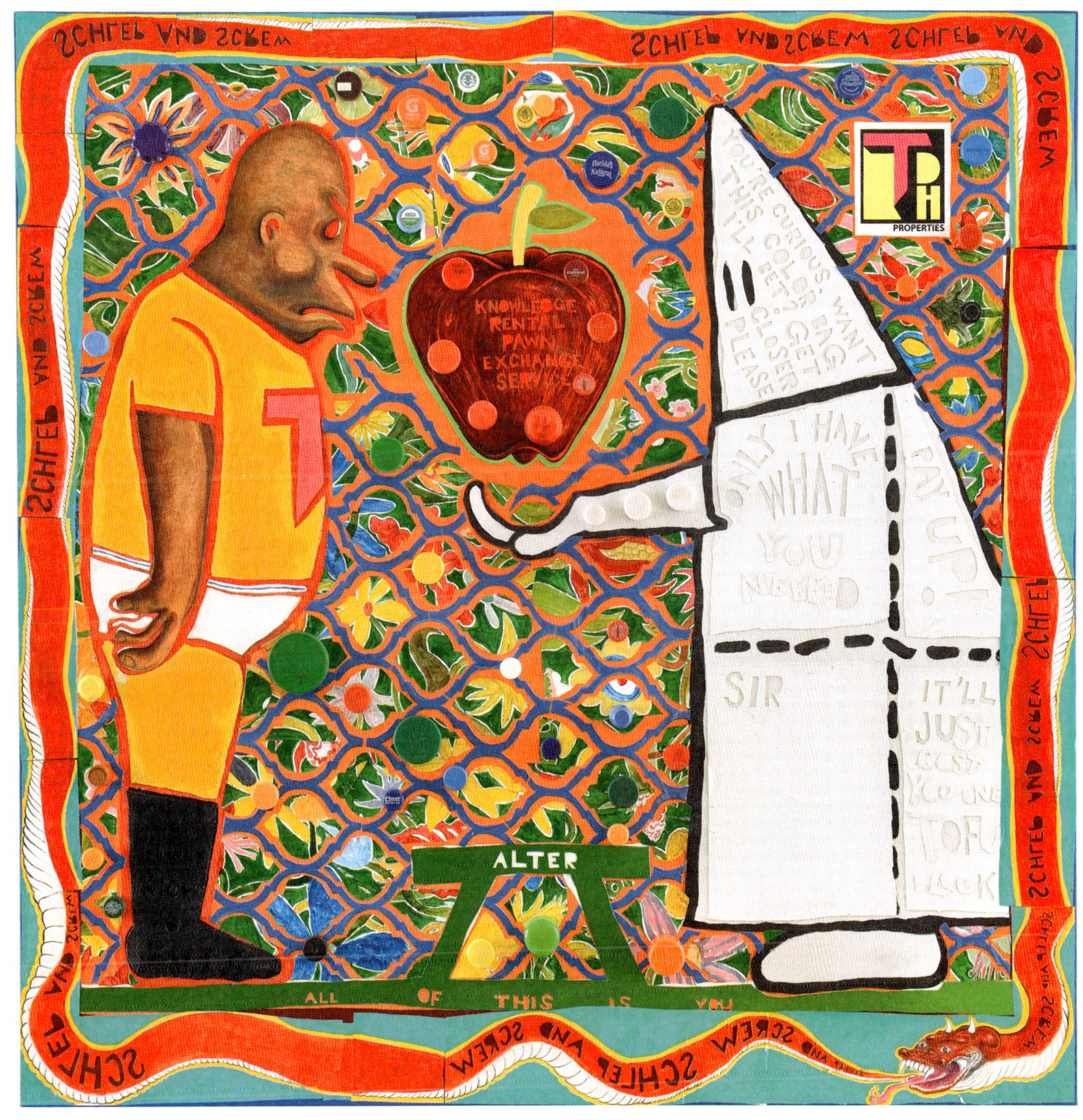

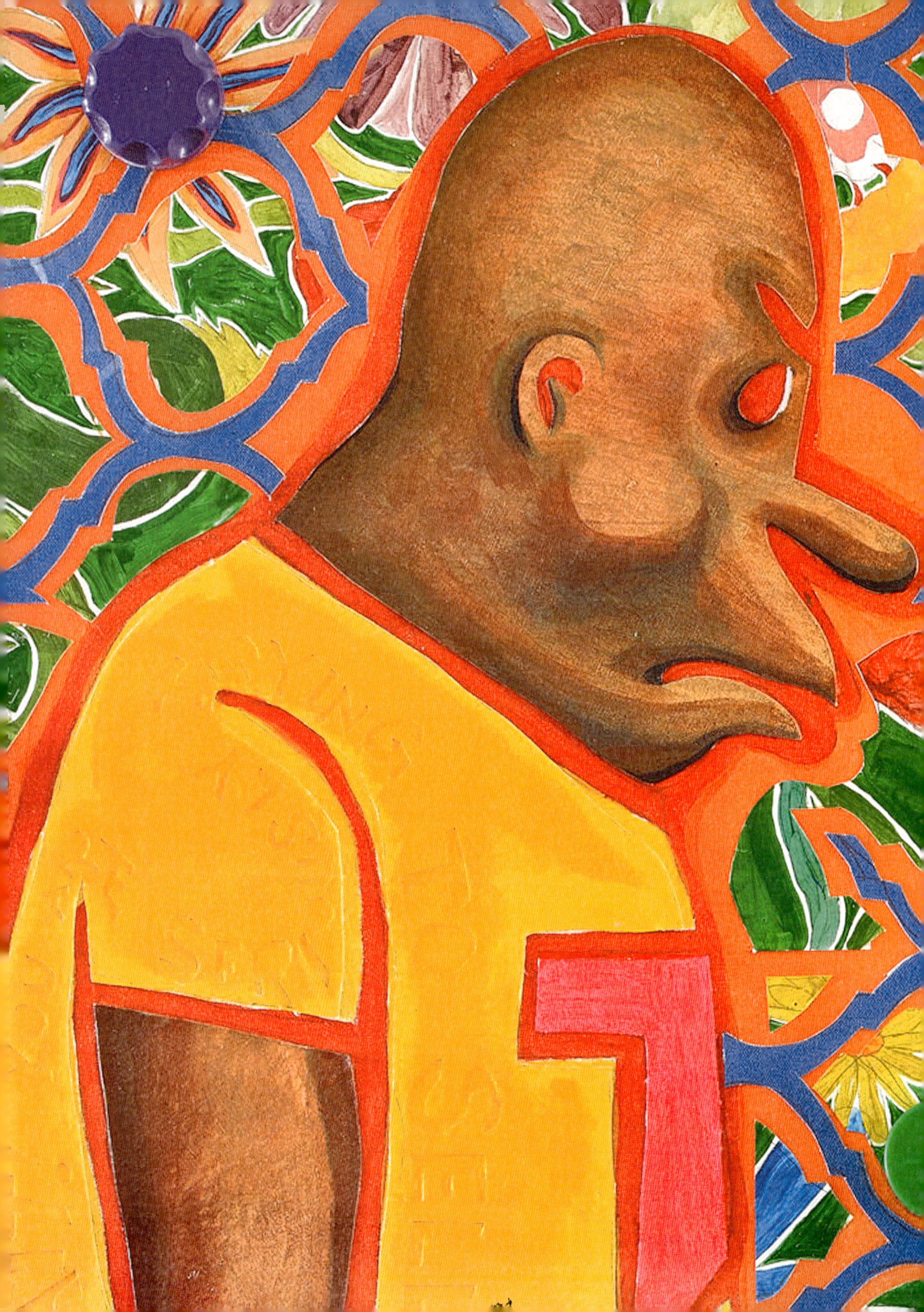

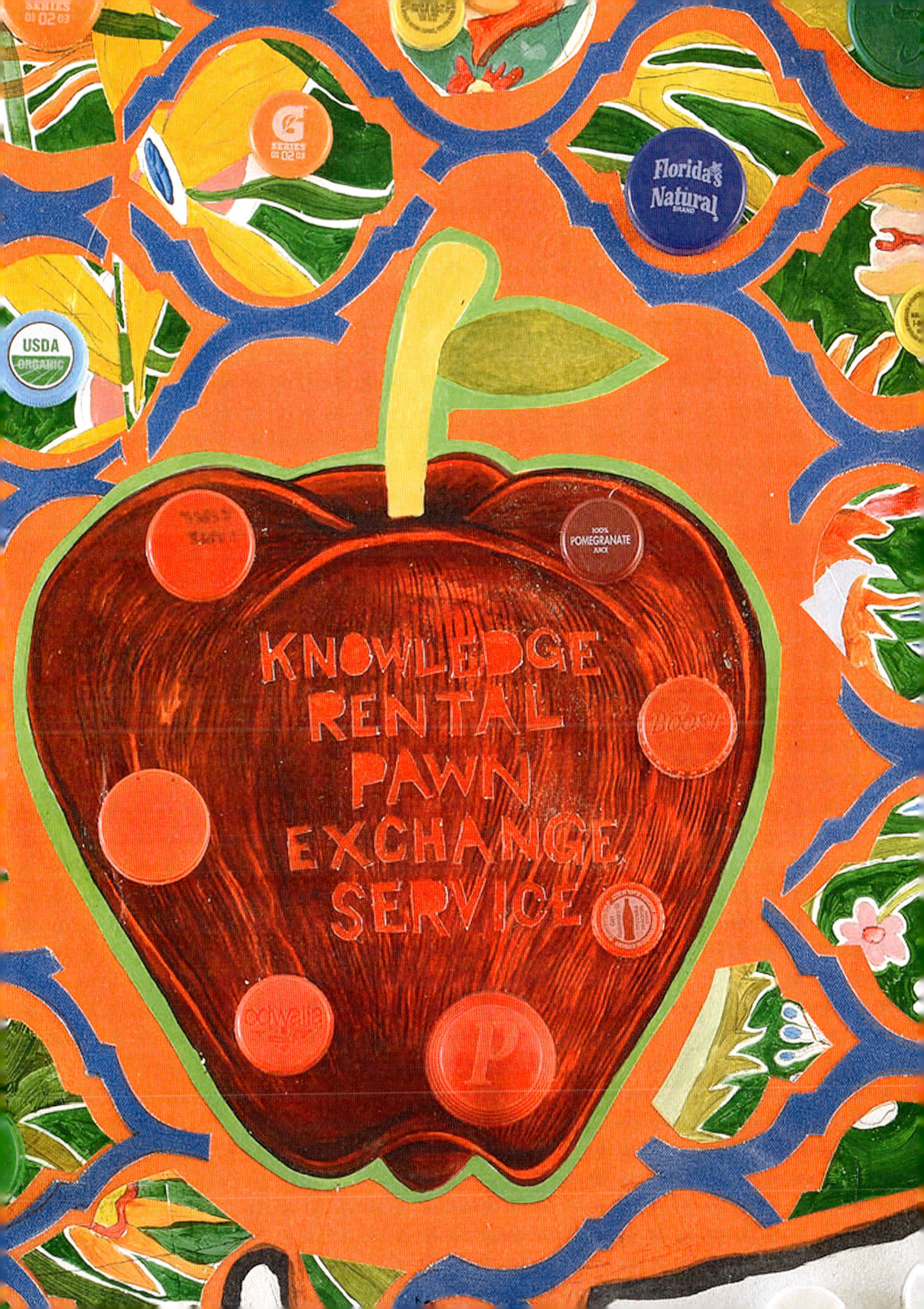
G SERIES 01 02 03
Florida's Natural BRAND
USDA ORGANIC
100% POMEGRANATE JUICE
KNOWLEDGE
RENTAL
PAWN
EXCHANGE
SERVICE
odwalla
P

Trenton Doyle Hancock
SKUM: Just Beneath the Skin, 2018
Acrylic, graphite, plastic bottle
caps, and paper collage on canvas,
60 × 60 × 4 in. (152.4 × 152.4 × 10.2 cm)
Collection of Lisa and Stuart
Ginsberg, New York

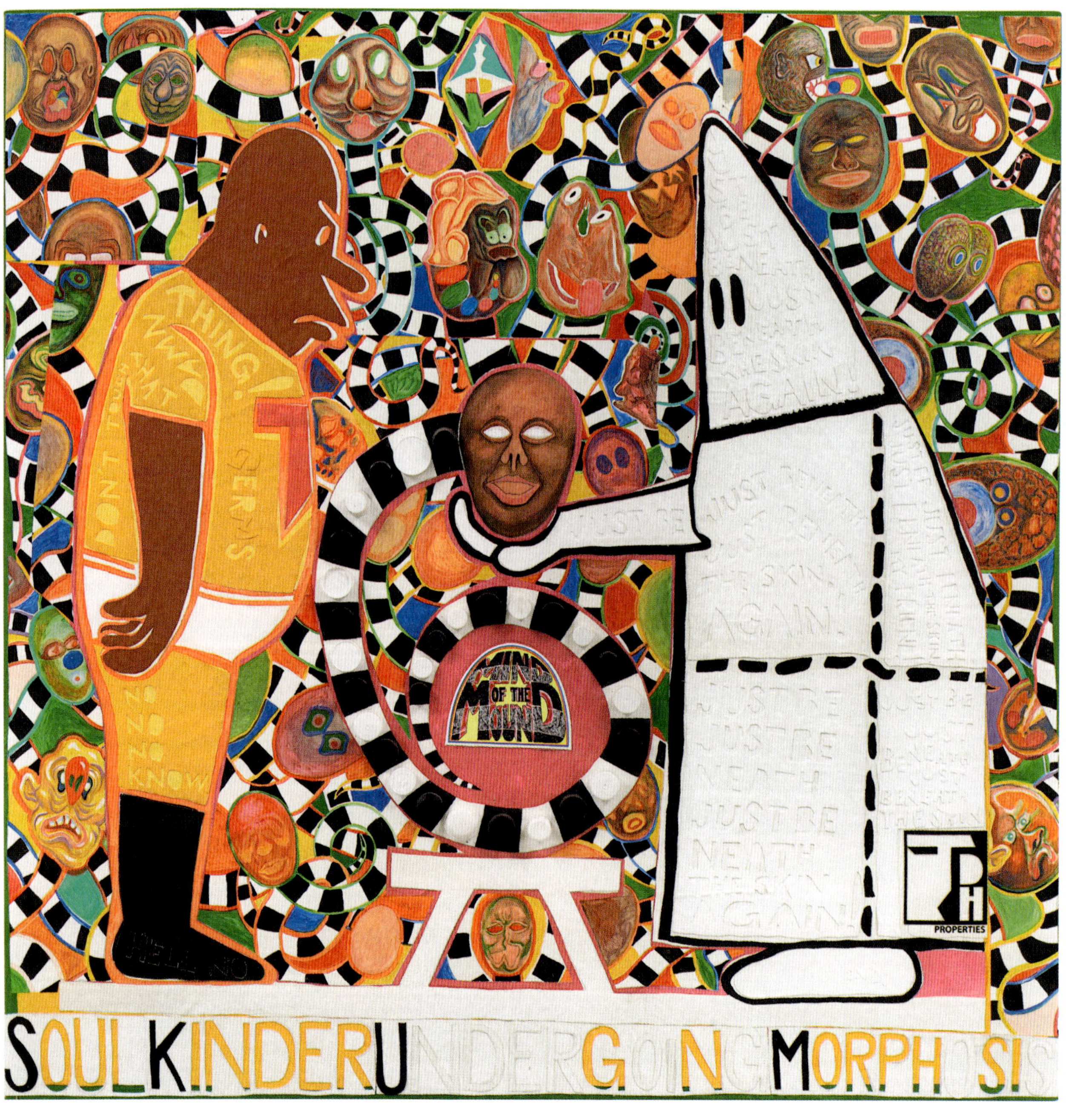

Hancock's "star of code switching" is a fascinating item: like a weirder, more menacing version of the Star of Invincibility, the beady-eyed power-up from Nintendo's *Super Mario Brothers* video game, it also refers to the Vulcan salute, the splayed hand gesture associated with the benediction "live long and prosper" that first appeared on *Star Trek* in 1967. Both are perfect parallels for the type of charm that might grant access to longevity and power in Hancock's imagined world. It is interesting to note that the Vulcan salute was invented by the Jewish actor who played Spock in the original TV series; Leonard Nimoy based it on his memory of the distinctive priestly blessing he had observed at synagogue as a child. Embedded in the DNA of the hand shape Hancock used to signify the nature of code switching is a story about assimilation and the ever-evolving identity of symbolic forms—which dovetails directly with Guston and Hancock and their interrogations into the conditions under which one might be able to pass in and out of whiteness, as the practice of code switching implies.

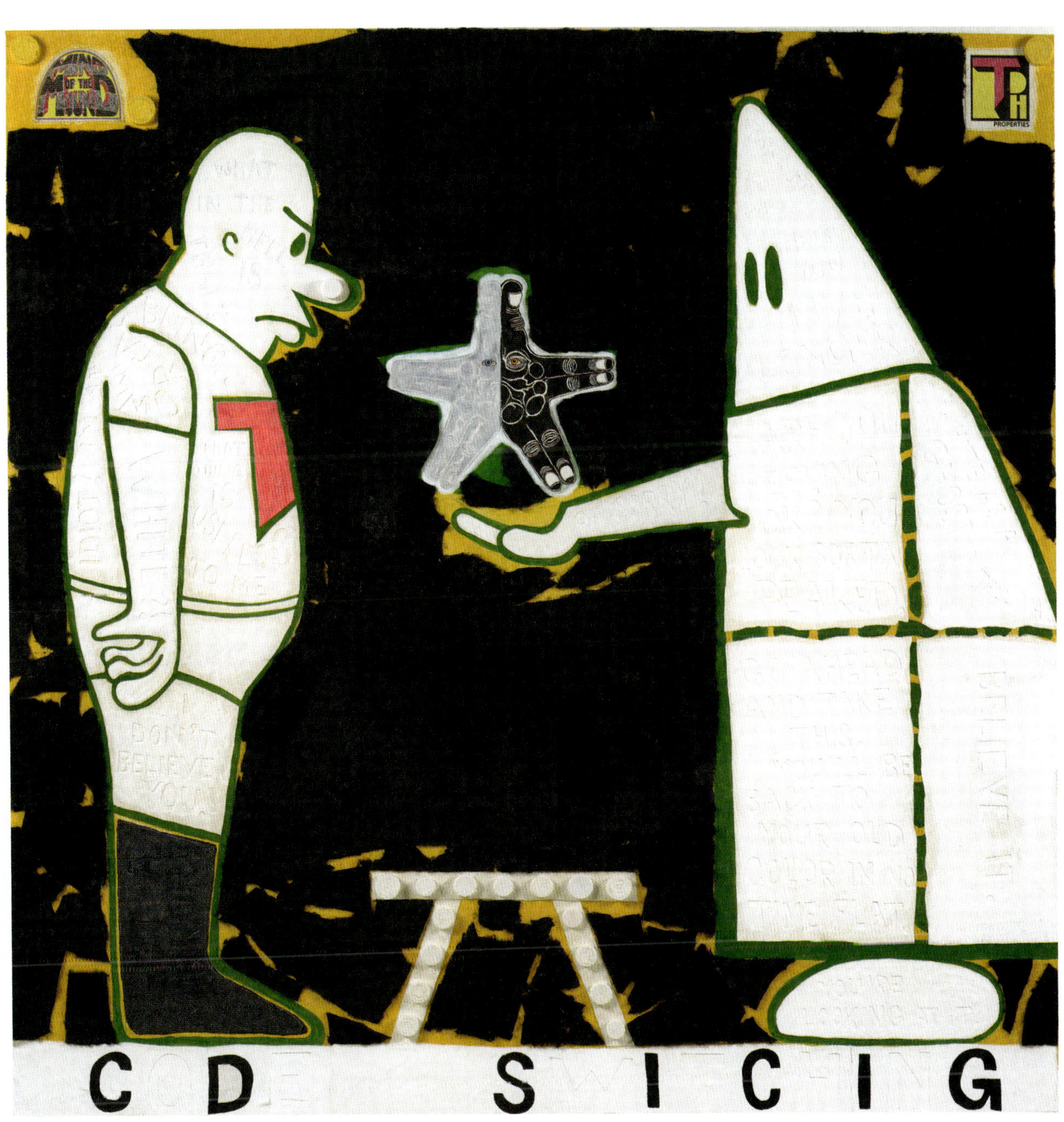

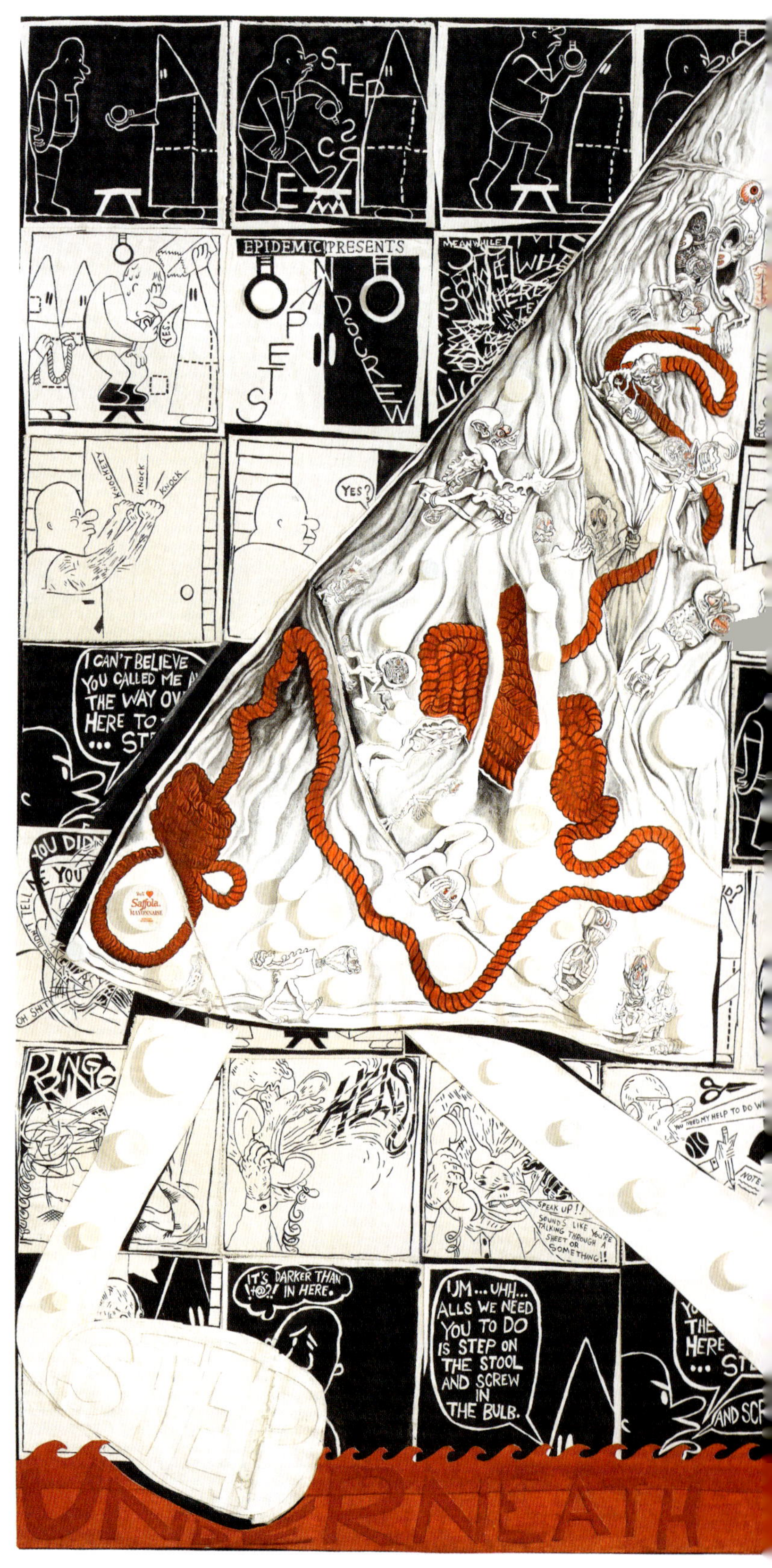
"STEP"
EPIDEMIC PRESENTS
SCREW
YES?
KNOCKETY KNOCK KNOCK
I CAN'T BELIEVE YOU CALLED ME ALL THE WAY OVER HERE TO ... STEP
YOU DIDN'T TELL ME YOU ...
RING RING
HEY
IT'S DARKER THAN HELL IN HERE.
UM...UHH... ALLS WE NEED YOU TO DO IS STEP ON THE STOOL AND SCREW IN THE BULB.
SPEAK UP!! SOUNDS LIKE YOU'RE TALKING THROUGH A SHEET OR SOMETHING!!
STEP
UNDERNEATH

Trenton Doyle Hancock
*Step and Screw Part Too Soon Underneath
the Bloody Red Moon*, 2018
Acrylic and mixed media on canvas,
90 × 132 × 5 in. (228.6 × 335.3 × 12.7 cm)
Collection of Mandy and Cliff Einstein,
Los Angeles

"This work highlights a chase scene between antagonist (Guston's
Klansman) and protagonist (Torpedoboy), each wearing specifically
American outfits (Klan garb and a football uniform, respectively).
I wanted to suggest a new American flag, its stripes being panels from
Step and Screw! My Moundverse antagonists, the evil Vegans, are
revealed to be puppeteering the giant Klansman."

—Trenton Doyle Hancock, March 2024

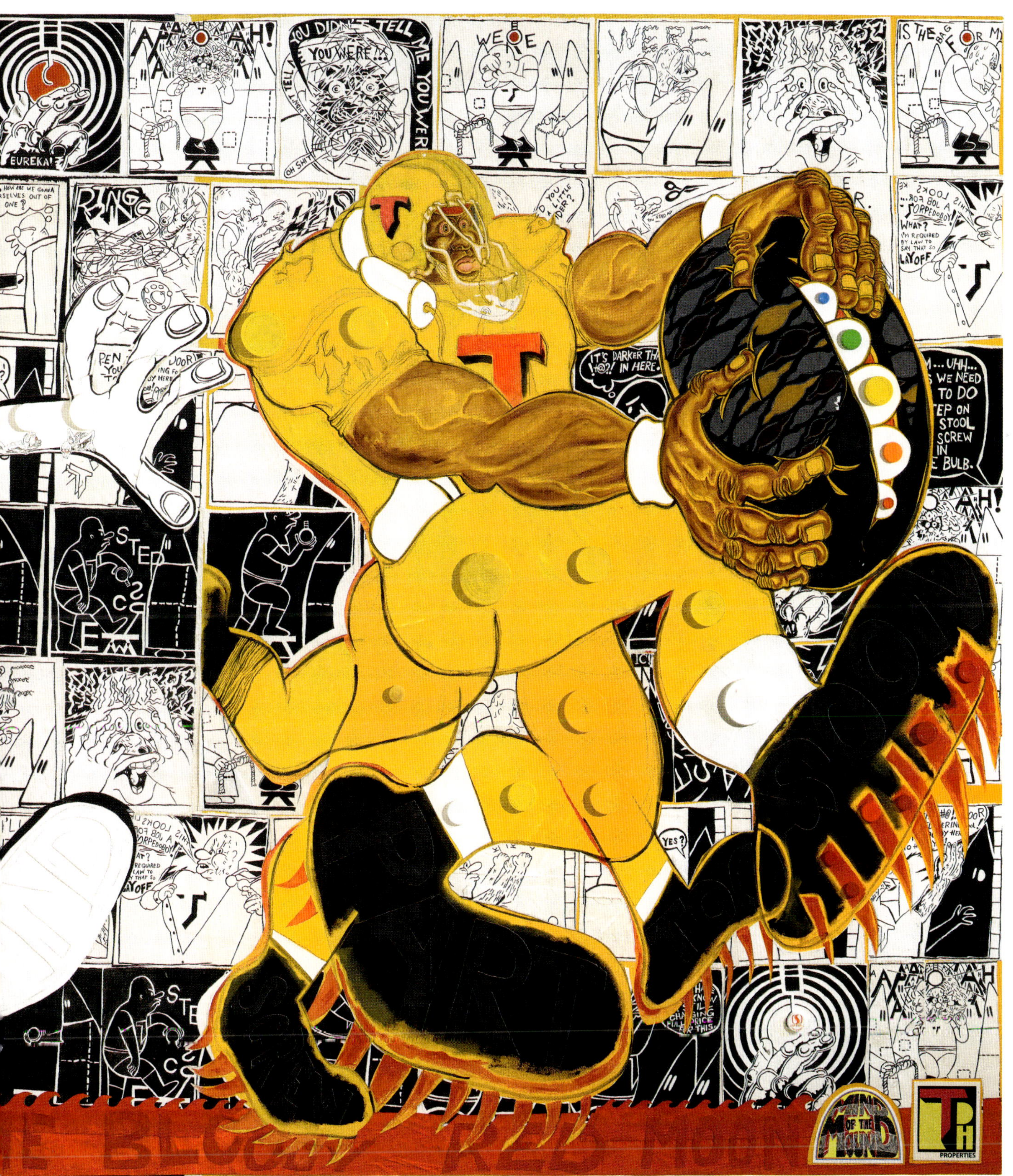

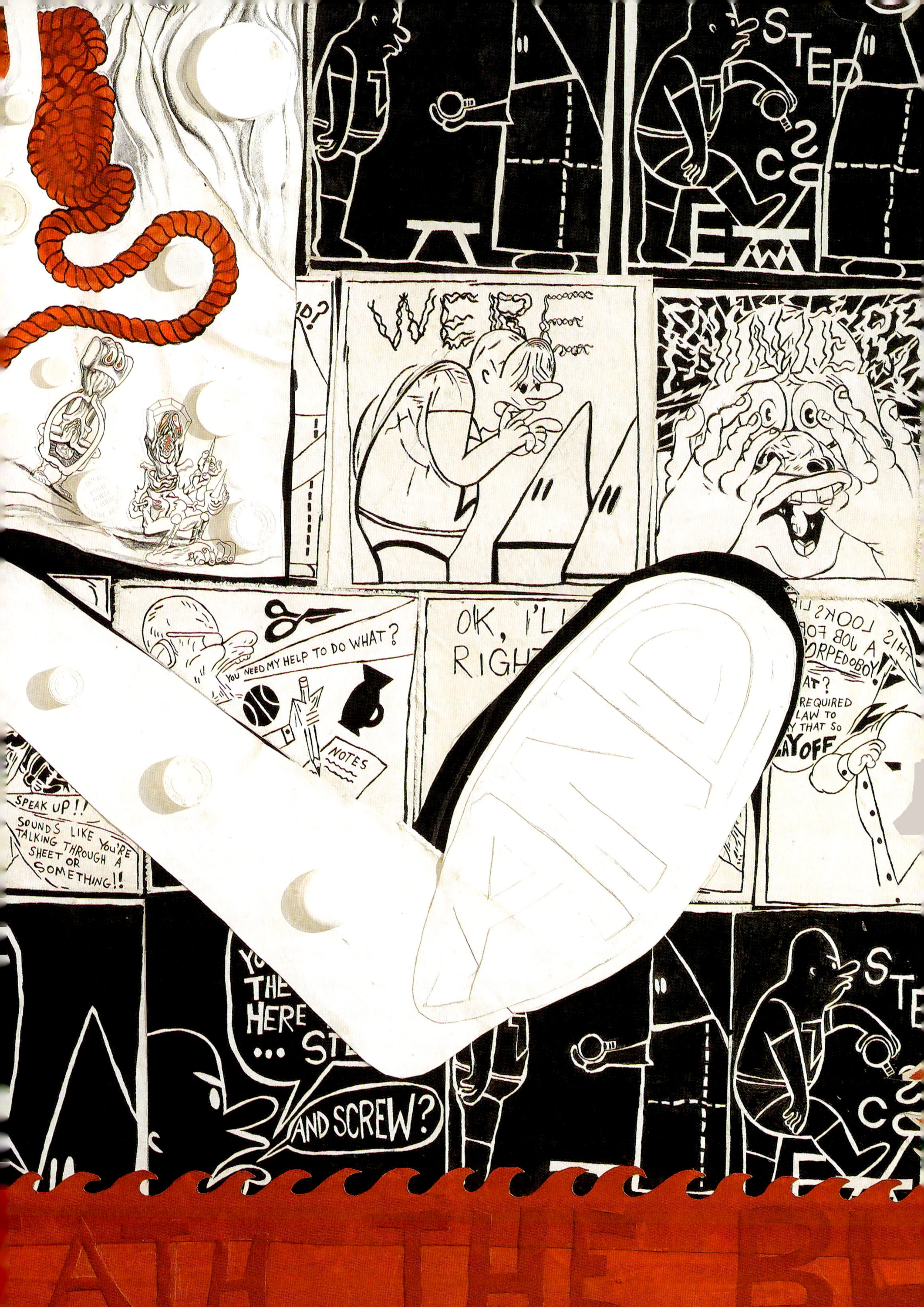

STED
SC

WERE

OK, I'LL
RIGHT

THIS LOOKS LI
A JOB FOR
TORPEDOBOY!!
AT?
REQUIRED
LAW TO
Y THAT SO
AYOFF

YOU NEED MY HELP TO DO WHAT?
NOTES

AND

SPEAK UP!!
SOUNDS LIKE YOU'RE
TALKING THROUGH A
SHEET OR
SOMETHING!!

YO
THE
HERE
... ST

AND SCREW?

STE
SC

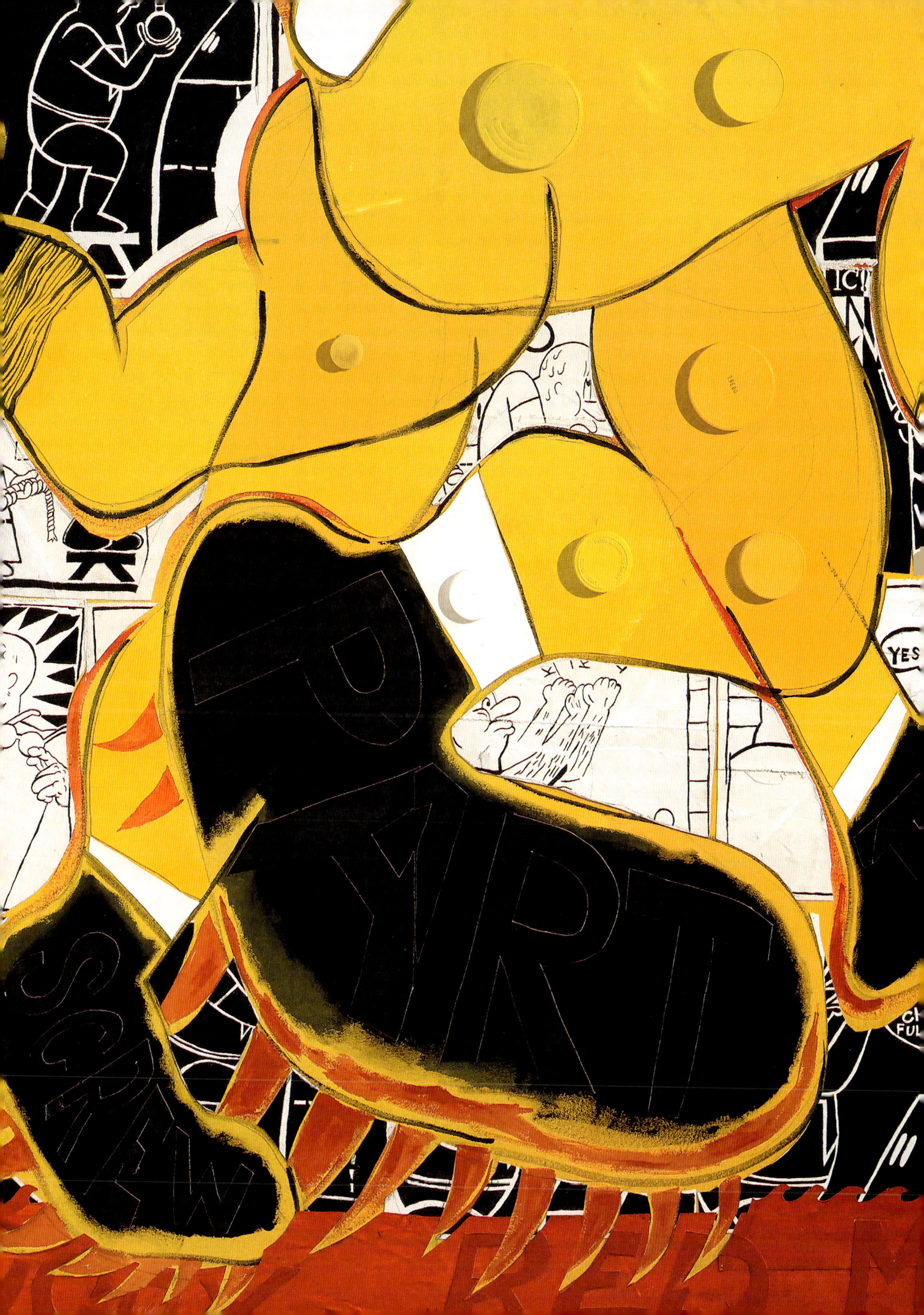

ICT
YES
P
YR
SCREW
CH
FUL

Trenton Doyle Hancock
*Line Up Featuring Torpedoboy and
TDH Properties*, 2021
Acrylic, paper, synthetic fur, and fabric on
canvas, 108⅛ × 72⅛ × 2¼ in.
(274.7 × 183.3 × 5.6 cm)
Collection of the artist

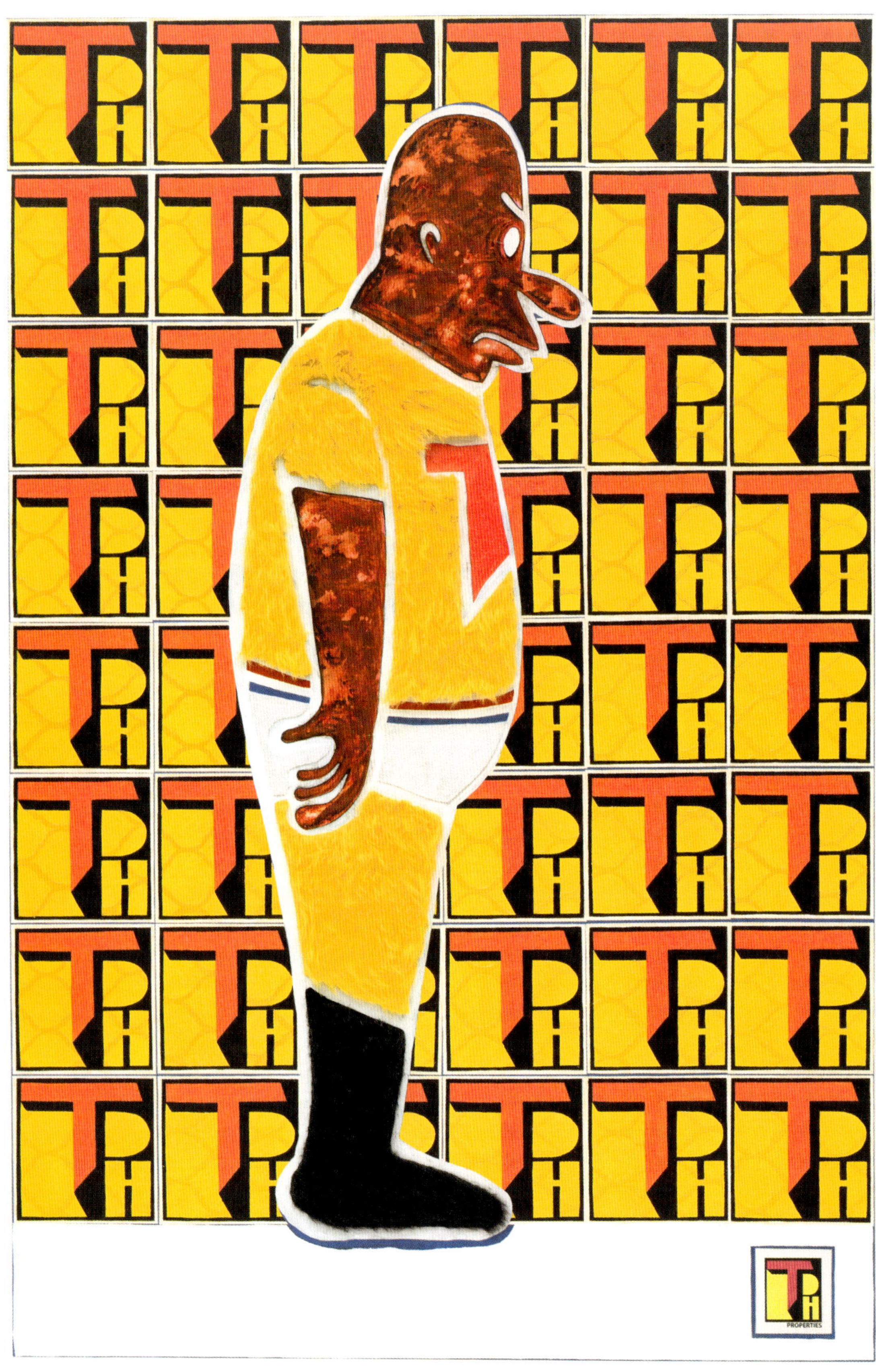

Trenton Doyle Hancock
I Didn't Even Get to Say Goodbye, 2021
Acrylic, paper, and plastic
on canvas, 72⅛ × 108¼ × 2¾ in.
(182.9 × 275 × 7.1 cm)
Private collection, London

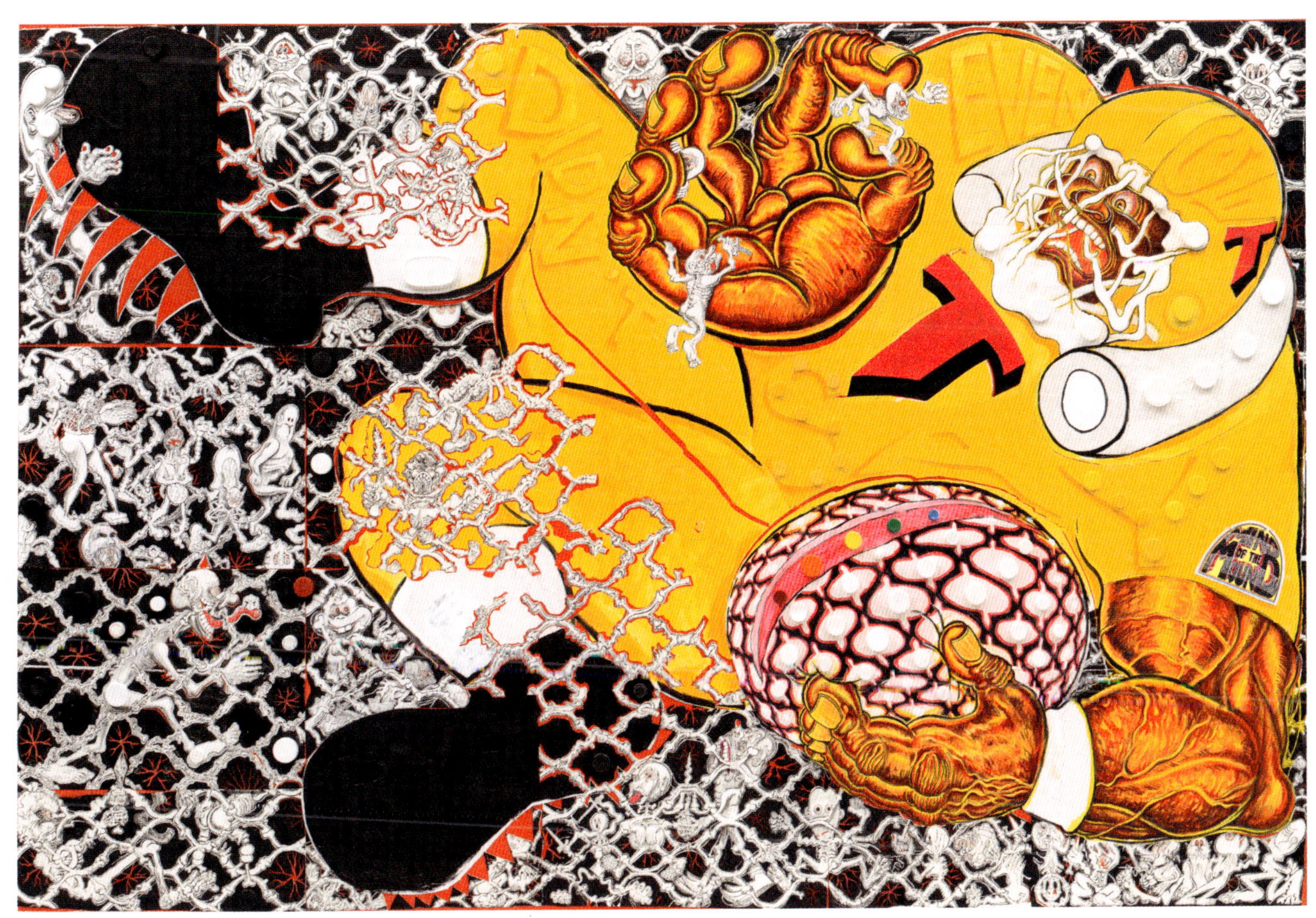

The tension between Torpedoboy's engagement with the Klan and his opposition to their villainy is palpable in many of Hancock's compositions. According to the artist, "Torpedoboy goes inside the hood to try to get into the mind of the enemy, but we are always in danger of slipping past the point of no return, where we become the very thing that we're fighting against." Because Hancock watched Quentin Tarantino's neo-noir crime thriller *Reservoir Dogs* (1992) around the same time he discovered Guston's paintings of the Klan, the two are inextricably linked in his mind—dual explorations of what it means to go undercover and what happens if you go too far.

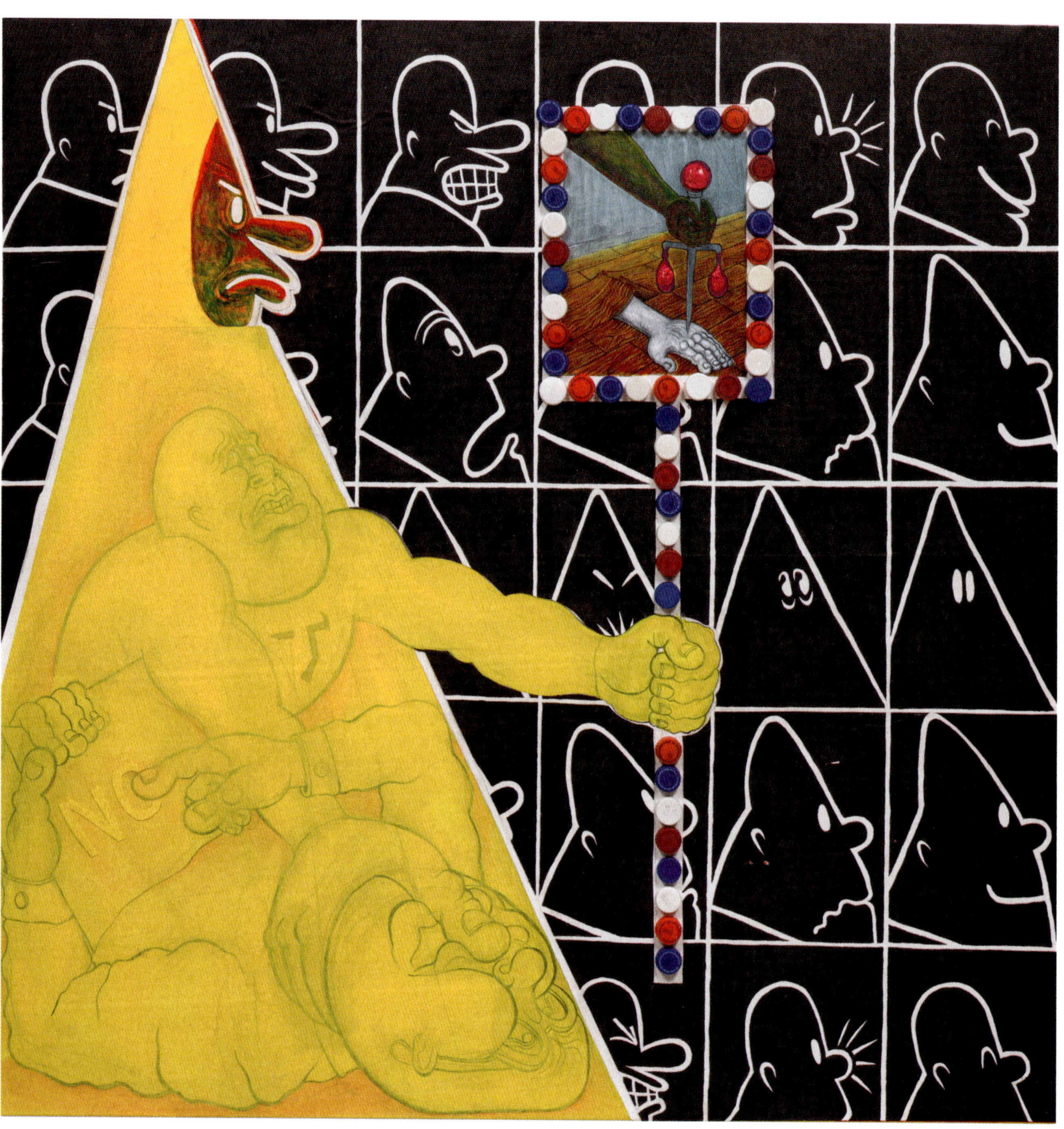

Trenton Doyle Hancock
The Midas Touch, 2022
Acrylic, graphite, ink, paper collage,
and plastic bottle caps on canvas,
60 × 48 in. (152.4 × 121.9 cm)
White Levin Family Collection

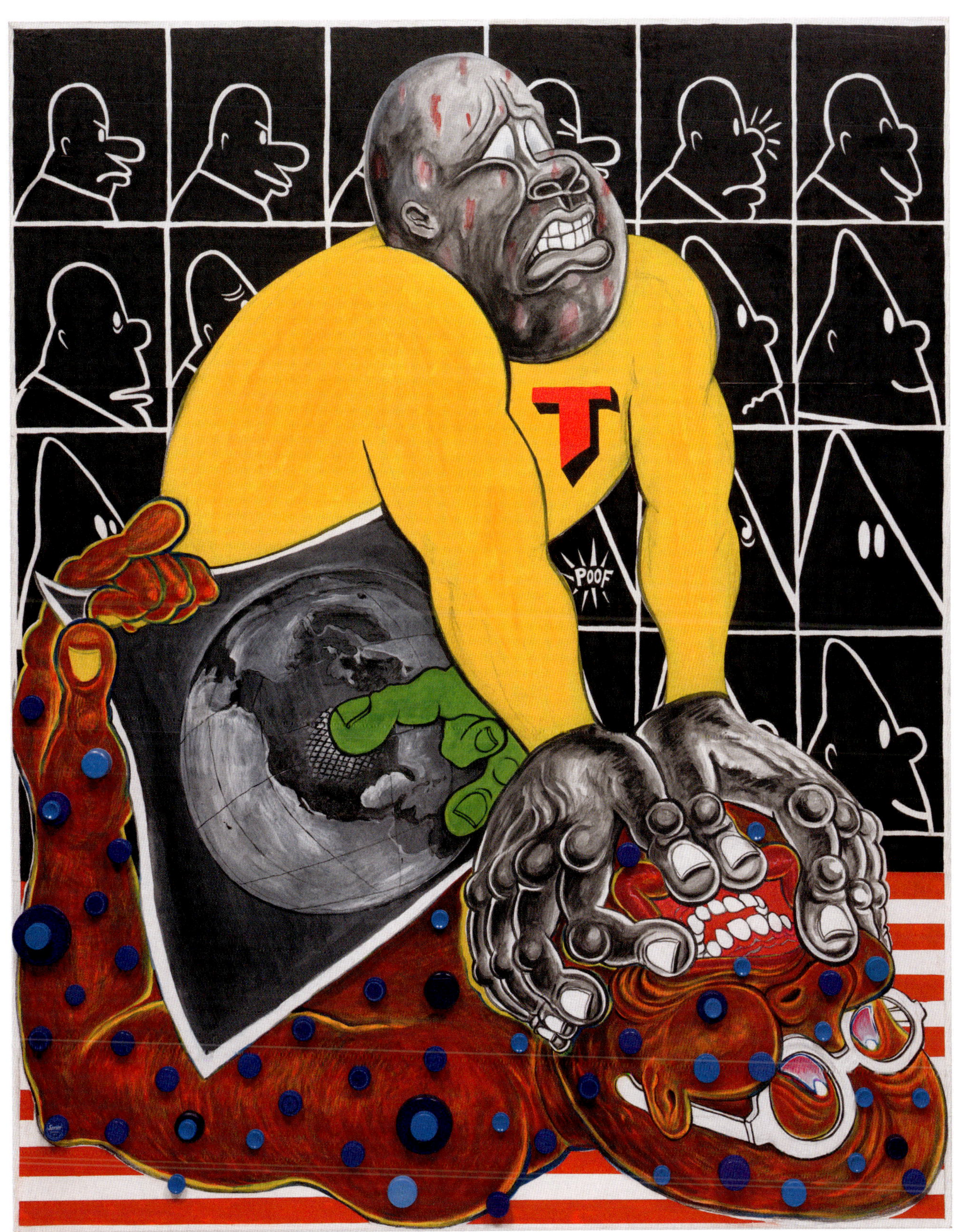

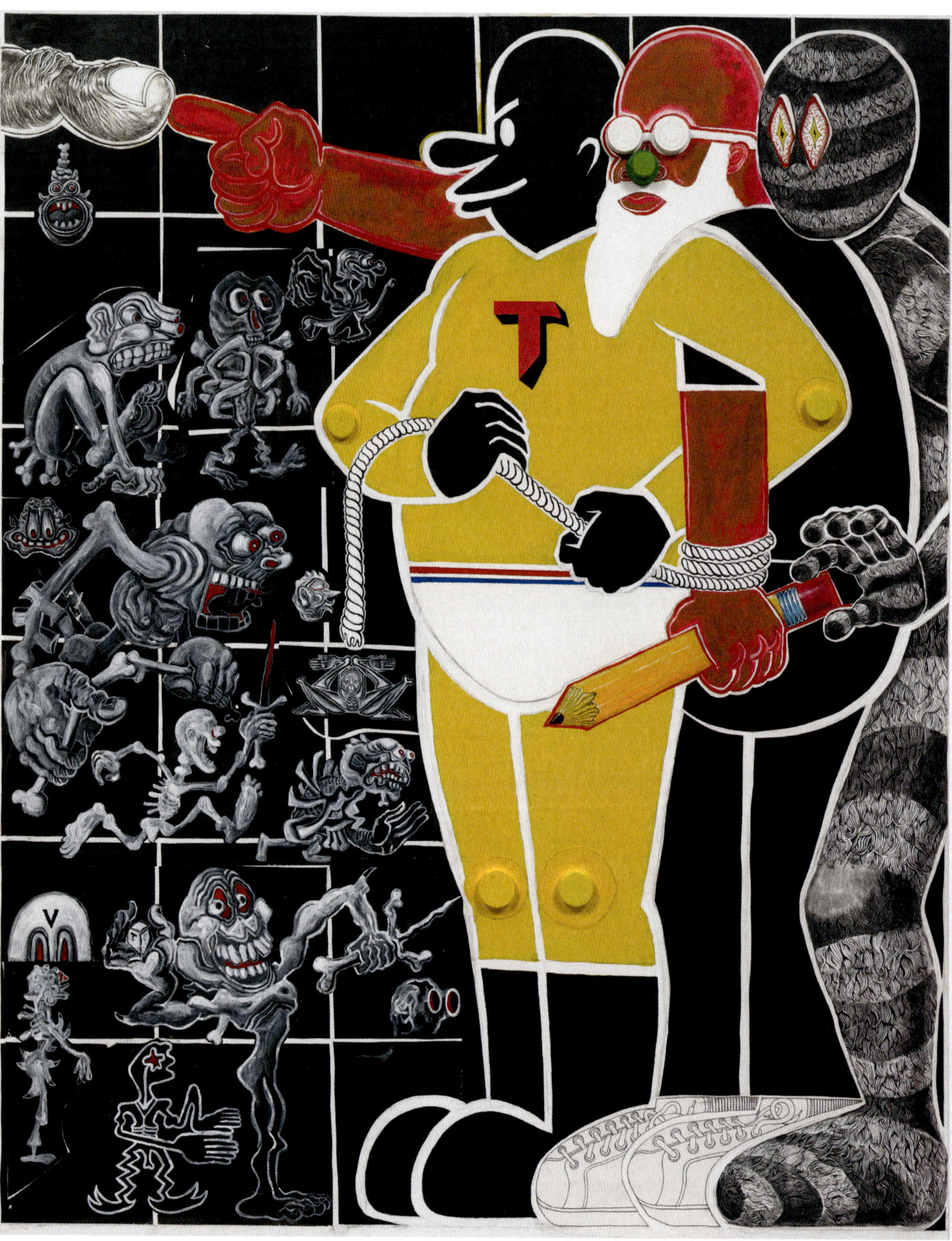

Trenton Doyle Hancock
It Takes Three or Four to Even the Score, 2022
Acrylic, graphite, ink, paper, canvas collage, and plastic bottle caps on canvas, 60 × 48 × 2 in. (152.4 × 121.9 × 5.1 cm)
Collection of the artist

"This painting is a portrait of my three split selves: Torpedoboy, the Artist, and the Bringback. Torpedoboy projects boundless potential; the Bringback, the mystery of memory and desire. The Vegans are the goblin-esque characters. They represent religious extremism and its dangers, and they are aligned with the finger of God at top left."
—Trenton Doyle Hancock, March 2024

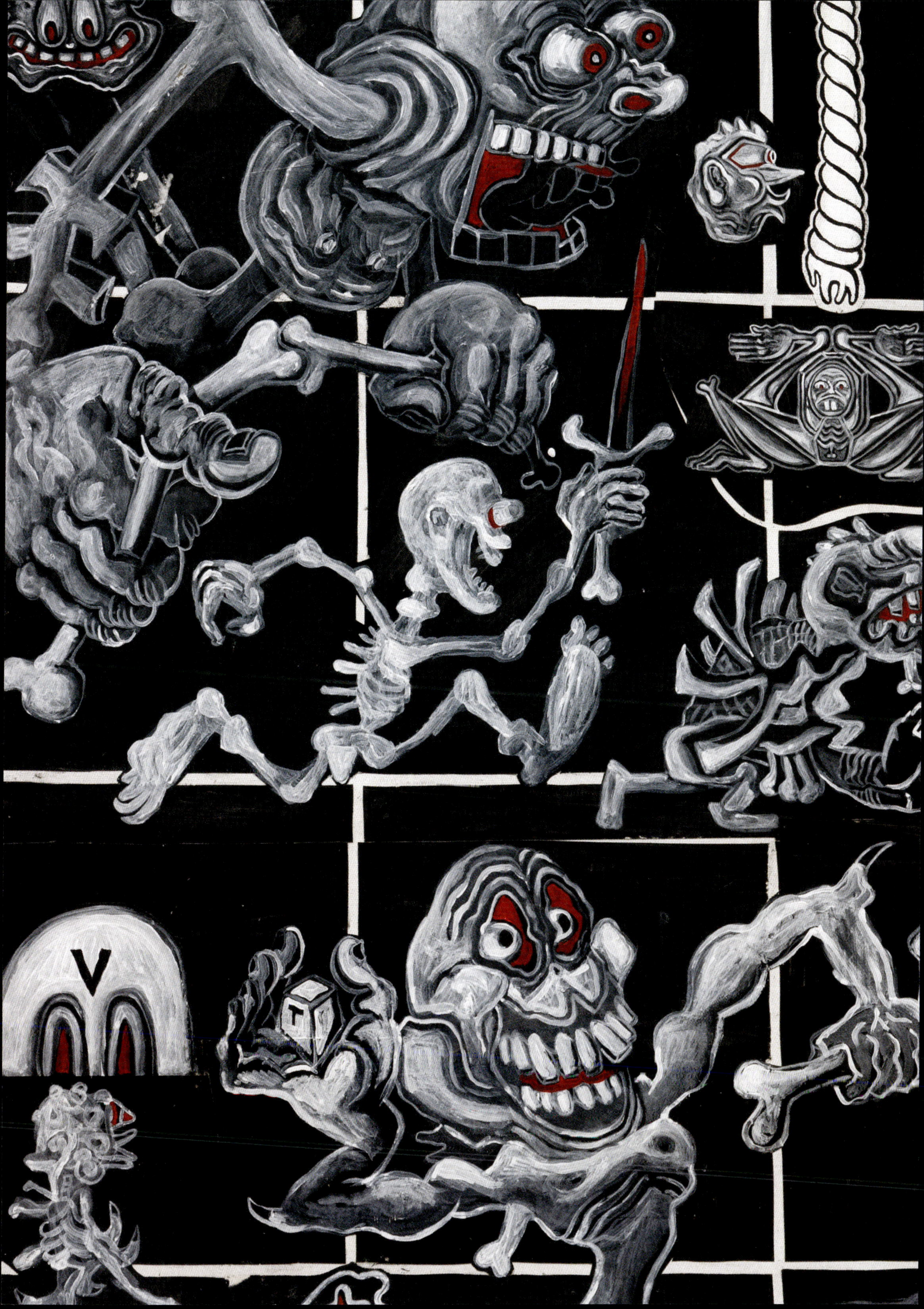

Trenton Doyle Hancock
*Step and Screw: West End Scrap (Four
Foot Furry Face Off)*, 2021
Acrylic and synthetic fur on canvas,
48 × 48 in. (122 × 122 cm)
Museum of Fine Arts, Boston

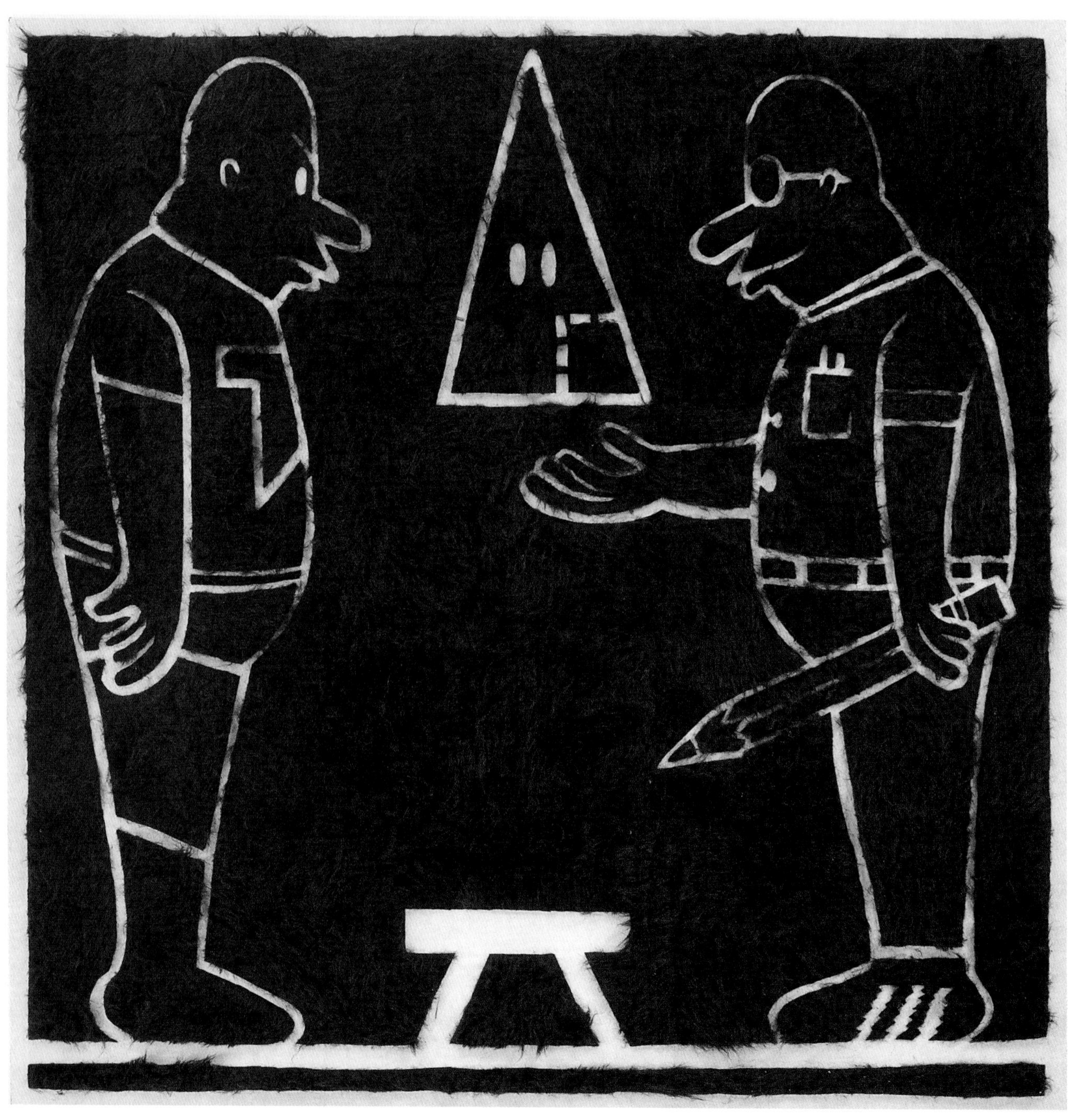

Trenton Doyle Hancock
Globetrotters, 2023
Acrylic and synthetic fur on canvas,
72 × 54 in. (182.9 × 137.2 cm)
Collection of the artist

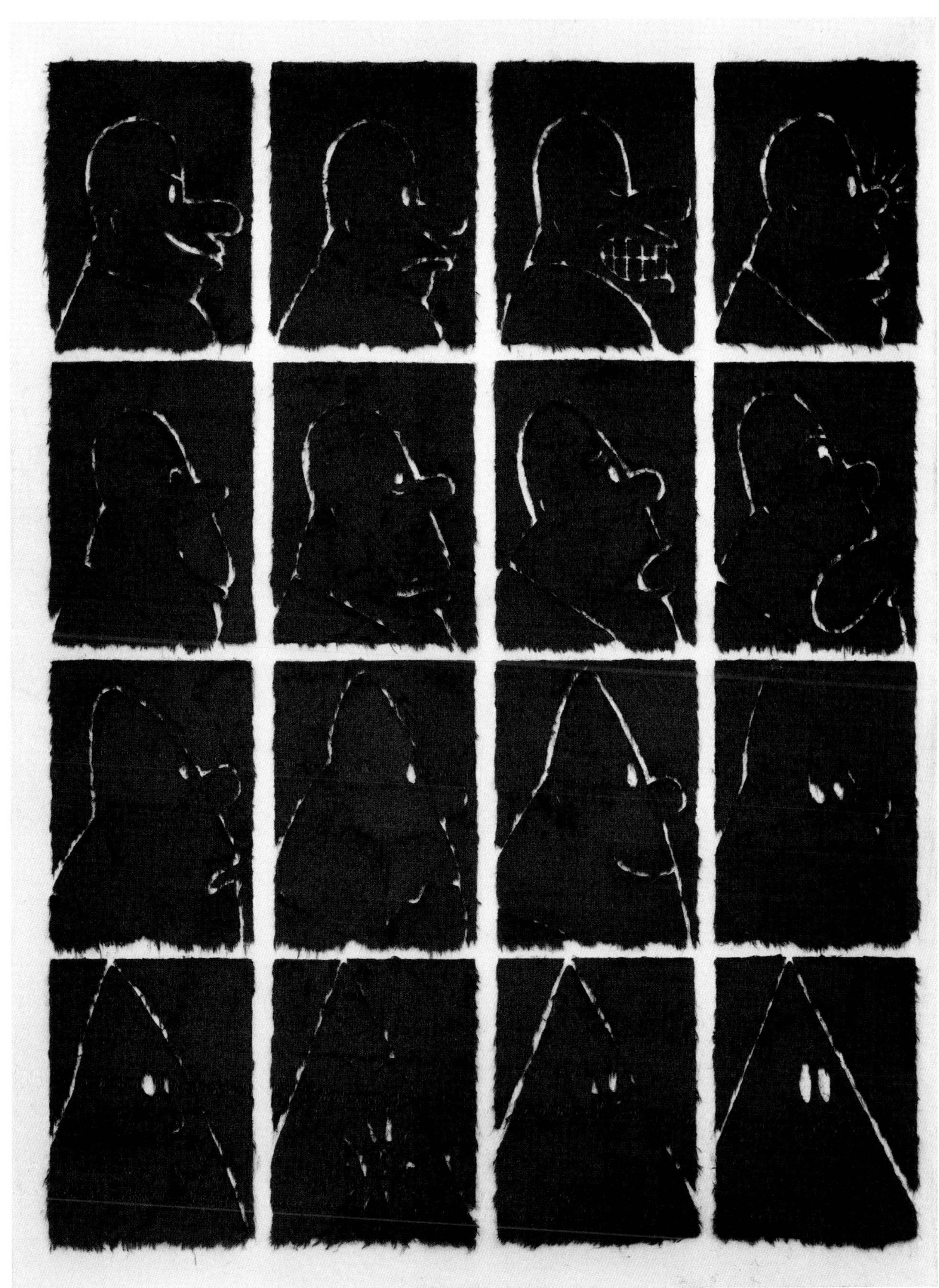

There may be a limit to the time one can spend exploring the psychology of evil. As Hancock puts it, "What the hell am I doing with these Klansmen if I'm not there to kill them?" In his most recent paintings, he does just that. This homoerotic send-up of the pottery scene in the film *Ghost* (1990) shows a mutual seduction between the Klansman and Hancock's Artist. Together, they fantasize about the Klansman's demise in the drawings they prepare on the table, while the hooded tormentor grips the turned-on lightbulb in the Artist's lap. The title recalls Eazy-E's 1987 debut single, "Boyz-n-the-Hood," a nod to the importance of rap in Hancock's political awakening.

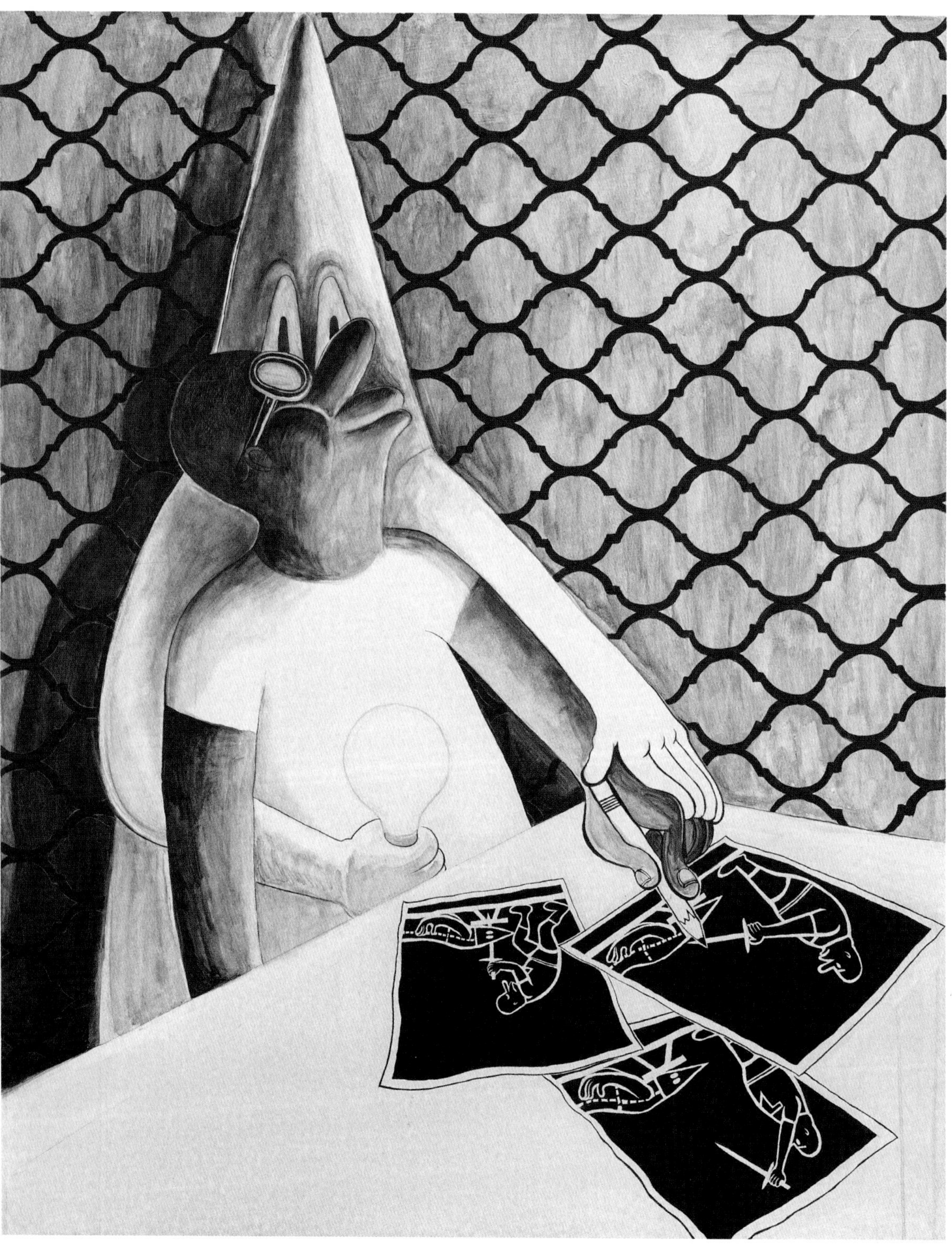

In *Lights Out*, Torpedoboy definitively ends his tentative affair with the Klansman, thrusting a sword through the hood of his aggressor. At a certain level, the painting acts as a symbolic patricide. "Guston often spoke of 'ghosts' in the studio, voices of predecessors requiring exorcism," says Hancock. "At some point, you have to stop the chase and confront those voices." Still, he notes, "It's an exorcism, but of course, the conversation continues. He's the artist I can't get away from."

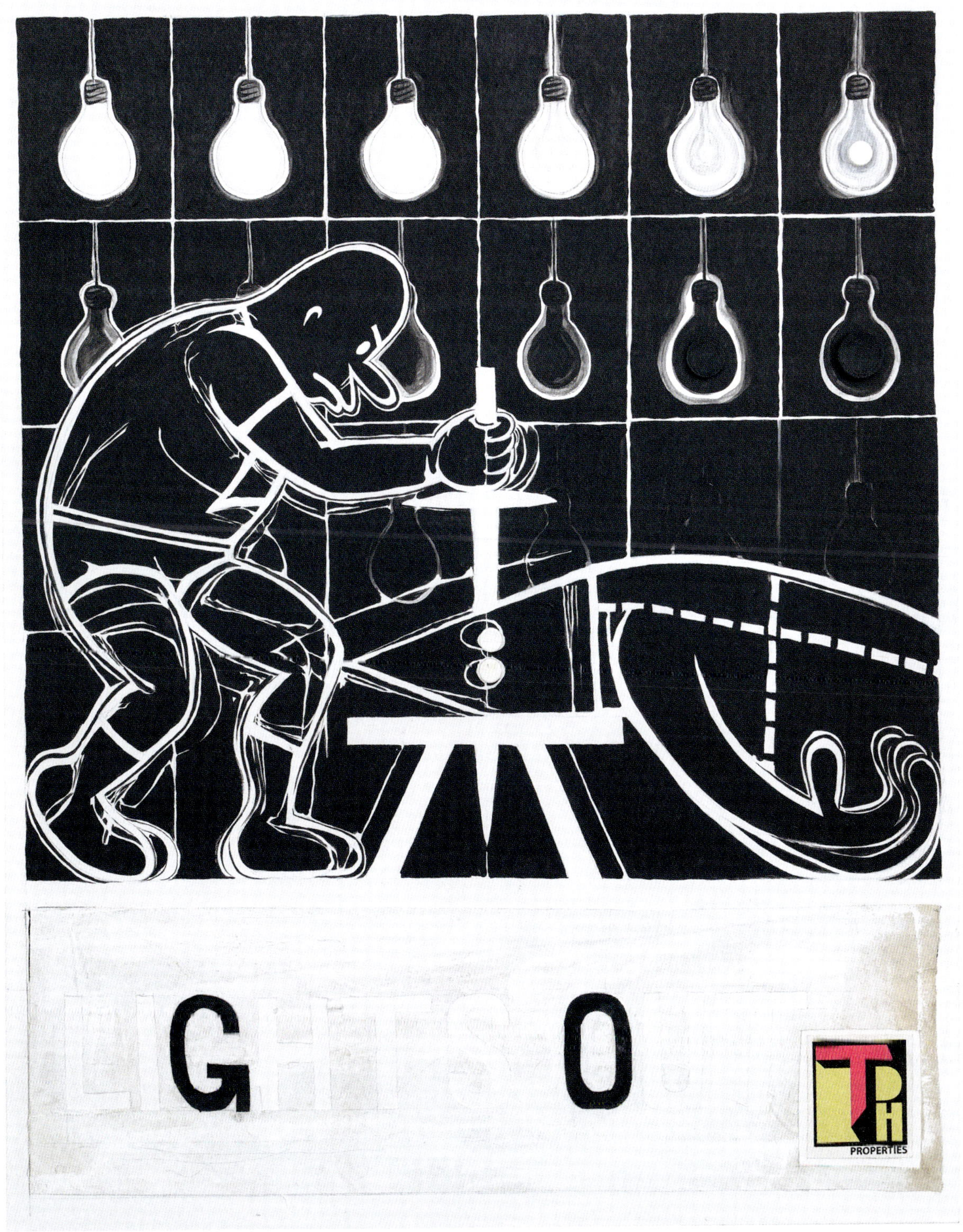

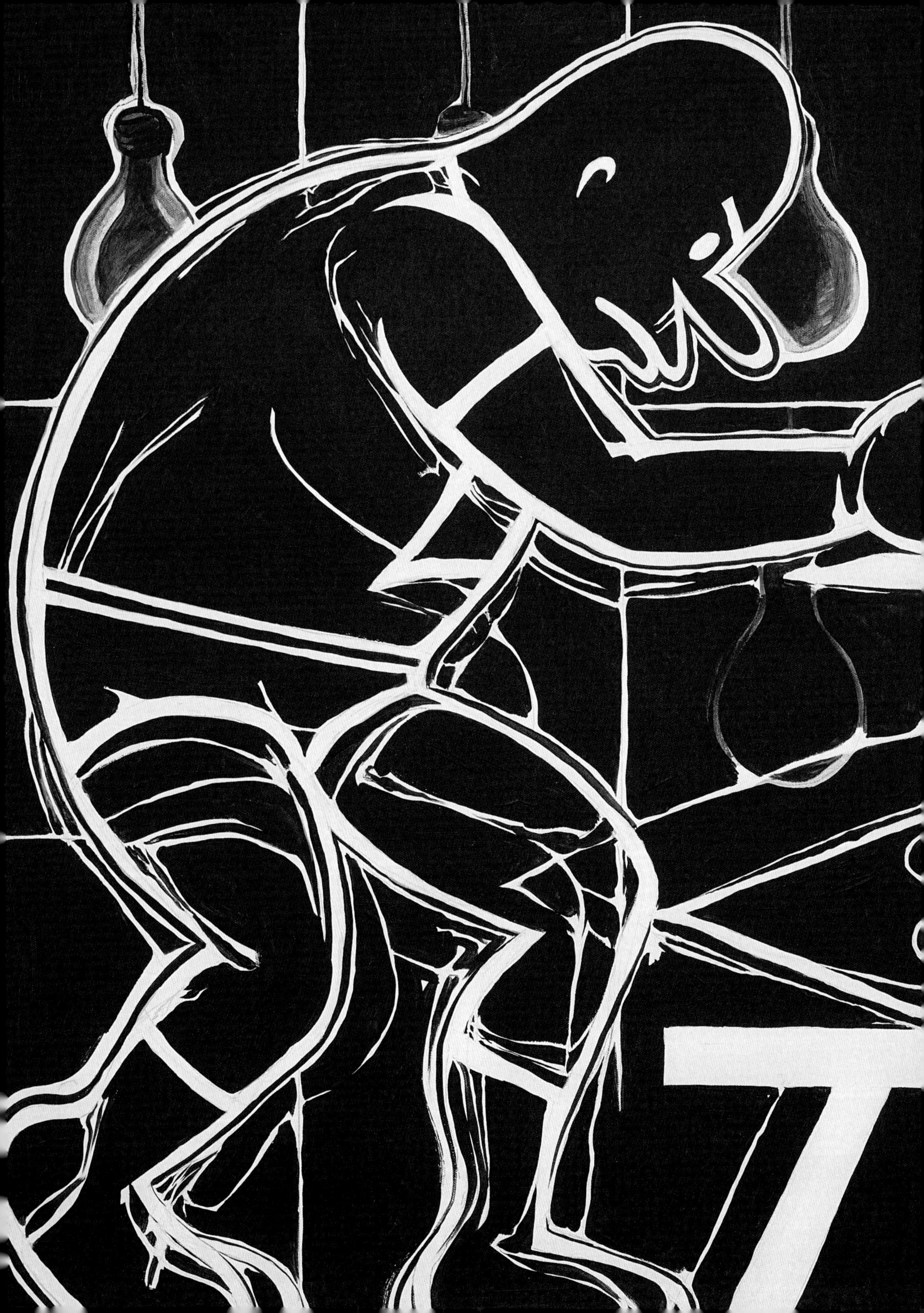

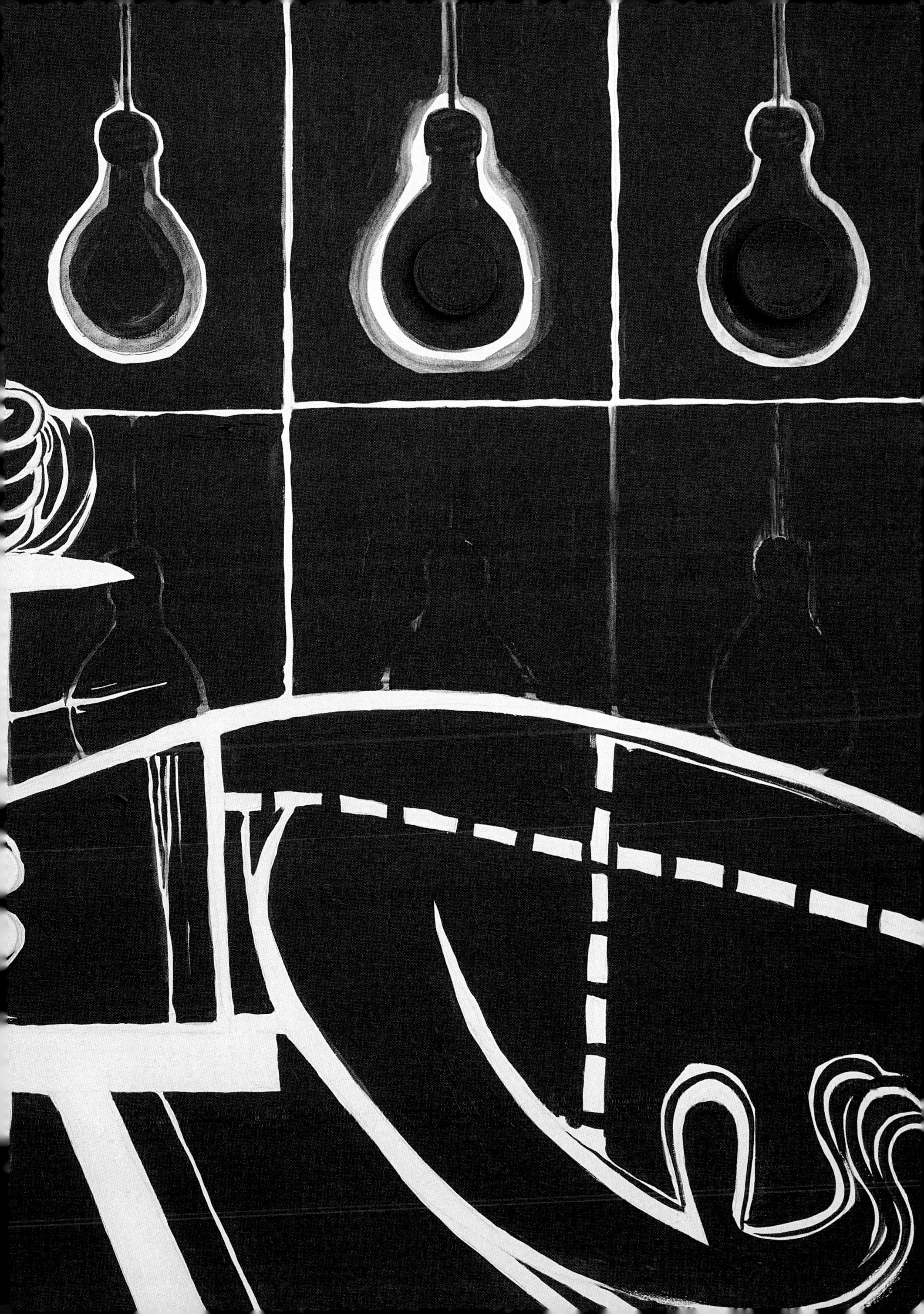

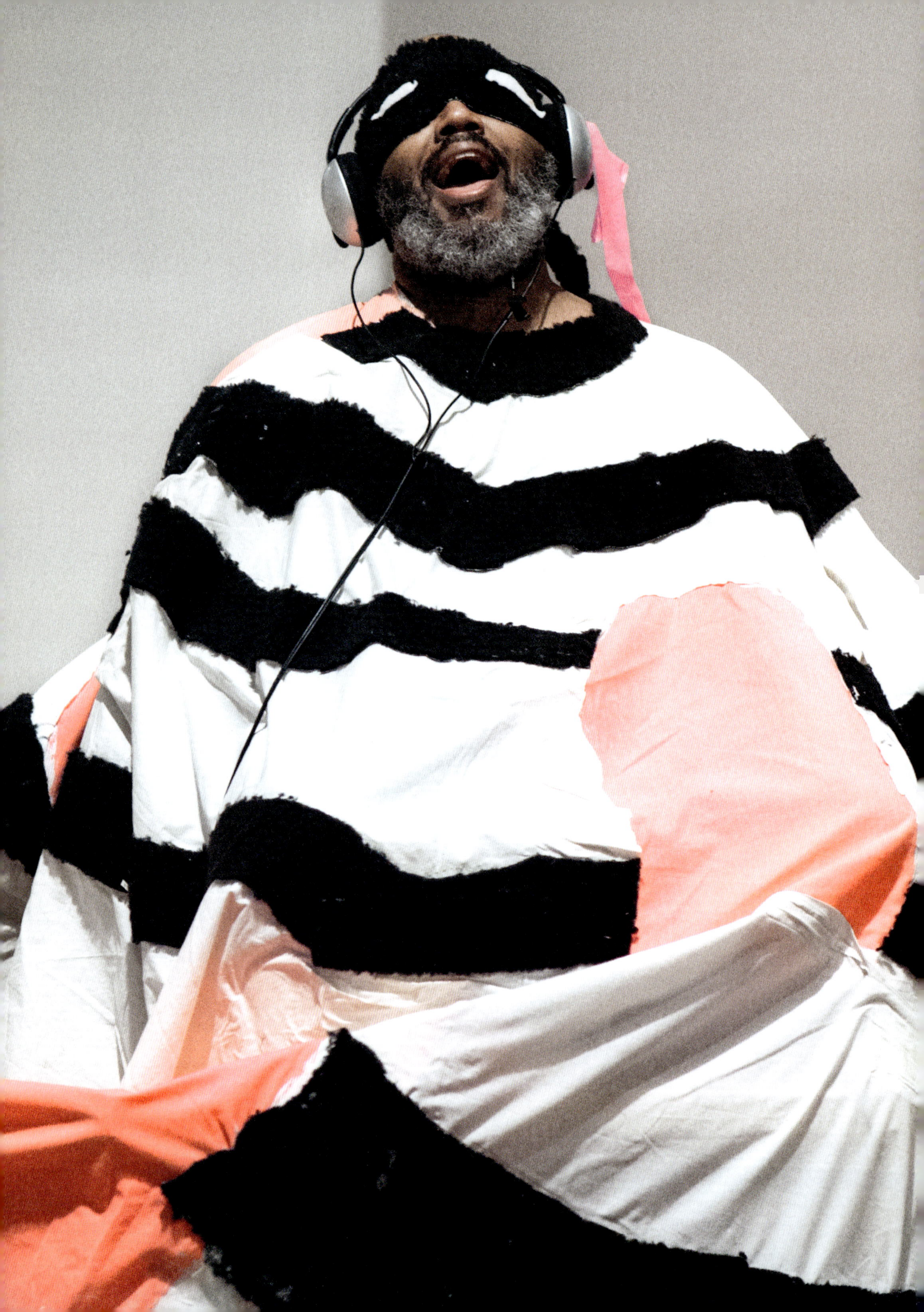

TRENTON DOYLE HANCOCK IN CONVERSATION WITH VALERIE CASSEL OLIVER

Valerie Cassel Oliver:
Can you talk about when and where Philip Guston entered into your life and your practice?

Trenton Doyle Hancock:
I was introduced to Philip Guston in 1994, when I was an undergraduate at East Texas State University. I came to that school already having my associate's degree from Paris Junior College, where, for a photography class, I had started an investigation about a cloaked character who wore a noose and wielded a hammer (see p. 43). It was sort of a self-portrait. I felt like I was doing something edgy and probing, in the spirit of Surrealism, though I didn't quite understand what it was.

Coming from a place like Paris, Texas, even though I didn't experience overt instances of racism, I knew that those sorts of things were happening, and my parents had told me about their own experiences. But I was born in the mid-1970s, so I was afforded a life that was sheltered from a lot of that. Most of the heavy lifting in the Civil Rights movement had been done by my parents' and my grandparents' generations. It wasn't until I was much older that I started to peel away those layers, or have them peeled away for me.

Some of that came to a head in this photo project. I became a lynched character. I started drawing more characters like that, and Klan-type characters—again, not yet understanding fully what I was doing. When I got to East Texas State, a professor named Thomas Seawell saw what I was doing and asked if I knew about Philip Guston. I'd never heard the name before. He happened to have a Guston book in his office and he let me thumb through it. I was amazed to see someone else working with the same kinds of tropes and symbols. It was coming from a cartoonish place, where I myself had a strong foothold, so the graphic language he was working with was something I was already interested in, as was the subject matter. I fell in love immediately with the work.

VCO: You see this in a more conscious way in the *Step and Screw!* series, particularly in light of where you come from. Paris, Texas, holds a position of great lore with regard to violence enacted on Black bodies.

Trenton Doyle Hancock performing *Devotion* at the Contemporary Arts Museum Houston in 2013 as part of the touring exhibition *Radical Presence*

TDH: Yeah, *Step and Screw!* was some years later. You and I had just worked together on the *Radical Presence* exhibition. I had loosened up my performative muscles and voice for that show. And it was during that show that I was invited by the NAACP chapter in Paris, Texas, to be a keynote speaker. My grandmother, who was ninety-something years old at the time, introduced me as the speaker. I had heard her speak so many times, and now I got to be up at a podium, addressing her. It was this beautiful, full-circle thing we were able to do. Afterward, back at home, I spoke with my mother and grandmother—not like parents to a child, and I don't want to say as equals, but they did talk to me like I was an adult. And they told it like it was. I had already been doing some research into the lynchings in Paris and had some specific names and dates to give them, to cross-reference what they knew. Of course, they knew every one, and they came at it from a very personal, subjective place. One event that is legendary is the Henry Smith lynching, in 1893. That's the one that happened at the fairgrounds. It was such a heinous crime that it made national headlines. *The New York Times* reported on it. And I was able to speak frankly to my mom and grandmother about this brutal event. My grandmother explained that Smith's body was dragged down the street that her house was on—the very street I played on as a kid. The whole town is smeared with this sort of cursed memory.

VCO: When the hooded figure emerged in your work, was it a precursor to the character of Loid? Or was he always that particular character?

TDH: The hooded character that evolved into Loid came from the same photo project. I knew the idea had power, that it wasn't just a one-off thing. I continued to look at the image and redraw it, repaint it, transform it, and I knew that I would continue to come back to it. He actually split into two different beings. The Loid character is a brutalized Black man with a sheet over his head. He wears a noose and wields a hammer, and you can always see his Black skin. There is a paradox of him wearing the sheet but also being undeniably of African descent.

VCO: So, he is an oppressed being, but also an oppressed being who oppresses?

TDH: Loid ends up being a spirit of vengeance. At some point I started drawing Klan characters more akin to Guston's Klansmen. By the time I got to *Step and Screw!*, the expression was very pure. I spoke specifically about these hooded Klansmen as everyone knows them now, as members of a terrorist organization. The way Guston drew them, he deflated them a bit. He turned them into buffoons, rounded off their sharp edges.

That's where I hit the ground running with the character, who faces off with my cartoon character Torpedoboy, a Black superhero. I wanted to see what that looked like, to have these two characters confront each other in a picture plane. That was the beginning of *Step and Screw!*

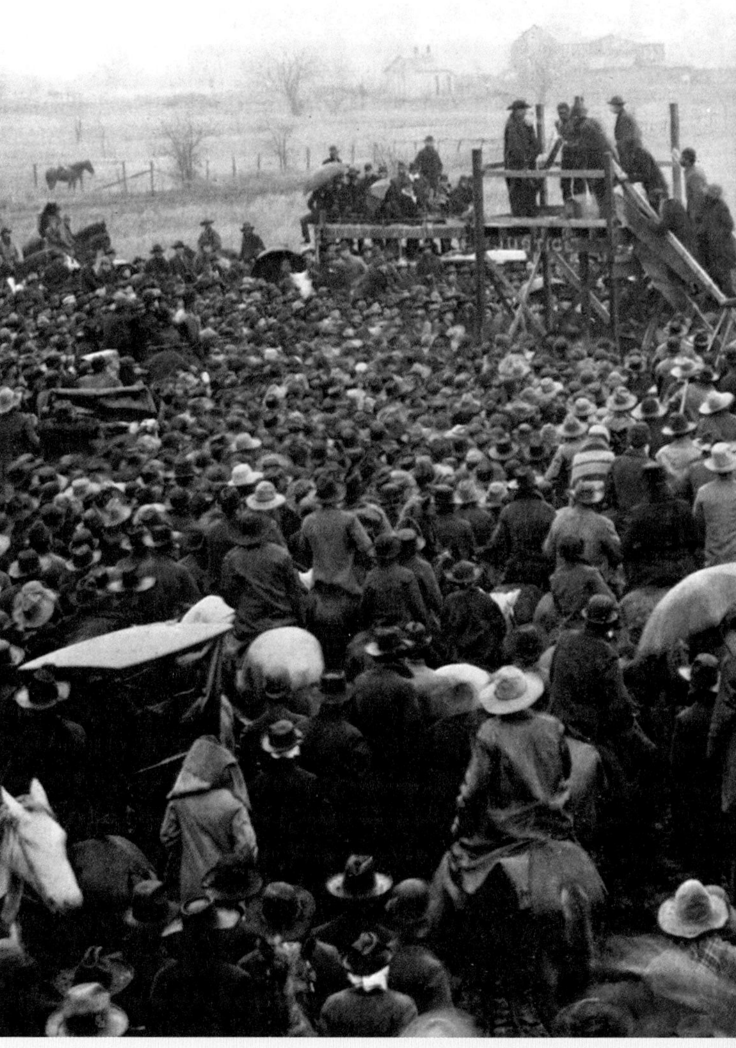

The public lynching of Henry Smith in Paris, Texas, on February 1, 1893

VCO: *Step and Screw!* debuted in the exhibition *Skin and Bones, 20 Years of Drawing* at the Contemporary Arts Museum Houston (CAMH). It was presented in a structure reminiscent of the interiors in which we see Guston's Klansmen congregating, replete with a dangling lightbulb, and which required visitors to walk through and experience. There were thirty panels that not only had Torpedoboy square off with Guston's Klansmen, but the installation also included a timeline that conflated what was happening in your own life with past and present events. Can you speak more to this idea of bringing in a timeline? Because in many ways it served to situate Torpedoboy and his world as a stand-in for yourself and the world that has an impact on you as a Black man.

TDH: The impetus to start the timeline came somewhat out of left field. I have a combination lock that my mom bought me when I was in the sixth grade, for my locker. I still remember the combination: 6, 16, 22. I had the lock there on the table, and I happened to glance over at it as I was starting the project. I was looking for a way to peel back layers of time and I thought, Maybe 6, 16, 22 is a date. That would be June 16, 1922. I looked up what happened on that day, which led me to the biography of Henry Berliner, a Jewish engineer who helped develop a version of a helicopter. And I think he died on May 1—my birthday—but four years before I was born, so I had two things that I felt were a sign from God.

That got me thinking that maybe Torpedoboy wasn't always me. Maybe he was a spirit or an energy that had to embody a corporal form on Earth. And when that body dies,

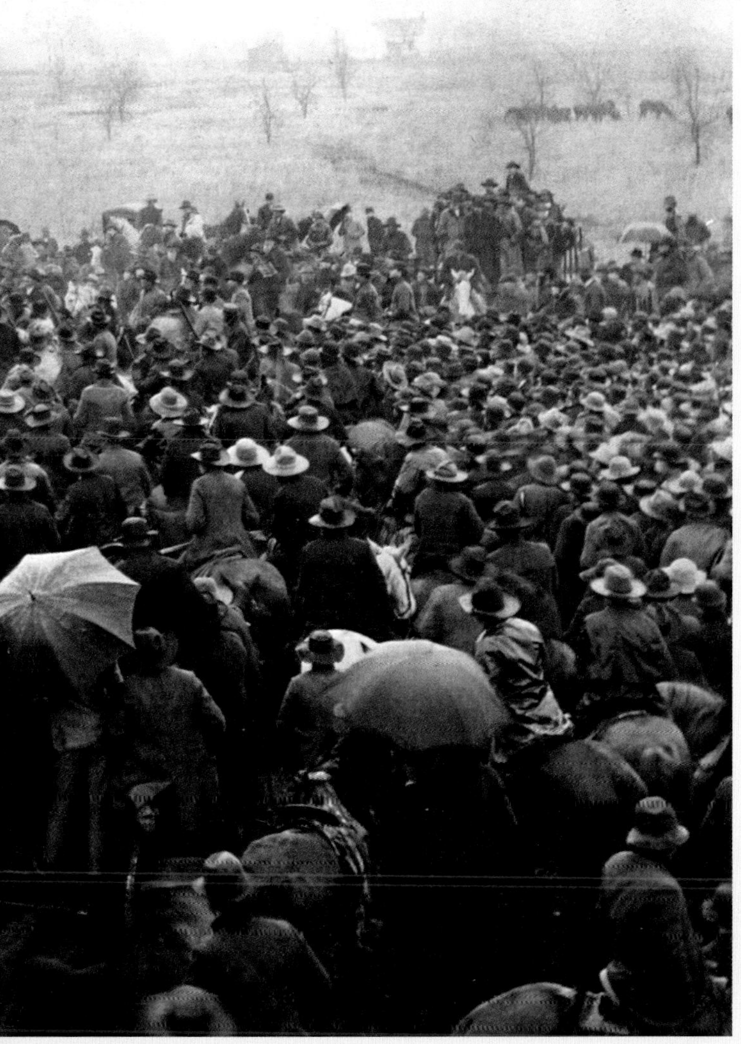

ANOTHER NEGRO BURNED

HENRY SMITH DIES AT THE STAKE.

DRAWN THROUGH THE STREETS ON A CAR—TORTURED FOR NEARLY AN HOUR WITH HOT IRONS AND THEN BURNED—AWFUL VENGEANCE OF A PARIS (TEXAS) MOB.

PARIS, Texas, Feb. 1.—Henry Smith, the negro assailant of four-year-old Myrtle Vance, has expiated, in part, his crime by death at the stake.

Every since the perpetration of his crime this city and the entire surrounding country has been in a frenzy of excitement.

When the news came last night that he had been captured, that he had been identified by B. B. Sturgeon, James T. Hicks, and many others of the Paris searching party, the city was joyful over the apprehension of the brute.

Hundreds of people poured into the city from the adjoining country, and the word passed from lip to lip that the punishment should fit the crime, and that death by fire was the penalty that Smith should pay for the most atrocious murder and outrage in Texas history.

"Another Negro Burned—Henry Smith Dies at the Stake," *The New York Times,* February 2, 1893 he enters another body to continue. Maybe *I* was Henry Berliner once, or Torpedoboy was Henry Berliner before me. Maybe that's even how he learned to fly, in the helicopter. That was my logic as I started to tie everything together, and I just started pulling dates. When was Philip Guston born? When did he die? When were my mother and father born? Who taught me how to draw (it was my Aunt Fan Fan), and when was *she* born?

Some of the most important dates that made their way into the timeline concerned the lynching history of Paris, Texas, and of the South in general. Hearing my grandmother talk so defeatedly about racism throughout her ninety years made me so angry. What could I do about it? That was the fuel that got *Step and Screw!* off the ground. All these other things helped shape it, like thinking about Guston and about these random dates that I thought had some kind of magical significance in my life. But the documentary aspect of it very much felt like the obligation that drove the project.

VCO: I understand that the iteration of *Step and Screw!* that we showed at CAMH has since been acquired by the Menil Collection. Can you talk about the presentation you did there in 2019 and how you expanded the series? Is the project ongoing?

TDH: At the end of the first series of panels, Torpedoboy ends up trapped in a house. He gets on a stool to screw in a lightbulb, and when he turns on the light, he sees that he's surrounded by Klansmen, but in a comical way. Yes, he's in peril, but it's sort of like Dudley Do-Right. How will our hero get out of this one? It ends on that kind of cartoon cliffhanger. We're all used to seeing the characters snap back, ready for a new adventure. Torpedoboy is no different.

That's how I started the next fifteen panels (see pp. 98–101). He's on the stool and gets the idea to bargain for his life. He thinks, Well, if this is how I'm going out, I should get a last meal. So, he asks the Klansmen for a bowl of ground beef. Since they've got him where they want him, they figure the least they can do is feed him. But what they don't know is that large quantities of meat for him is like spinach

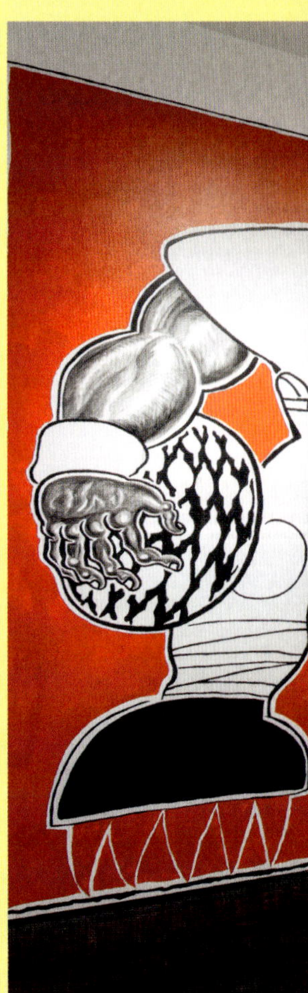

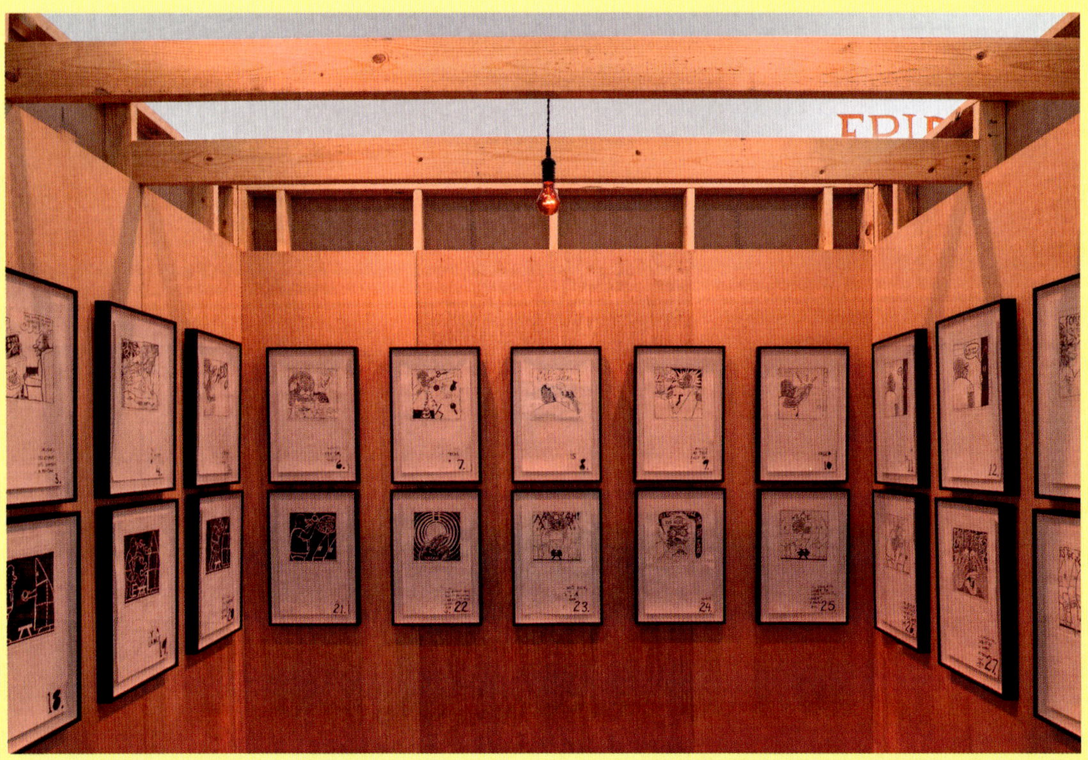

Installation views of *Contemporary Focus: Trenton Doyle Hancock*, featuring *Epidemic! Presents: Step and Screw!*, 2014, and *Epidemic! Presents: Step and Screw!, Part Two*, 2019, at the Menil Collection, Houston, 2019

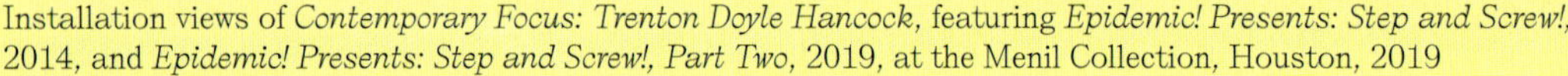

for Popeye. It turns him into a super being. He goes into what's called "meat form" and morphs into a giant football player. It's his war armor. He's ready to take them all on.

The new images offer you the catharsis you don't get in the first thirty panels of *Step and Screw!* You get to see him smash and step on and do all the things you want to do to white supremacy.

VCO: The scale of the first thirty panels was about nineteen by twelve inches; the next fifteen panels have only been shown as murals so far, correct? And then aspects of *Step and Screw!* also moved onto canvas?

TDH: Yes. After Torpedoboy is lured into the house, he meets the Klansman, who orders him to get on the stool. That's what I call "The Exchange": the Klansman hands over a lightbulb. A lightbulb can, of course, represent an exchange of ideas, but the way that it's drawn, it could also be a bomb or a vial. It also directly relates to Guston's use of the lightbulb. The shed in which this exchange takes place is also connected to a space of trauma for him, because Guston found his father hanging in a shed.

So, there's a lot of meaning in the Klansman's gesture, which I took as a sort of "pregnant" situation in which anything could happen. At that point I started making over-life-size paintings of the isolated moment when Torpedoboy and the Klansman face off. I started to substitute other things for the lightbulb. An apple allowed me to explore ideas of original sin and the Garden of Eden. That became quite a colorful painting, with a serpent wrapped around as a frame, speaking nonsense to Torpedoboy (see p. 103). Instead of a timeline at the bottom, I presented the conversation between the characters, carving it out of the canvas itself onto their bodies, almost like tattoos. It felt right that these two characters were enacting things on each other's bodies. It's a civil conversation yet it requires a violent intervention with the medium. You also have to get quite close to the painting to read the dialogue, which seemed an exciting way to draw people in.

I eventually broke away from the strictures of that specific architecture and those two characters. It became more filmic in terms of how the narrative started to move forward.

VCO: Returning to the idea of Guston "flattening" or deflating the Klansmen into buffoons—there is a kind of absurdity that you play with in your work as well, creating a space of humor.

TDH: One of the cues I took from Guston was his ability to identify with, or perhaps go undercover as, a Klansman. You get the sense that

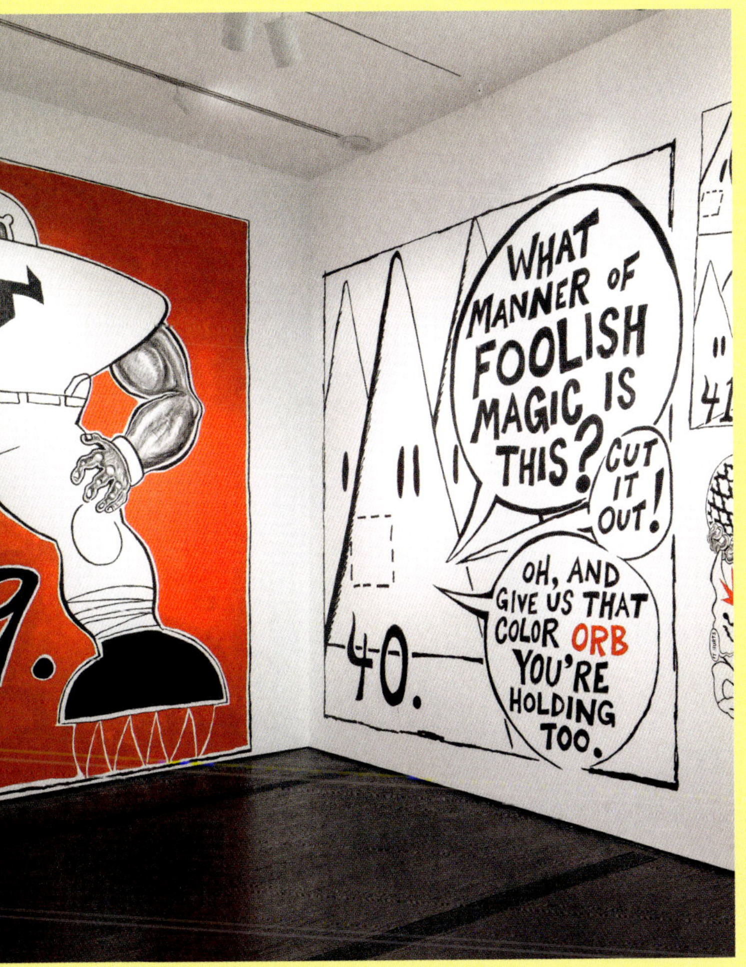

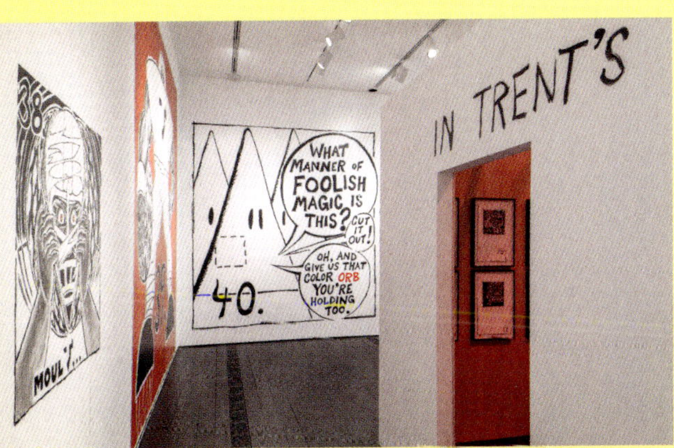

he was infiltrating the organization in order to blow it up from the inside. That's what his paintings are—a bomb ready to explode but which never quite gets to the place of explosion. There's a tension there.

If you follow Guston's career, trace it all the way back to his earliest work from the 1930s, he originally painted a much more naturalistic, terrifying Klansman (see pp. 20, 21, 42). But I think, as he grew older and dealt with the paradox of being both an artist and a politically aware being, he began to question his obligations as a painter. It became a sort of absurdist adventure—an ironic conundrum—wondering what painting could actually achieve. So perhaps you deal with it with a bit of humor. I think both the Jewish and the Black communities are masterful at turning pain into something more digestible through comedy.

It took me a lot of time—decades—to understand that trauma enacted on the Black body as projected onto the canvas doesn't have to be solely about the contract between Blackness and whiteness in America. I am in control of my own abjection and of my own self-deprecation. I tried to find my way into a new, multifaceted kind of humor—humor plus sadness plus maniacal laughter. It doesn't always have to be about the failed contract with the American enterprise.

VCO: That speaks to a kind of evolution by which we, as Black individuals, now feel freer to be our complex selves rather than just one half of a binary. There have always been complexities and paradoxes to Black lives, but the ability to explore them in a real, unlimited way is freeing.

TDH: I totally agree. I think us seeing each other fully becomes the key to progress, really. And to self-healing.

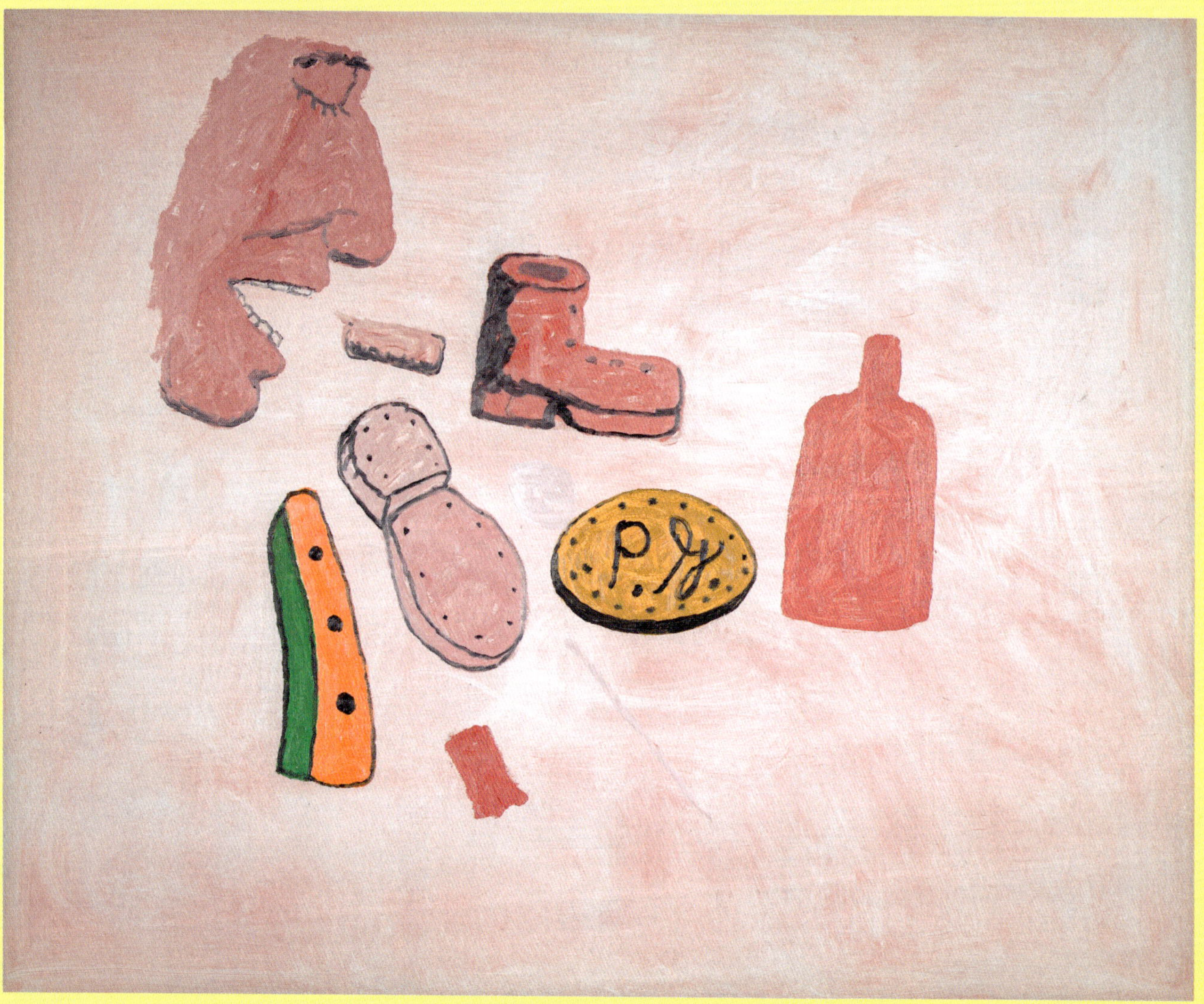

Philip Guston, *Painter's Forms*, 1972, oil on panel, 48 × 60 in. (122 × 152.4 cm). Private collection

 There are spaces in Guston's paintings that isolate or almost dismember the body in order to convey information or to focus on specific things. I see in some of your work, not so much a dismemberment of the body as a focused exaggeration of it. Can you talk about the synchrony of these strategies, dismembering and exaggerating?

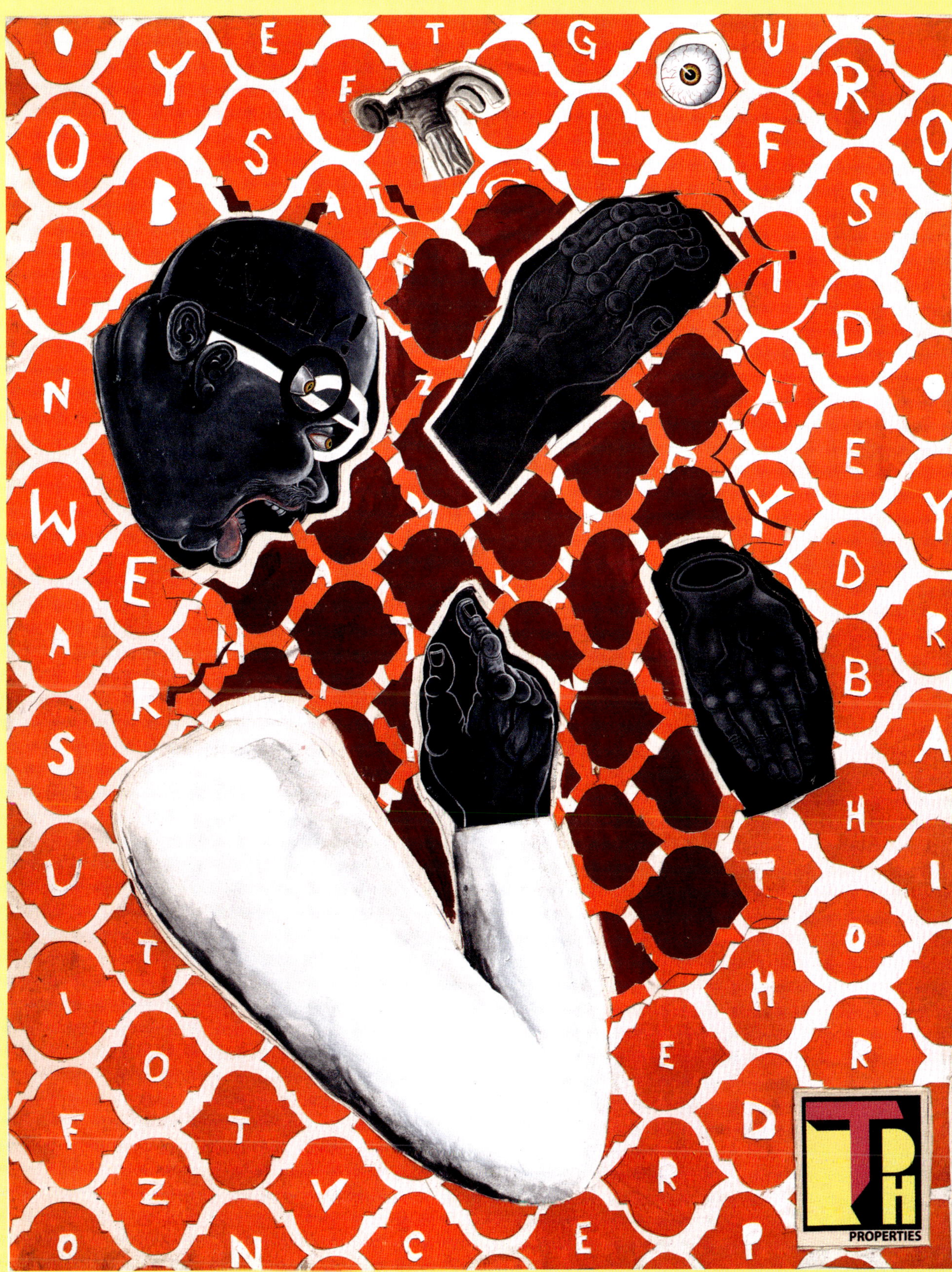

Trenton Doyle Hancock, *Finally!*, 2016, mixed media on canvas, 48 × 37½ × 1½ in. (121.9 × 95.3 × 3.8 cm). Private collection, Aventura, Florida

TDH: I think Guston and I both scavenge the interior subconscious. How does the brain operate when you shut off your daytime machine and go on autopilot? What does it do with those fragments of life? I've definitely begun several bodies of work where the narrative called for a device that helped promote an atmosphere of paranoia, or hiding, or running for your life. How do you do that—make it explicit through imagery, without writing it down? So I started having characters peek out from behind things, or perhaps just show an arm poking out from stage left or stage right, so you're not seeing the full body. That speaks to a kind of dismemberment, a fragmented reality of fear, trauma, and paranoia.

It's been something of a through line in my work. In the 1990s I did a lot of disembodied heads and hands and things like that, floating around the picture plane. And I think it has something to do with the fragmentation of the Black body. Being separated from culture, from family, from a source, and having so much of that be lost to history—not knowing where you come from. In the 1990s, when there were no race studies at my school, I had to figure those things out for myself and read what I thought was relevant. Like James Baldwin. I learned how he, as a Black intellectual in America, was unable to reach a position on nationalism or patriotism that his white counterparts were able to do rather easily. I thought, Here's the smartest guy of any color I've ever read, yet he's unable to participate fully in this enterprise of being an American. I started to understand that there's just a fragmentation you're subject to as a Black being in America. I had no choice but for that to rear its head in my work.

VCO: Yes, the Black body itself can be considered a literal space of dismemberment, but also one of activism and awareness. Your earlier work shows Black beings in striped clothing reminiscent of the incarcerated (see pp. 136, 139), which renders the Black body a space of activism. You align perfectly with Guston in that respect, and I wonder whether that is conscious—as John Coltrane said, "We're all dipping from the same well." At the same time the differing realities of where Guston's work and your work emerged from are ever-present. How do you truly conclude your relationship or dialogue with Guston—exorcise it, so to speak?

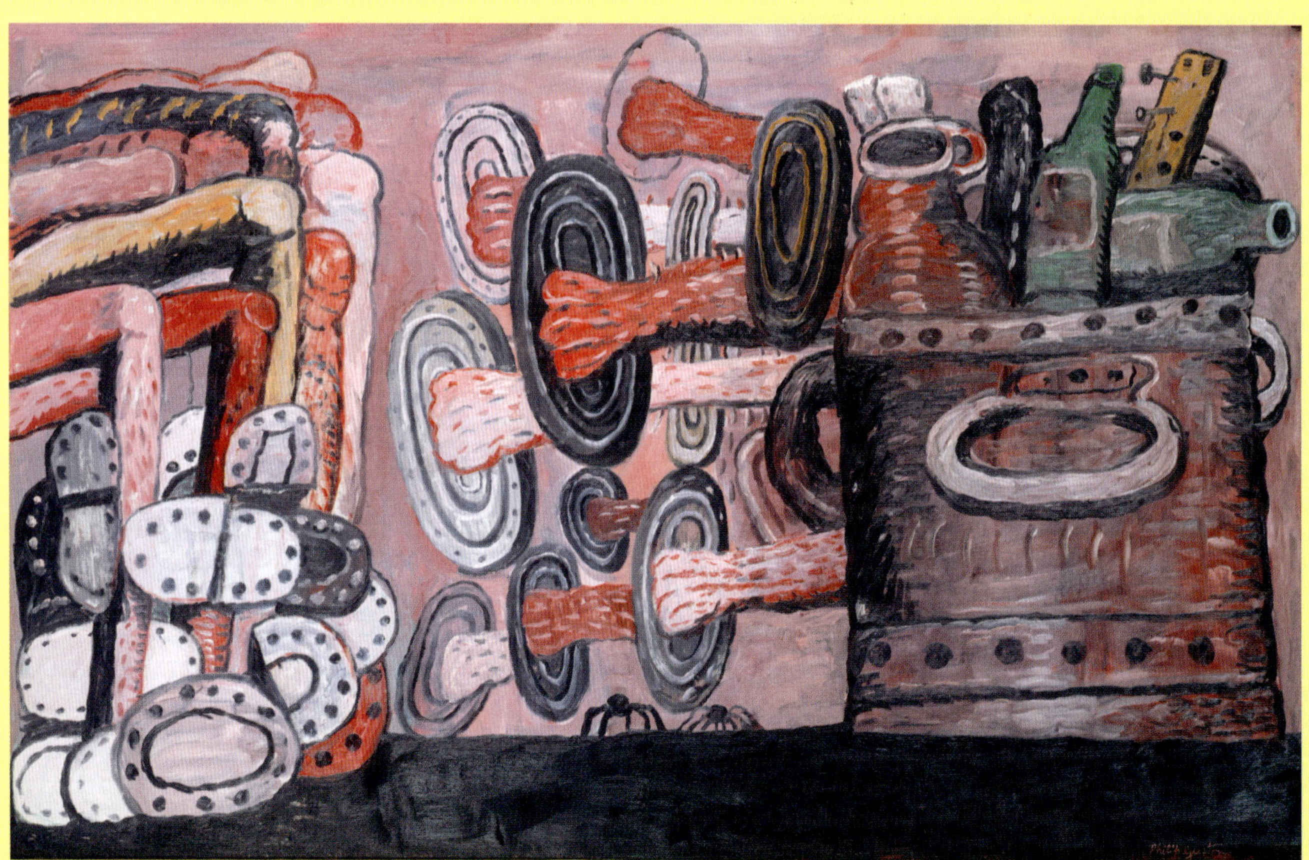

Philip Guston, *The Street*, 1977, oil on canvas, 69 × 110¾ in. (175.3 × 281.3 cm). Metropolitan Museum of Art, New York

TDH: I know that's not possible. It's more likely he'll just go underground for a bit and then come back in an even more intense and explicit way.

Being able to participate in the recent *Philip Guston Now* retrospective—a worldwide refocusing on his work—was a dream come true, to see so much of his work in one place and to learn from the diverse voices speaking about him. It might be time to go back to the studio fueled by these exhibitions and essays and whatnot, but then to put the Klansmen to sleep in a semipermanent way. As much as I love that work, it has to drive off into the sunset. In a Freudian way, you've got to kill that father figure.

VCO: So many artists enact patricide—kill the very thing that gives them a source of life, artistically. For so many years, you have walked in step with Guston, so to now come to a point of patricide seems apt. But until you reach that point, given what you were saying about *Radical Presence* and how it opened up a performative impulse for you, I wonder whether the Klansman and Torpedoboy could manifest in a performative way.

TDH: I think that would be very interesting. It almost seems necessary.

VCO: There's so much rich material to work from, and the framing of the narrative in the panels lends itself to the cinematic. It's almost like you've already created a storyboard.

TDH: Very true. All the heavy lifting has been done, so animation could happen easily, or some combination of animation and live-action

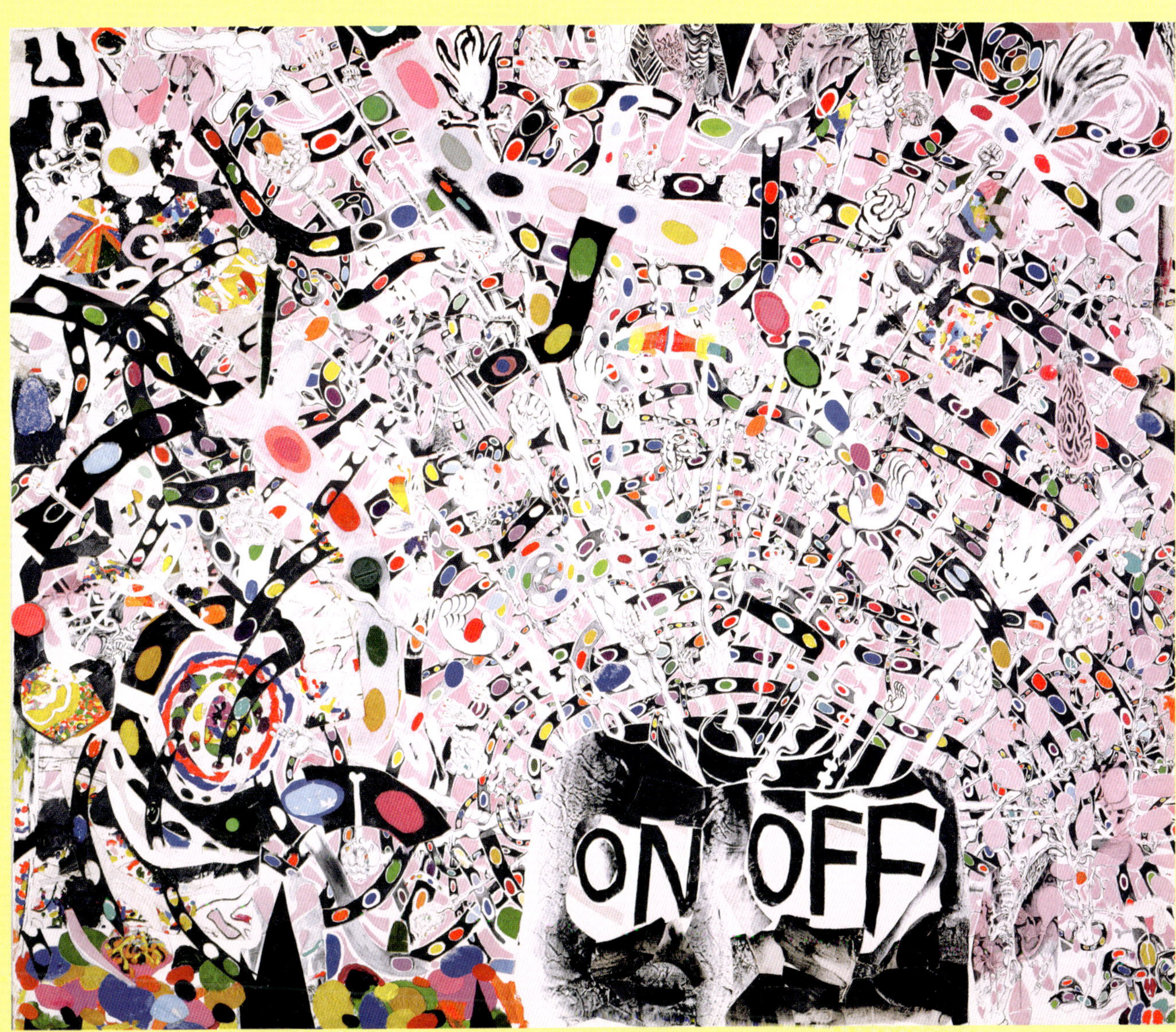

Trenton Doyle Hancock, *The Second to the Last Great Hurrah, Symphony Masquerades as War*, 2006, mixed media on canvas, 90 × 108⅜ × 6 in. (228.6 × 275.3 × 15.2 cm). James Cohan, New York

performance. I've definitely opened up pathways in the past several years to having a multidisciplinary, multimedia platform for these bodies of work.

VCO: Now more than ever, the relevance of such work seems to be at an apex, because we've come back to a point where people are enacting violence with greater impunity.

TDH: I believe so, too. We have come to a place where the understanding is, Well, nothing has really changed, has it? Although the advent of the digital era has allowed people to report and to document crimes and injustices, so it's at least understood as a truth—a constant—that needs to be addressed and fixed.

I would also say that people don't simply take things at face value anymore. People have been conditioned through a kind of irony—through comedy, through humor—to understand that there are layers to things. I think the general public today *does* have a more nuanced understanding of where things stand, politically and artistically, that maybe they didn't have in 1968 or '69 [when Guston was making his late Klan pictures].

VCO: In terms of this exhibition, what do you feel would be most relevant for people to understand after seeing your work in conversation with Guston's?

TDH: I would hope that people come away with an understanding that people can come from different backgrounds and yet share a language that speaks to their traumas; that they can use art—specifically, painting—as a way to deal with it, but also as a weapon to protest against it. I hope they see that art can be a platform to talk about the liminal aspects of language, saying things that are beyond words, and that those things oftentimes are communal.

I would hope that people can look at both my and his graphic output and realize that, between these paintings—"between the gutter," as a cartoonist would say—there is a space where time is amorphous and we are eternal beings, connected beyond time. I want the exhibition to speak to that truth, and also to the topical realities that both Guston and I, and that victims of white supremacy, continue to face.

Trenton Doyle Hancock, *The Second to the Last Great Hurrah, Symphony Masquerades as War*, 2006 (detail; see p. 133)

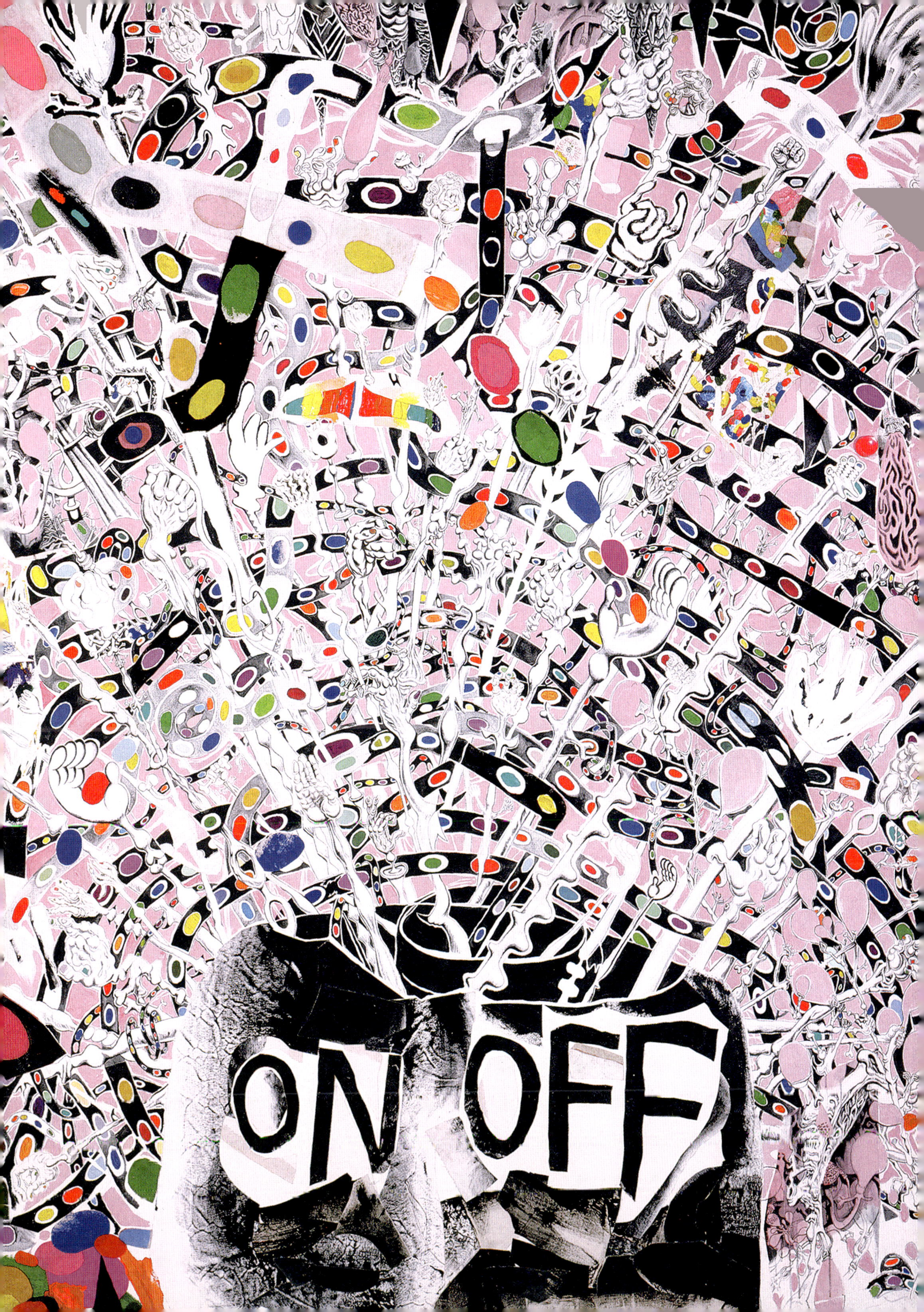
ON OFF

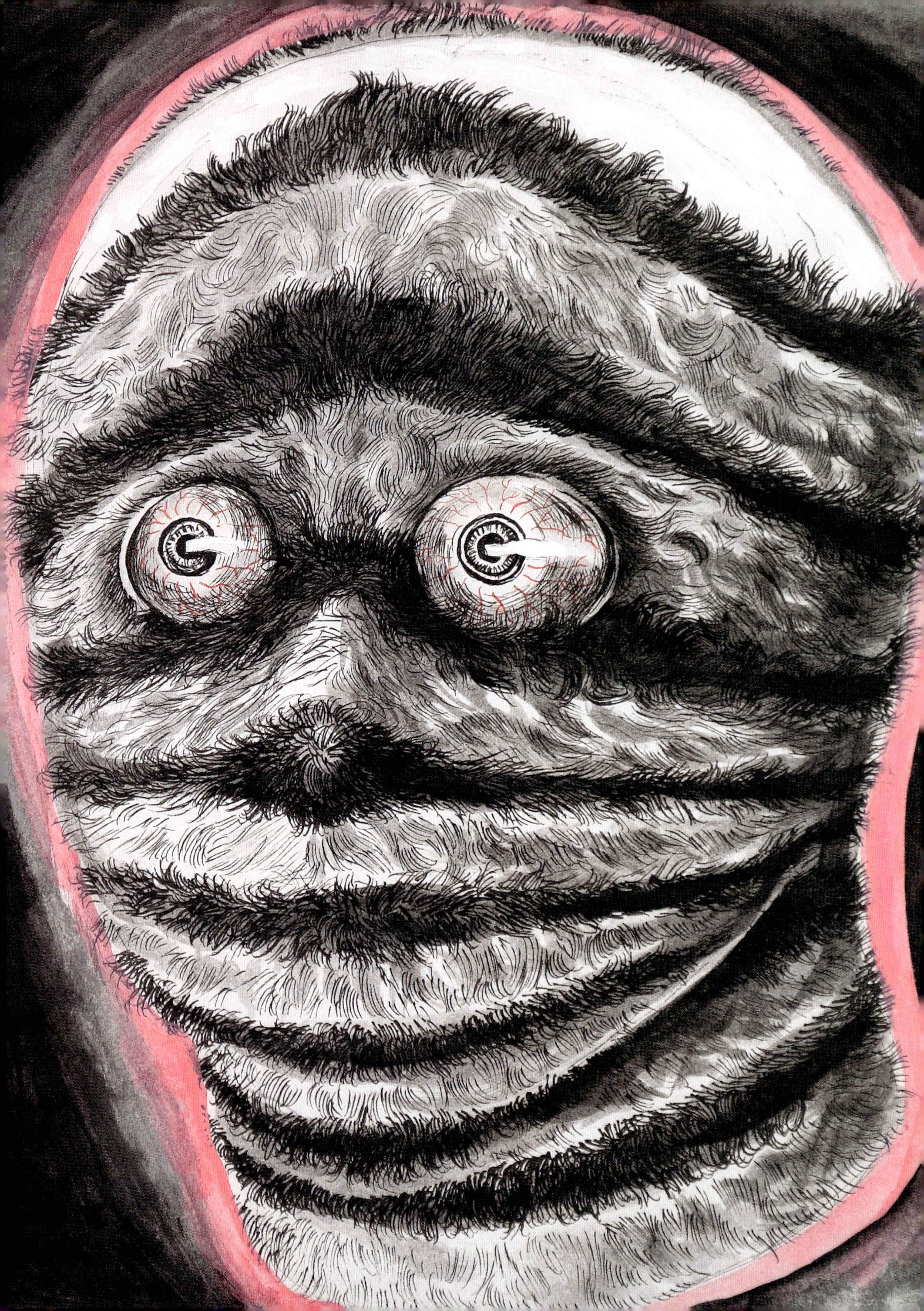

TRENTON DOYLE HANCOCK IN CONVERSATION WITH ART SPIEGELMAN

MODERATED BY REBECCA SHAYKIN

Trenton Doyle Hancock, *. . . and then it All Came Back to Me* (detail), 2011, mixed media on paper, 9 × 8 in. (22.9 × 20.3 cm). Collection of KAWS, New York

Rebecca Shaykin:
Let's start with an open question to both of you: when did you first become aware of Guston's work, and how would you describe his influence on your art over time?

Art Spiegelman:
Sometime in the mid- to late 1970s, I can't remember where. I was a slob snob: if it wasn't on newsprint, to hell with it. I thought painting was a con—you make it big, so you can charge more. But Guston's work crept up on me until eventually it was a done deal when I saw the Nixon drawings [the *Poor Richard* series].

If I can sidetrack for a second, Trenton, this morning, I read the *Moundverse* comic in [the catalogue to your recent solo exhibition at MASS MoCA]. It was such a relief to me that there was a comics section. What I understood from it is, I've got a giant mound, it's called comics. Mine don't extend into toys like yours do, and I have a few other, smaller mounds, but comics is the main one.

Growing up, I got excited about what comics could do when they weren't just trying to get a gag out of you. (Although I do like gags a lot. Humor is a basic weapon in making things.) I read about the early history of comics. Anytime I'd get an encyclopedia, I'd look up cartoons and comics, and if they weren't in there, I'd look for anything close. Which predisposed me to certain painters, including Picasso, because he just seemed like a talented cartoonist who had figured out the con.

When I first saw Guston's late work, I thought, He's a member of the tribe, one of us. Even if he was excoriated for that work and horrified when people called him a cartoonist. That's not what he wanted, but it was my way in. [And with the Nixon pictures,] the deal was complete, because, like I said, comics are my mound, so if I can fit an *artiste* into that mound, it just gets bigger.

Those pictures were the first thing I saw after September 11, a show uptown [at McKee Gallery]. I hadn't been out of my neighborhood for weeks. When I got there, the elevator opened and there's this big American flag. Having seen [the flag] in a different context in the days leading up to that, I thought, Oh, give me a break. But as soon as I got into the gallery, I thought, Yeah, this is the America I can like. The works were so clearly inspired by [George] Herrlman, who's like the god-king of early comics. Nixon becomes Krazy Kat at a certain point! It was all mapped out at a scale I could understand, in a language I could understand. They were almost full-scale comics narratives, except that, other than the title, they didn't have language. But they're visual stories, for sure. Guston was deep diving into the comics that obviously influenced him when he was young.

Trenton Doyle Hancock:

I never harbored a distrust of painting. In fact, it was always the opposite for me. I too was obsessed with encyclopedias as a child, and I often pored over the images of classical and modern paintings. I imagined that all the various images made by a hundred or so different artists were conflated into one omnivorous hand. It was all the same to me, with no hierarchy, and I trusted it all. So when I learned of Philip Guston, I trusted his images to teach me things. It was through Guston that I first learned of George Herriman, who for me provided a refraction point toward appreciating comics from the early twentieth century.

I grew up looking at comics, too. Not *Mutt and Jeff* and *Krazy Kat* like Guston did, but more superhero stuff and whatever was in the funny papers, like *Garfield*. In the 1980s, *Garfield* was everywhere. It was very American, like apple pie. Jim Davis [Garfield's creator] did this thing called *Garfield: His Nine Lives,* which was amazing. It was a really sophisticated breakdown of the character, and a departure from the stuff you would see on Sundays in the paper. It was conceptual, [riffing on the idea that] a cat has nine lives. So it was actually about reincarnation. Davis delegated the different lives to different artists. I saw it when I was ten years old. I didn't fully understand it, but it might have been my first entry point: here's this thing I know and love, comics, and here's this abstraction or furthering of it, deepening the world building. I was recently able to talk to [Davis] about how much that meant to me and how it loosened me up for *Raw*. When I saw *Raw*, it felt in some ways familiar, because I had seen this other thing earlier.

AS: It all depends on the stuff you were exposed to. The artists of my generation maybe had richer soil. It was pretty natural to be looking

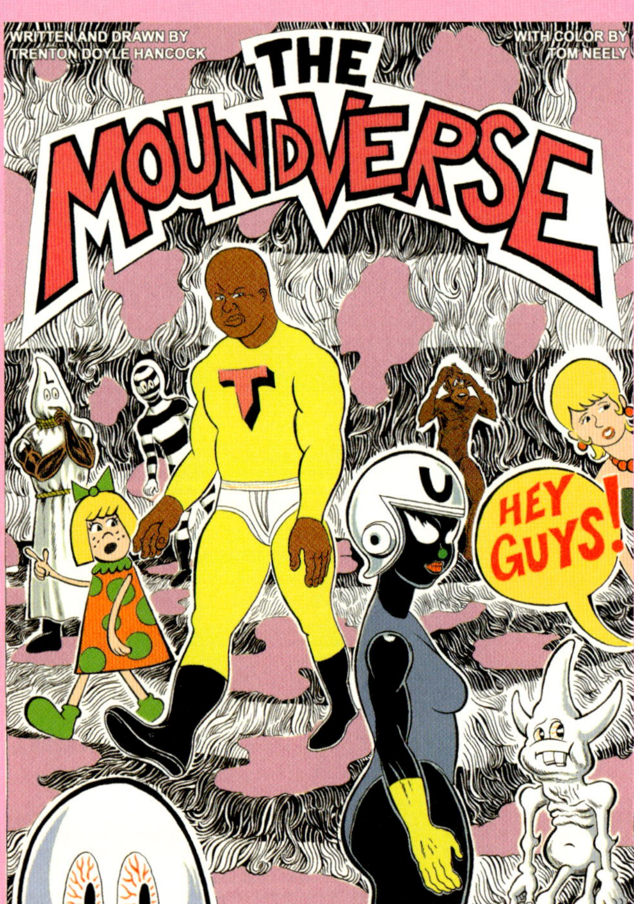

Cover of Trenton Doyle Hancock's *Trenton Doyle Hancock Presents The Moundverse*, 2018– , an ongoing graphic-novel project

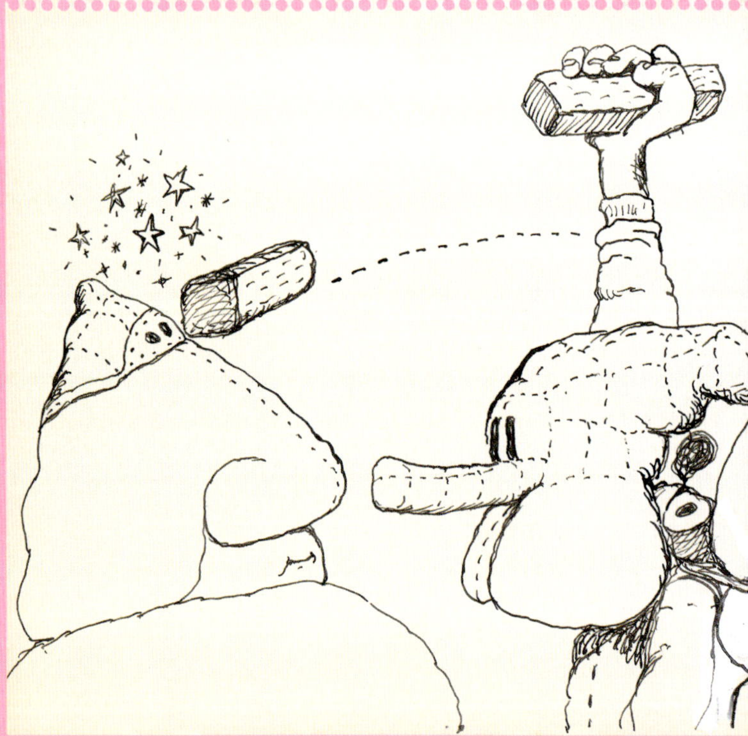

Philip Guston, untitled, from the *Poor Richard* series, 1971, ink on paper, 10¼ × 13⅞ in. (26.7 × 35.2 cm). Private collection

at *Krazy Kat* and *Mutt and Jeff* and *Mad*. When my son was seven, he had the *Krazy Kat* books but was equally interested in *Garfield*. So kids are "ambi-taste-rous," too. I'm not going to try to squelch that.

TDH: Yeah, you guys were recycling stuff and kind of chopping it up and reusing it. So when I saw *Raw*, I thought, Here are guys who are a bit older than me, taking existing comics and running them through a postmodern machine and just *playing*.

RS: Trenton, I know *Mad* was important for you as well, and even before you knew about *Raw*, you had known about Art's work through Garbage Pail Kids, right?

TDH: Yeah, Garbage Pail Kids was my introduction to your work. Of course, I didn't know it was your work at the time. I was eleven years old, and I feel like I was the exact target audience for Garbage Pail Kids. I was attracted not only to the abject nature of the cards, but also to the puns used throughout the series. However, I was most impressed by the intensity of the illustrations and how such seemingly trivial material was treated so majestically. Like most parents, my mother *hated* those cards and, being a rabid Christian at the time, proceeded to burn my whole collection. A trauma that I'm still recovering from!

AS: I started Garbage Pail Kids, I shaped it, but I never did one of the finished drawings, just a couple of rough doodles to show what the idea should be. I found the artist who was really perfect for it, John Pound.

I had this analog computer in my brain, trying to figure out, Okay, Tide detergent, what are we going to do with that? Change the first letter, change the vowel, and soon it was Toad detergent, for cleaning your pet frog or whatever. Similarly, "cabbage" and "garbage" are close enough.

The first card was Adam Bomb. I knew that if we could make a second one, we could create a million characters. It proved a little harder until we got to Leaky Lindsay. From my years at Topps, I knew that snot sells.

TDH: In the mid-1980s things got grosser and grosser. It was the gross-out era, and I feel like you guys kicked it off! The look of children's media totally changed in the mid-1980s, based on the popularity of Garbage Pail Kids. The toy designer James Groman is the toy world's answer to Garbage Pail Kids. He designed My Pet Monster, Madballs, and many other toys in the 1980s, and defining traits of his character designs were warts, snot, and exaggerated facial features. The gross-out aesthetic was

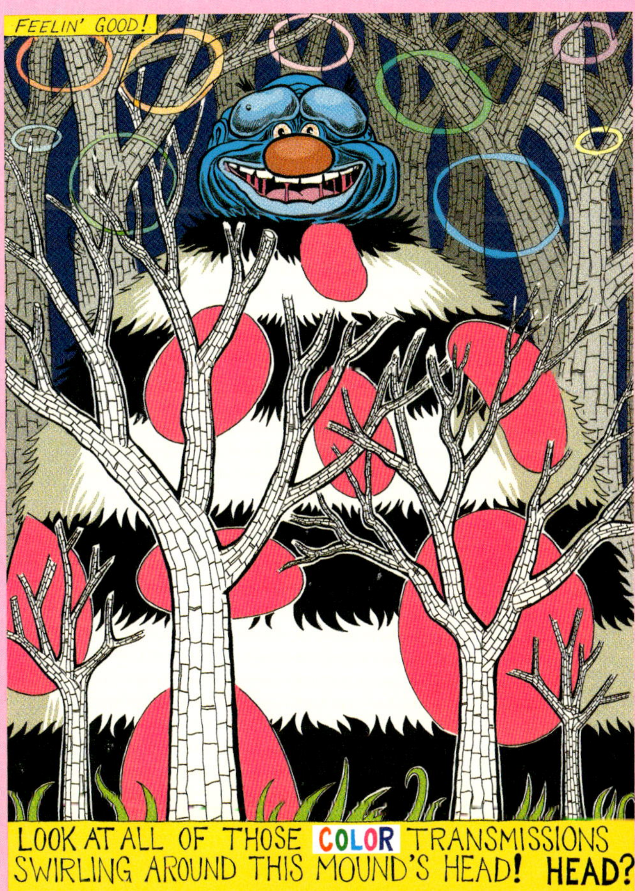

Excerpt from *Trenton Doyle Hancock Presents The Moundverse, Chapter 1: What is a Mound?*, 2018–

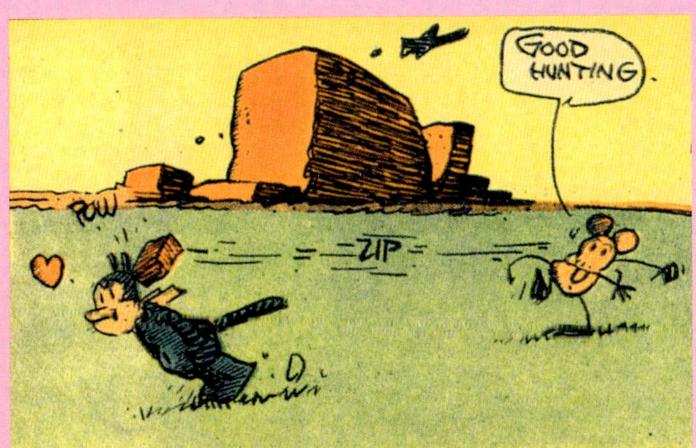

Krazy Kat, a character created by George Herriman, appeared regularly in newspaper comic strips and early animated shorts from the 1910s until Herriman's death in 1944.

so popular that whole films were greenlit to satiate kids looking for more boogers, farts, and bulging eyeballs.

Because I have a dark sense of humor, this media spoke to me and influenced my understanding of the world. When I was in painting school from the mid- to late 1990s, I gravitated toward painters who echoed the same sensibilities that I saw in the Garbage Pail Kids. There was a renaissance of young cartoon-based painters raised on a steady diet of *Mad*, Wacky Packages, Garbage Pail Kids, and Philip Guston. It was nice to feel as though I was part of a community of artists with similar goals. I began to rebuild my collection of Garbage Pail Kids cards, and I studied their construction. Specifically, I responded to the placement of the text, which acted as a title banner above the image and a caption below. I've often used these graphic devices in my own paintings. In the early 2000s, I started buying the actual Garbage Pail Kids illustrations directly from the Topps Company, to study the methods of the painting up close. I have amassed about twenty images so far.

RS: When did you discover *Underground Comix*? Before or after *Raw*?

TDH: Before, but not by much. When I was in junior college (I graduated in 1994), Rick Parker was drawing *Beavis and Butt-Head* comics for

Marvel. He kind of . . . *calibrated* his style to be more *Underground*-y. There was so much detail in it—detail where there didn't need to be. It was the first time I'd really seen anything quite like that in comics. I loved the way he would focus in on sections of drawings and pile on the detail.

AS: So [perhaps] that explains your own highly compact canvases. There's so much going on there. It's a concept that was invented by Harvey Kurtzman, who created *Mad* with his high school chum Will Elder. They had two words for it: chicken fat and eyeball kicks. It gave their comics a long half-life, because there's so much to keep discovering.

TDH: Yeah, totally. I was looking at every corner of the pictures in *Mad* and felt like, even if the material—the gag—wasn't funny, at least the picture looked great.

AS: But *Mad* was funny! I'm sorry to keep lording my longevity over you, but *Mad* was like nothing else on the fucking planet. And the magazine—the first version of it was unlike anything else since [the British satirists William] Hogarth and [James] Gillray in terms of how intense every picture was. Kurtzman was what made my life happen. That's when I said, Okay, I'm going to be a cartoonist. I don't know if I have any talent for it, but that's all I want to do.

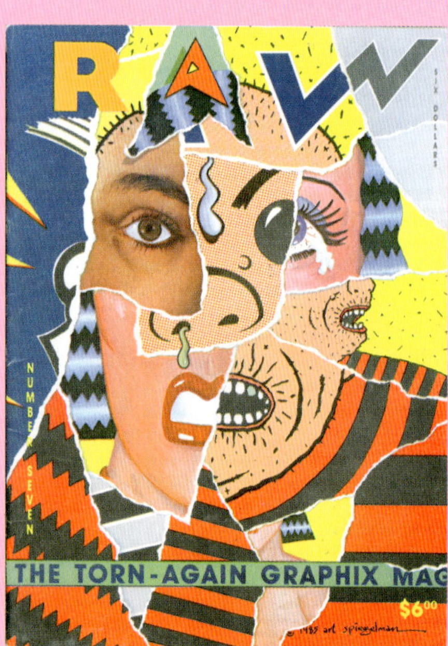

Raw, no. 7 (May 1985), with cover art by Art Spiegelman

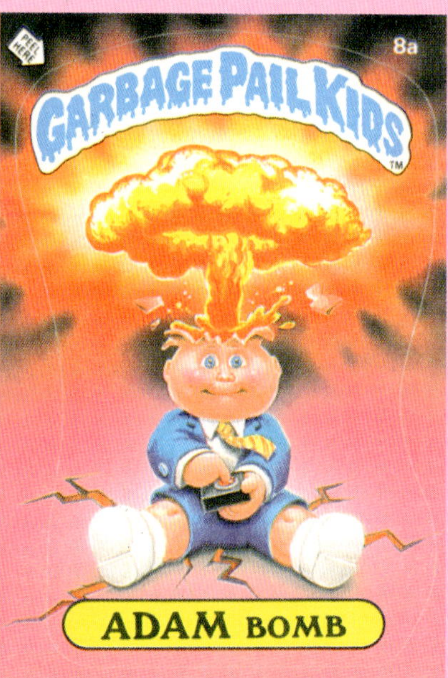

"Adam Bomb," Garbage Pail Kids trading card, 1985

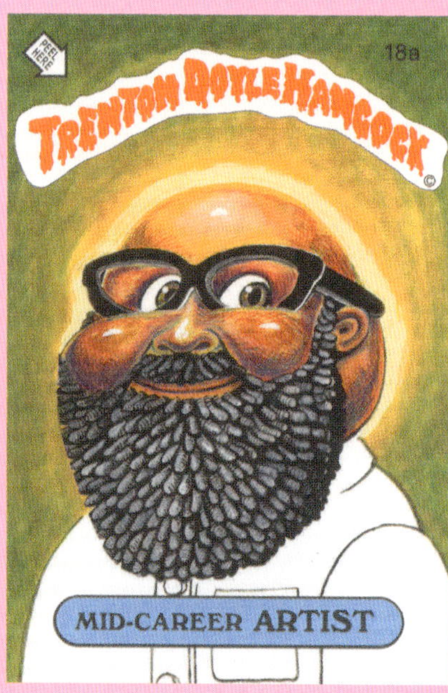

In conjunction with his exhibition at Contemporary Art Museum St. Louis, Hancock produced a limited-edition Garbage Pail Kids trading card with himself as subject.

RS: Trenton, when did you discover [R.] Crumb?

TDH: As a kid in the 1970s and 1980s, I saw "Keep on Truckin'..." printed everywhere, so I was aware of his style, but I didn't have a name to attach to it until college. That's when I started putting it all together—that this was a school of thought, that all you artists knew each other. And it all kind of came together in *Raw*.

AS: We actually didn't use Crumb until maybe the third or fourth issue [of *Raw*], because we didn't want it to be confused with *Underground Comix*.

TDH: I came to *Raw* in the 1990s, well after the print runs were over. I was just so excited about how diverse the selections were. It was the first place I saw Sue Coe's work, Chéri Samba's work, [Henry] Darger. Seeing all of them together, page after page.... I looked at the whole thing as a total package, as one artist. I thought, I love the way this looks so much, all of this together—that's what I want for myself. I want to diversify my hand in a way that, once I make it to maturity, I can go back and forth between something objectively stupid and something that feels absolutely, objectively sophisticated and important. To just ride that spectrum. So when people see what I do, they're not just seeing one thing, they're seeing a translation of a whole history of graphic representation through my lens.

So much happened for me in the mid-1990s. When I was at East Texas State University, it was still the exact same school that Gary Panter had graduated from, and Ric Heitzman, and Georganne Deen. And Lee Baxter Davis, he was sort of the ringleader, the center of the centrifuge. We all kind of spun off his crazy energy. I was there a few decades later, of course, but I recognized the legacy.

AS: I just discovered recently that there seems to be a common denominator between you and Gary.

TDH: When I realized that [Gary] was in *Raw*, I took the book to Lee Davis, and he's thumbing through it and says, Oh, Gary's in here. We're in his office and he opens a drawer, and he takes out the exact same images that Gary had made however many years ago. Gary had given Lee those prints as a gift, and there they were, reprinted in *Raw*. I took it as a sign. If I had any reservations or doubts before then about where I was supposed to be, it became super clear that I was in the right place. Coming from a Christian upbringing, where everything's about divine destiny, I felt like God had pointed me in the right direction. And learning about Guston right around that same time just felt right.

AS: And you discovered the "cartoon" Guston first?

TDH: Yes, the late paintings. I saw those images first, because a professor told me I should learn about this guy who also made these

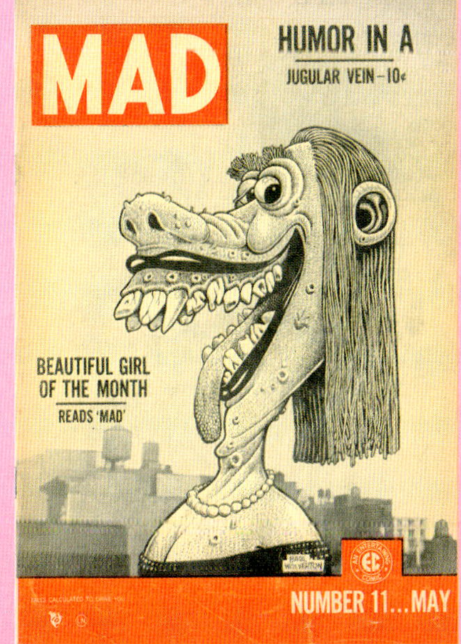

Mad, no. 11 (May 1954), with cover art by Basil Wolverton

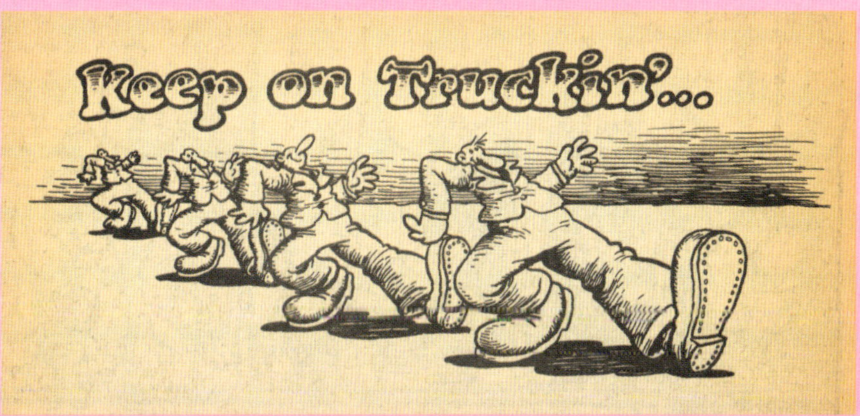

R. Crumb, "Keep on Truckin' ..." originally published in *Zap Comix*, no. 1 (1967)

Klan-like, hooded characters. I was already on a trajectory to use that material, but it was great to see how my artistic "grandfather" kind of revolutionized it.

AS: Trenton, you have said that you deprioritize text by "smuggling" literal content into painting. That speaks to a long history in art of decoupling words from pictures. It's getting down to something of a "pregnant" moment [one that conveys everything it needs to without the help of words]. Are you familiar with Frans Masereel and Lynd Ward?

TDH: No.

AS: Around the time of World War I, they were making woodcut novels, telling stories one picture at a time. It was silent storytelling, so each picture had to be a "pregnant" moment. You can go through the whole book with a clear conscience and not feel like you're eating an unkosher meal. It is fascinating to me how that approach can work on both the high side and the low side of the street: what comic artists are doing and what these books were doing.

Which leads me to ask—high art, low art, what's that all about? Why is there this ghettoized fence around comics? There are so many deep-rooted prejudices against comics, one of them being how they combine words and pictures. Anybody who could crack the code [like you, Trenton,] is really interesting to me. You've done an admirable job of figuring out, whether consciously or subconsciously, how to get there.

Another thing you do that interests me is include panels within panels in your paintings. You're left with implied narratives and hidden narratives that are only semiconnected, if not unconnected, to what's happening in the foreground.

TDH: Yes, the collage aspect of my work. There's a thing I talk about, a you-had-to-be-there kind of quality to a work. Comics, 99.9 percent of the time, are experienced in print, so you're not looking at the actual object; you're not seeing how the ink sits on the paper. That is a secondary or tertiary concern, or maybe not even a concern at all for a lot of comic-book artists. But for me, it's primary: you have to be there. It's a fake, mediated experience seeing a painting in a book.

Similarly, I think Guston thought of the painting as not just a picture but an object. If you can actually be in front of it, you can see how the paint is operating, and that, in a way, is an expression of time.

I've also talked about Guston's painting in terms of quadrants (see p. 59). Each section has to be interesting unto itself. So you *are* reading it, transposing [onto a painting] the language of how you would read a comic. And I think that's what led me to making the types of paintings I make. I saw a connection [with Guston] pretty immediately. He obviously loved comics, but he figured out a way to melt down the language and reuse it in this format.

AS: I think that's what Guston was trying to figure out with the *Poor Richard* series. He got scared of getting to that point where narrative would "eat" the pictures. He had to retreat. And that series culminates with one of his most amazing images, the giant portrait of Nixon. It distilled what he'd been doing in the *Poor Richard* book into one majestic, over-life-size painting.

What excites me about what we're calling Guston's "late" style is that he was willing to be scabrous and transgressive, because as far as he was concerned, nobody was going to look at his shit anymore. He had crossed the line. To have Dick Nixon just be a dick? What could be harsher? It's as angry and dismissive of this creep as a painting can be.

But there's also something really interesting in this picture, which is important for Guston's work in general: it has empathy. I know that's weird, because it's talking about what a subhuman horror show this guy was, with a claw for one leg and the other leg being grotesquely swollen. But Nixon has a tear coming out of his eye. On the one hand, it's making fun of his self-pitying personality. Yeah, I'm glad you're in pain, motherfucker! But then Guston pauses and goes, Shit, that must really hurt. So there's an empathy there, which he also extended to the Klan. And that's shocking, in a way. It's probably what caused the entire kerfuffle.

TDH: You're totally right about the empathy thing. You get a sense of that in the proportions and posture of the figure. He's forever in a hunched position, bunched like a contortionist in that space, and we all know what that feels like. Our entry into the painting is through his pain, whether you hate him or not or even know who he is. His villainy collapses under our own understanding of pain.

AS: That's as "pregnant" a moment as it gets, that painting. I got totally obsessed when I saw that stuff. What did Guston know and when did he know it? I don't remember which year, but in about 1968, Crumb's stuff, like *Fritz the Cat*, still had a cuteness to it. Then he had an LSD trip where he channeled Basil Wolverton (see p. 141) and it changed everything about his work.

    What we saw then was the return of the repressed. At the time, the highest form of the comic strip grew out of that whole "less-is-more" thing. *Peanuts* was the ultimate comic strip, because it couldn't have been more boiled down. But then, the untidiness of the *Mutt and Jeff* era came back, all that cross-hatching and scribbling—it was very low rent. It affected everything I was looking at. All of a sudden advertising, illustration—everything got infected by it. Milton Glaser's gang at Push Pin Studios was affected by Crumb very directly. And Saul Steinberg, one of the more rarefied cartoonists, found his own way through the barricades between high and low, drawing women with big asses and fat legs.

RS: So do you think Guston knew about Crumb's work as early as 1968?

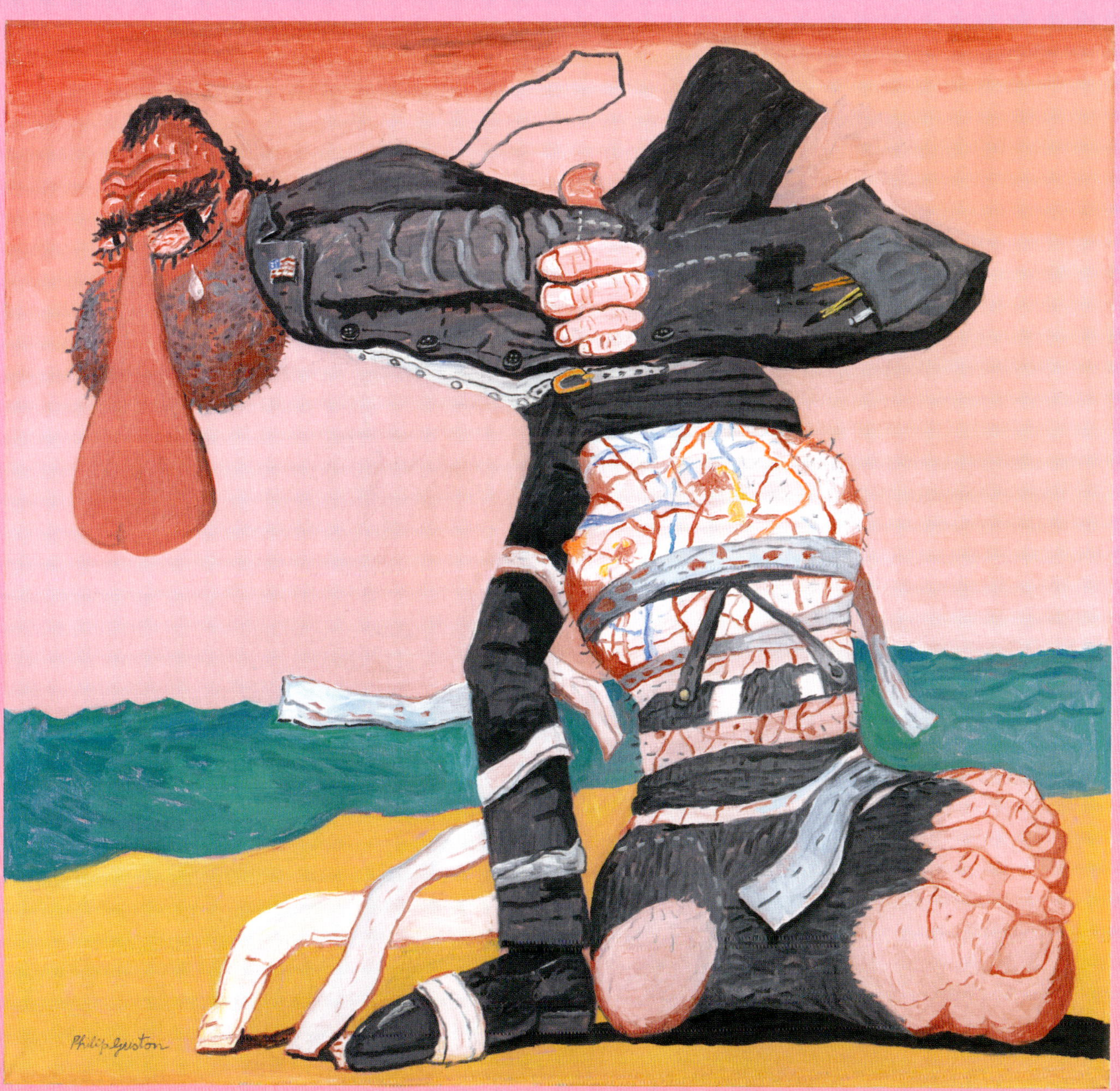

Philip Guston, *San Clemente*, 1975, oil on canvas, 68 × 73¼ in. (172.7 × 186.1 cm). Glenstone Museum, Potomac, Maryland

AS: I'm trying to find the smoking gun. Guston was always a cartoonist. He drew comics as a kid. And later he did caricatures of his friends, but those are a sophisticated kind of cartooning, they look nothing like that low-rent style. And then, all of a sudden, they become *exactly* that. They look uncannily similar.

My theory, which I can't prove, is that when Guston [began his late Klan paintings], underground newspapers were really big. And Crumb was in them pretty early on. I don't think Guston looked at Crumb and said, I can steal that. I think all he had to do was walk past it and it reminded him of his thirteen-year-old self, because he was looking at the same *Mutt and Jeff* stuff that had been important to Crumb.

RS: We've covered a lot of ground, but let's go back to what was said earlier, regarding the empathy you both see in the Nixon work and in the Klan pictures. Trenton, for you, there's often this exploration of a descent into hatefulness, but it is coupled with a kind of empathy for evil characters as you become them or inhabit their personas.

TDH: The idea of wearing a painting as a mask is something that interested me pretty early on. How do I tell the truth about who I am but also have a sense of privacy? It's contradictory, but I believe painting can address this issue quite well. I first experienced the masked nature of painting through Guston's work.

I saw what he was doing and wanted to do it, too. So it's kind of like what you were saying, Art, how *Mad* started you in a certain direction, like Guston did for me. I was at the very beginning of seeing myself as a painter who performed his own characters, and those performances were often first scripted as comics.

I was working for the school newspaper as the on-staff comic artist. I had to come up with something every week. I loved having that deadline on top of my other coursework, because if the painting thing didn't work out, I would have a portfolio to pitch to a newspaper. But then I figured out that I could put all of it together, the comics *and* the painting, and have this new thing. I thought, This is the microbe or the atom that's going to blossom into a full, rich creature. I knew that if I could take the graphic novel and reformat it to fit the proportions of a gallery, then I'd be doing something I hadn't seen before.

AS: It's interesting to hear you say that, because when we were trying to find artists for *Raw* that wouldn't just make it a larger-format *Zap Comix*, we were looking for cartoonists who weren't like any others we'd seen. Those who had found a new way of combining words and pictures. Like Gary [Panter], whose background as a painter allowed him to invent a different kind of comic. Gary's stuff looked like it belonged on a wall. And until I saw your work, it was as close as any comic I'd seen that could look good on a wall.

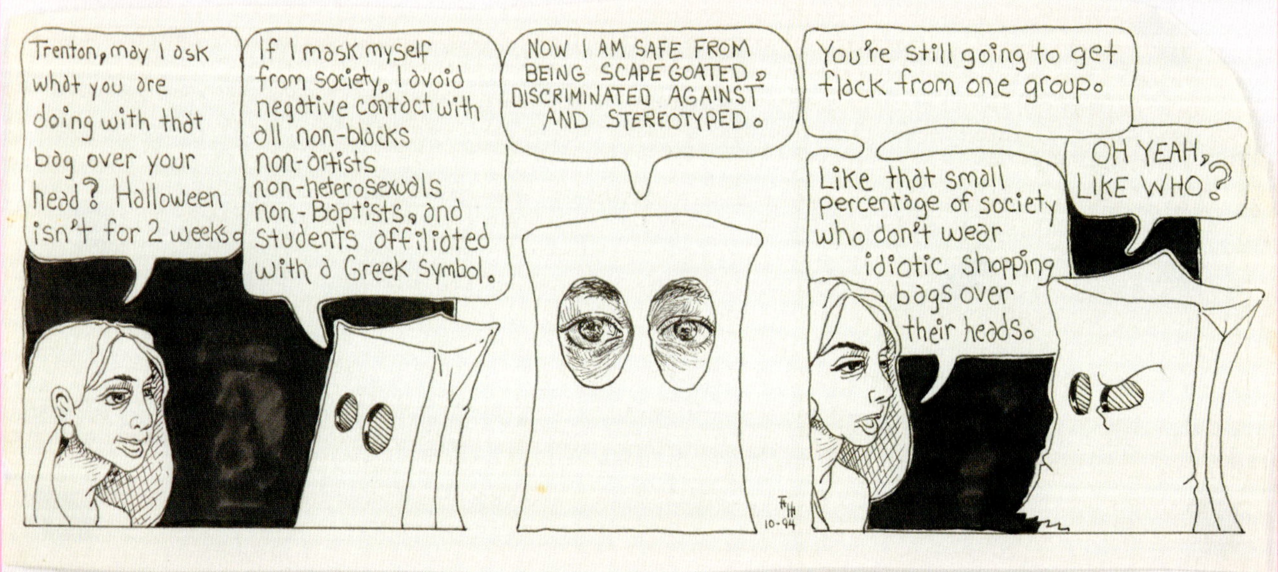

Trenton Doyle Hancock, "May I ask what you're doing with that bag over your head?" Originally published in October 1994 in *The East Texan*, the student newspaper of East Texas State University (now Texas A&M University–Commerce)

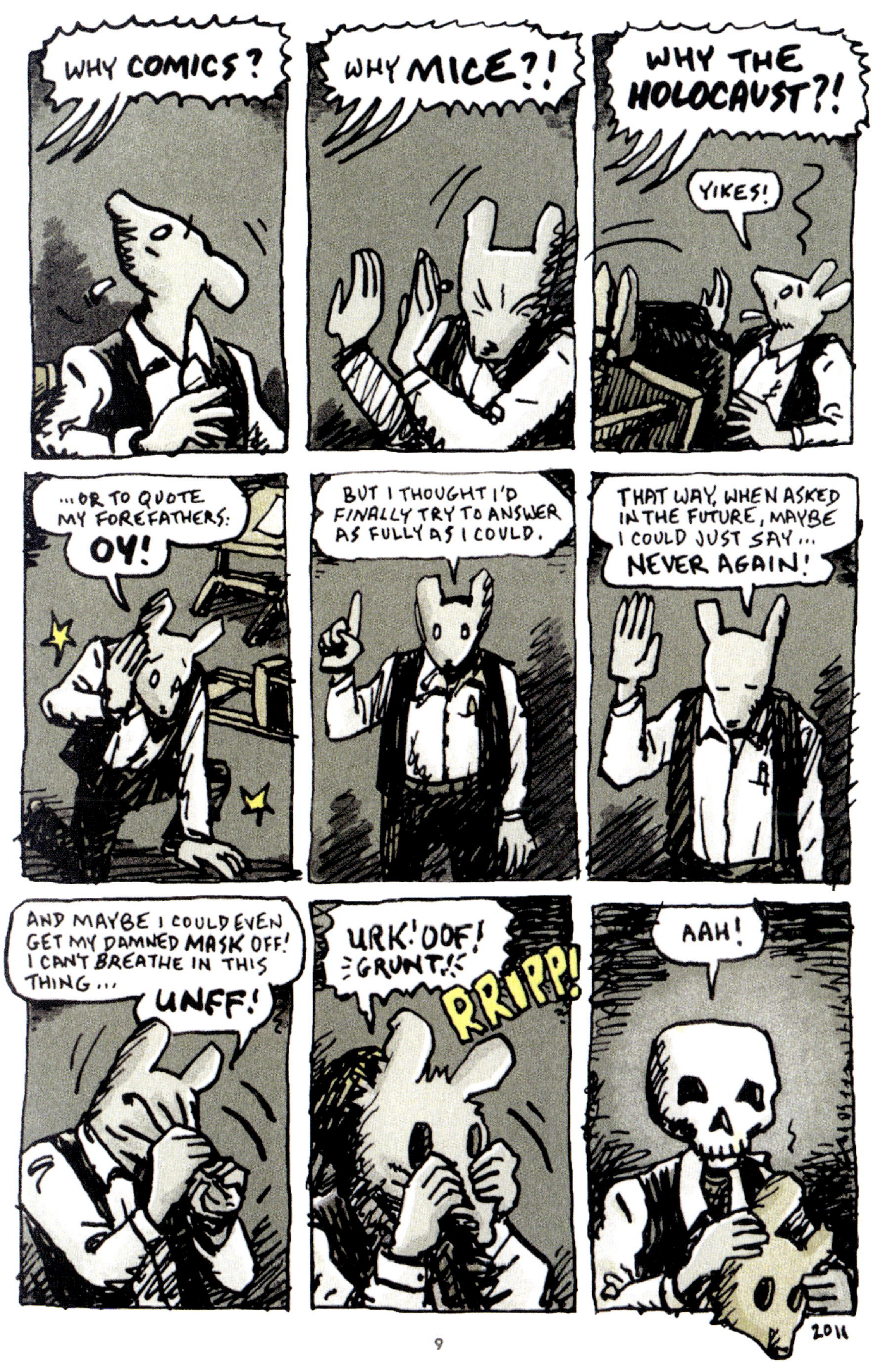

Art Spiegelman, excerpt from *MetaMaus: A Look Inside a Modern Classic, Maus*, 2011

TDH: Gary was also performative—wearing paintings he had made and fashioning them into masks.

AS: Let's hit on a word you've mentioned a couple of times and which is important to me, as well: masking. And not just the white sheet over the head. Comics themselves are a kind of masking. Did you ever look at any of those *How to Draw a Cartoon* books when you were little?

TDH: Of course, yeah.

AS: Back in the earlier days of those books, there was a whole section about ethnic types. A whole dictionary of [stereotypical] attributes that are pure racism. *You want to draw a Black person? It's easy!* And all of a sudden, you have proof of how racist comics are at their core.

It's distinct from other forms of racist stuff, like early cinema, *The Birth of a Nation* and shit like that. Because every time you see [overt racism] in a movie, you've got a Hattie McDaniel or a Stepin Fetchit or another real person behind it. And if you're looking at them with contemporary eyes, then you have to see how tortured that person is to be making a living that way, playing a denigrating role.

There's kind of a built-in contradiction that comes with the territory of comics. It's a form of masking. Thinking about Black representation in cartoons is what led me to the whole cat-mouse thing. It was my friend Ken Jacobs who pointed out that Mickey Mouse is just Al Jolson with big ears, and he compared that image to other racist cartoons of the time (see p. 152). And I think this idea is essential to your project, Trenton, and to my projects as well, especially the cats and mice. I was going to do something featuring Mickey-like mice and Ku Klux Cats.

I eventually chose to use anthropomorphized images to focus on my own family's history, when Jews were portrayed as rodents infiltrating society that had to be killed like rats. In fact, Zyklon B was a pesticide, a gas that was used in Auschwitz. So it's built in that, if you want to work with that vocabulary of comics, it comes with baggage.

Underground Comix burst everything open. All of a sudden, sex and violence were really overt. And (in big quotes now) "racist" comics, that was all fodder for the Crumb moment. Like his highly sexualized Angelfood McSpade character. I don't think Crumb was consciously being racist [in creating that character]; it was more like an exorcism. It was in the spirit of Lenny Bruce's famous bit that used every ethnic slur, repeating the n-word over and over to shock. Because it's the suppression of those words that gives them the power, the violence, the viciousness. Bruce repeated the word over and over until

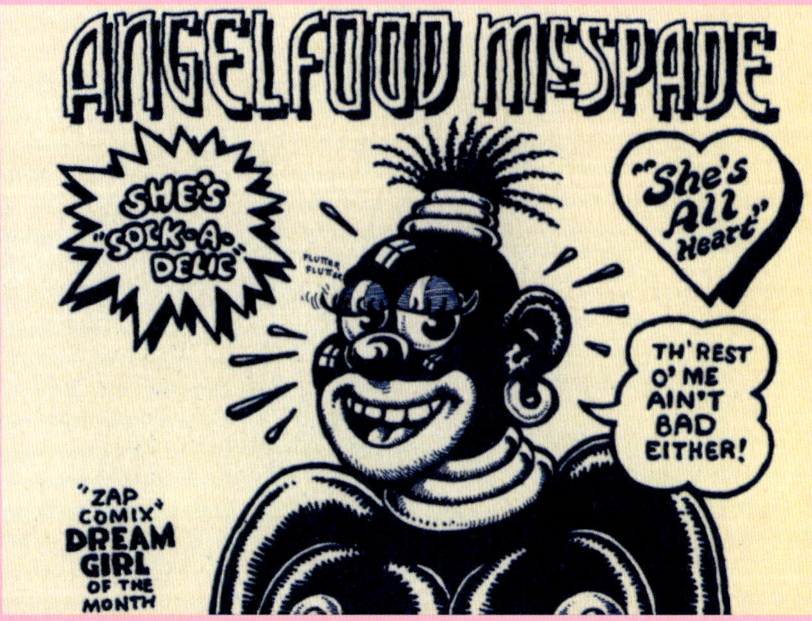

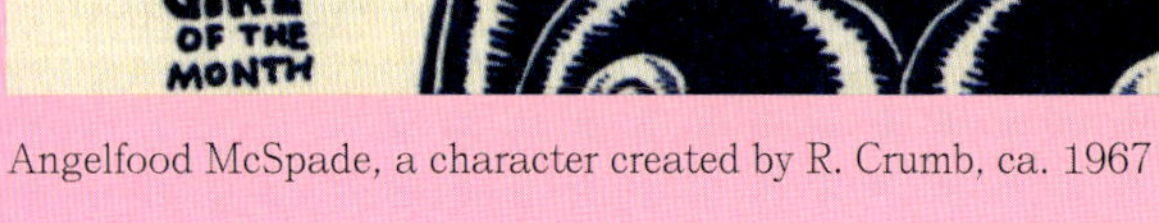
Angelfood McSpade, a character created by R. Crumb, ca. 1967

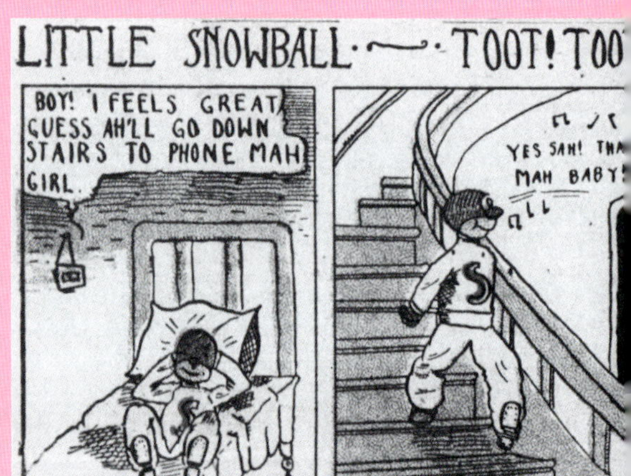

it became meaningless, and ended by saying that someday, you'd never be able to make some six-year-old Black kid cry because somebody called him a "n—" in school. I'm not saying that worked, but Crumb's project—and it was a very important one in the evolution of the comics medium—was to look inside his own head and not let shame stop him from inventorying what had been planted there. The vocabulary of cartooning can be toxic. Like Guston with the "Little Snowball" comic he did as a kid—he wasn't being a racist, he was just trying to be a cartoonist.

TDH: The keyword is "consciously." As for Guston, he made those cartoons when he was a child, and I would imagine that he was mimicking the representations of Blackness that he saw from adult, white comics artists. Thankfully, he grew to have a more complex understanding of the humanity of being Black in America, as he related it to the rigors of Jewish life.

As a child, watching old *Looney Tunes* . . . I'd see the savage with the crockpot in the jungle, Bugs Bunny inside it. Those sorts of images became ingrained in me as a kid. But as a three- or four-year-old, I didn't yet identify. I didn't say, Oh, that looks like my brother or my mom. But I got used to it. I was programmed to think that, if a cartoon character ends up in the jungle, they may run into a dark-skinned character with a bone in their nose that's putting someone in a pot. Yet I didn't associate this with real people.

AS: You didn't take it personally.

TDH: I didn't then, but now I look at it and realize that the programming hasn't gone away. Just as racism hasn't gone away—it just morphs into something else. It finds new forms, because it wants to stay alive. It's like an organism. It just doesn't want to die. I'm fascinated by the sentience of racism.

You say that Crumb and Guston weren't racist. And I love them as much as the next artist. But at one point, they surely harbored prejudicial ideas that came out on the page. For Crumb in particular, his Angelfood McSpade character might actually be a feminist, anticolonialist commentary, but it's so layered with fetishism that, for me, that potential is canceled out. It becomes very difficult to see the racist tropes as ironic.

It's important that we're able to see a fuller history of Black comics artists and see how they actually wanted to be represented. In 1950 Fawcett Comics published a series called *Negro Romance*. It was drawn in the popular, pulpy style of the Black illustrator Alvin Hollingsworth, who drew idealized images of Black couples as opposed to stereotyped imagery. Artists like Ollie Harrington, Jackie Ormes, and Charles Johnson were all powerhouses, graphically and intellectually

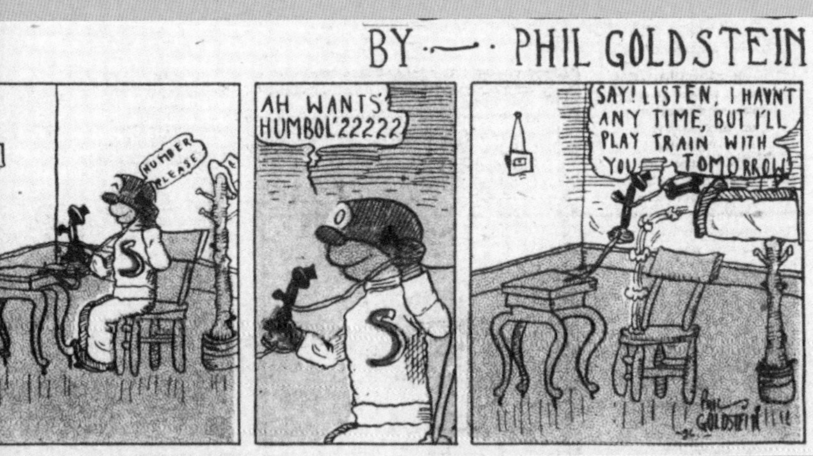

"Little Snowball—Toot! Toot!," an early comic strip by Philip Guston, published in the *Los Angeles Times*, June 27, 1926

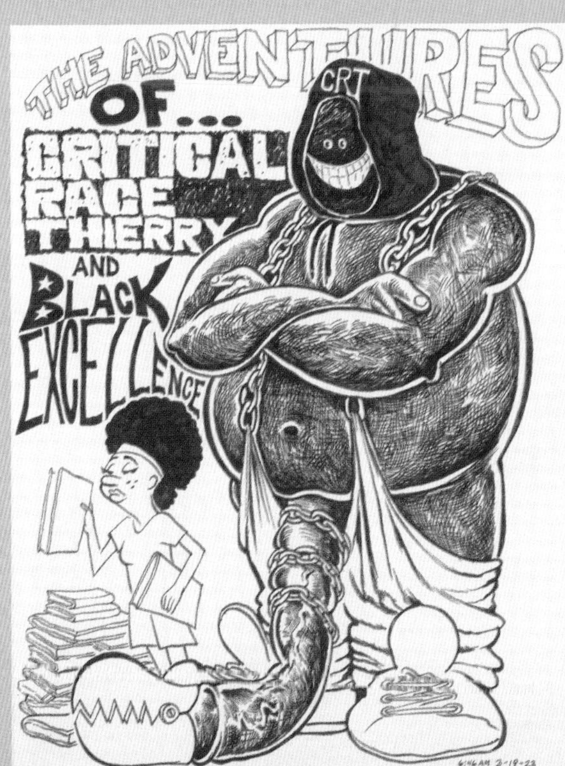

Trenton Doyle Hancock, *The Adventures of Critical Race Thierry and Black Excellence, brought to you by White Conservative Nightmares Productions*, 2023, ink on paper, 11 × 8½ in. (27.9 × 21.6 cm). Collection of the artist

speaking, and their work was made largely to express the concerns of modern Black Americans. George Winners's *New Yorker*–esque gag cartoons appeared in *Ebony*. His work was a comical look into the homes of a growing Black middle class. Thankfully, the work of all these comics artists is gaining more recognition. And let's not forget that George Herriman was indeed Black, and that his comics have only recently begun to be reexamined through the lens of codified Black American commentary. Aside from Herriman, who for so long was able to pass as white, there wasn't an equally popularized Black voice in comics (underground or otherwise) to counter the narratives we were seeing from white artists. One had to look to literature (noncomic), music, and stand-up comedy to hear equally probing, provocative, and popular Black voices.

Comedy has been a way for both Black and Jewish people to process trauma, and the importance of humor has been key to the equilibrium of both communities. Landing the joke was as much about educating your community about ongoing conditions as it was about therapy. Like many of the aforementioned artists, I use comics and humor to convey complexities and contradictions of American life, and as a Black commentator I've found it important to be in charge of my own comedic abjection and to never let representation slip into buffoonery. We're in a post-postmodern world, where things are looked at through a meta lens. We see so many different layers of identity, and I think it's only through this new way of looking that we can keep Crumb's older work in the dialogue. However, his more recent works featuring illustrations of Black blues artists are beautifully nuanced and naturalistic, and they provide a counter to his Angelfood McSpade character.

AS: When talking about Klansmen and [other problematic] stuff, this should be part of how we come to understand it. [If you were to consider the Jewish psychiatrist and social crusader Frederic] Wertham, the first time he saw a comic book . . . he was horrified. His first initiative was against racism in comics, and it led him to do a book called *Seduction of the Innocent* [in 1954]. It became a best seller, because everybody was beginning to panic about comics, the first medium aimed directly at children. And it led to the actual burning of comic books.

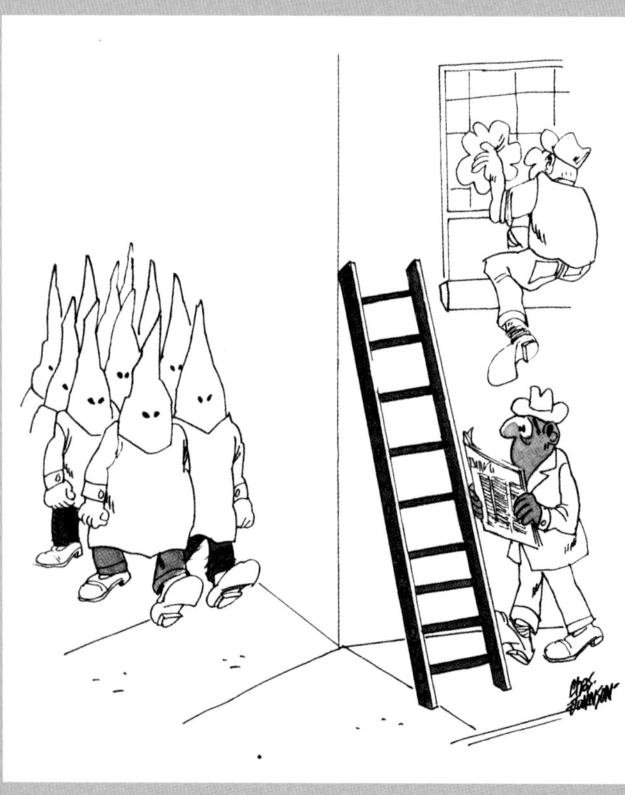

Charles Johnson, freelance cartoon, ca. 1968–75

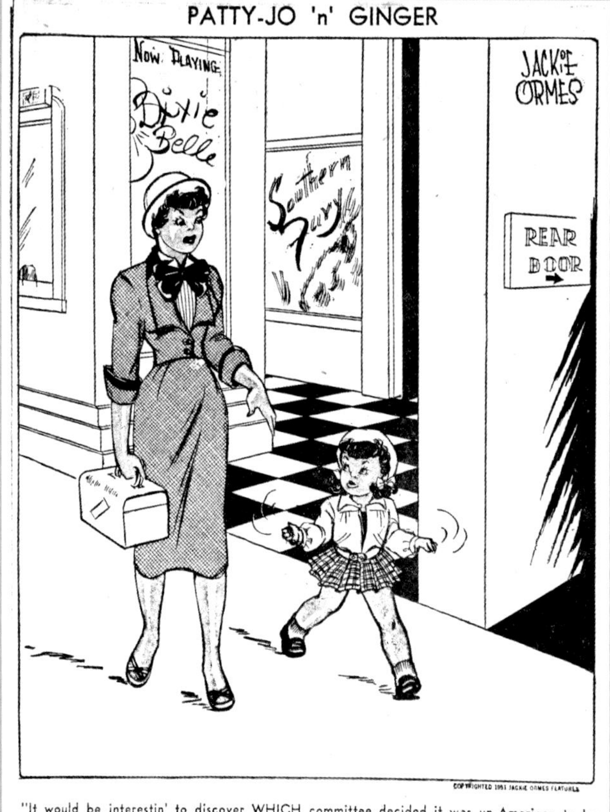

Jackie Ormes, "Patty-Jo 'n' Ginger," comic strip for the *Pittsburgh Courier*, April 7, 1951

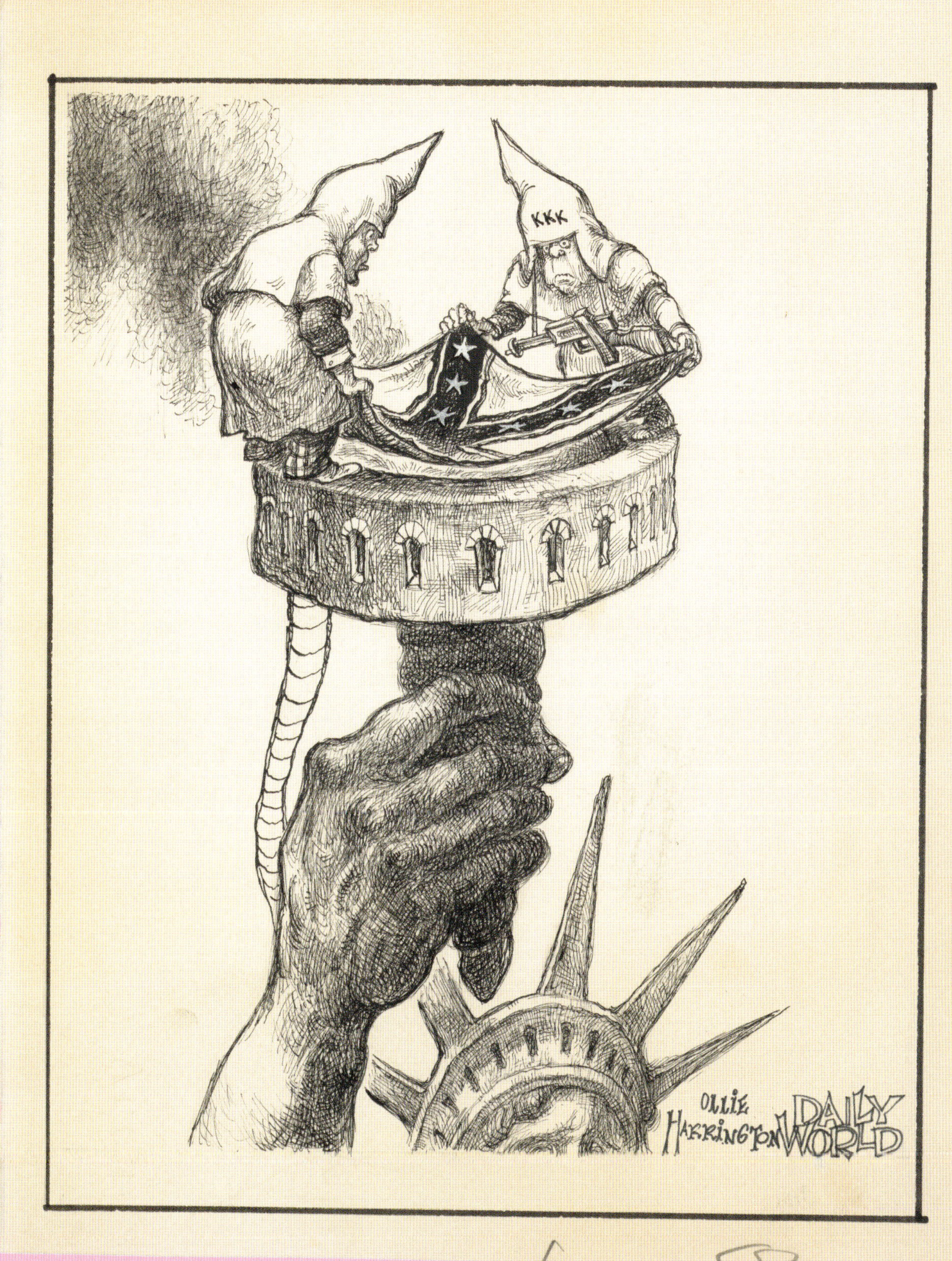

Oliver "Ollie" Harrington, political cartoon for the *Daily World*, January 1, 1981

RS: Trenton, do you think Wertham's research had anything to do with the toys or Garbage Pail Kids your mother destroyed, thinking they were conduits for evil?

TDH: Well, I think the "satanic panic" in the 1980s is connected to McCarthyism and similar moments in time. Every ten years, someone's burning a pile of something.

Even with the most innocuous of the [Garbage Pail Kids] cards, I think my mother saw something subversive. Coming from a Christian fundamentalist household, she was very affected by televangelists and the false warnings they were feeding her about these visual symbols.

AS: Speaking of visual symbols, Trenton, you touch on an important notion: we're both in the icon-making business. America's a very Protestant country in its roots and aesthetics, and as a result it has a strong aniconic tradition. It's why comic books are *still* being burned, in a sense. America has a history of being wary of pictures. Picture books are always the first target, and graphic novels get the greatest scrutiny, because you don't have to read the whole book to say, There's a naked woman's breast in this book. I don't want Junior seeing that.

After *Maus* came out, [the writer] Adam Gopnik compared it to *The Birds' Head Haggadah*, which I hadn't known about. The Haggadah tells the story of Passover, and one is tempted to illustrate it, but how do you do that without using graven images of people? This one ingeniously uses birds' heads in the place of human heads, because they aren't an image of God anymore, they're just birds. Cartooning comes from that same attempt to find an escape clause that lets imagery back in—that actually lets you make something through masking.

TDH: My early art history lessons were through the encyclopedia, because we had those at home and I had no museum to go to. As I mentioned before, I loved the painting section of these books, and I'd thumb through all the Renaissance stuff, all these images from Catholicism. I was getting the same imagery in song and scripture at church but specifically through a Black, rural lens of a certain generation. I kept [the two versions] very separate for a long time—here's the art-historical version

of Jesus, and here's the Jesus that I'm getting from my folks, which is a whole different ballgame. My family's version was attached to salvation and justice, and to having somewhere to be free after you're not free for so many years here in America.

It was up to me to reconcile [these two understandings] and to ask how academia and the art world had extracted and eliminated all the components I was taught to understand about Christian symbology. At university it wasn't at all about the lessons and parables. We were just looking at Christian imagery as paint. Or because it demonstrated the golden mean. It was just the formal

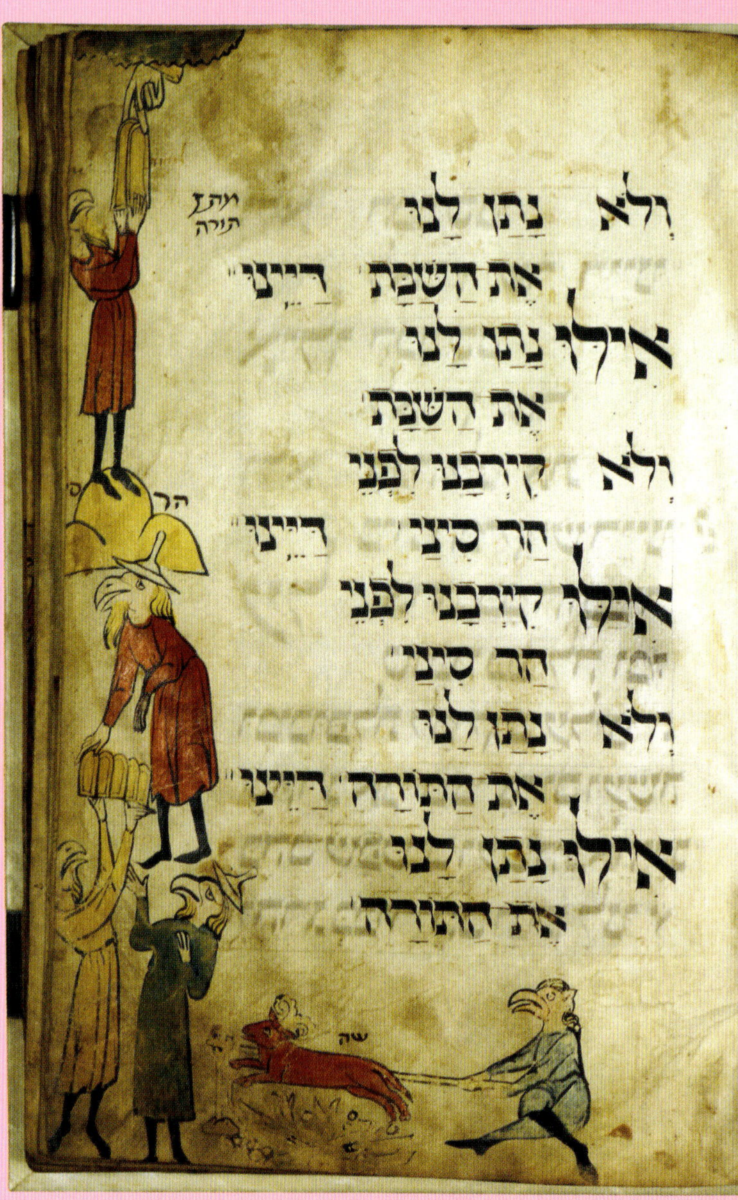

The Birds' Head Haggadah, South Germany, ca. 1300, ink and tempera on parchment, each folio 10⅝ × 7⅛ in. (27 × 18.2 cm). Israel Museum, Jerusalem

stuff. I wondered how it could be so different in the two spaces. One space was pretty white, cold, without singing or shouting. The other space, where it was warm and about the stories and the utility of the image, was the Black space for me. It racialized and kickstarted my understanding of these two segregated versions of Jesus. That got me onto a journey about how white America and Black America think of religion, Christianity in particular, and what that might mean for one's contract in the American enterprise. It's something I'm still focused on, and I think it's what led to *Step and Screw!* I saw Guston as a way to bring that conversation down to earth.

AS: Yes, like Guston's *The Studio*, an amazing picture of a masked Klansman drawing a Klansman. What's underneath that hood? Guston demythologizes the Klansman, making him a schlubby, chain-smoking version of himself. He's inhabiting the hood, recognizing his own implication in it, which is why it's more interesting to me, ultimately, than the Angelfood McSpade picture. I don't think Crumb was conscious of any of this, but Guston certainly was. He accepted his own complicity and all the guilt that comes with that, which even led him to deal with what it meant to change his name to a more Christian name.

Have you seen *Binky Brown*?

TDH: Yes, by Justin Green.

AS: He was drawing about his Catholic guilt, and it was so autobiographical that it invented autobiographical comics as a category. Which, I think, helped pave the way for you to have an

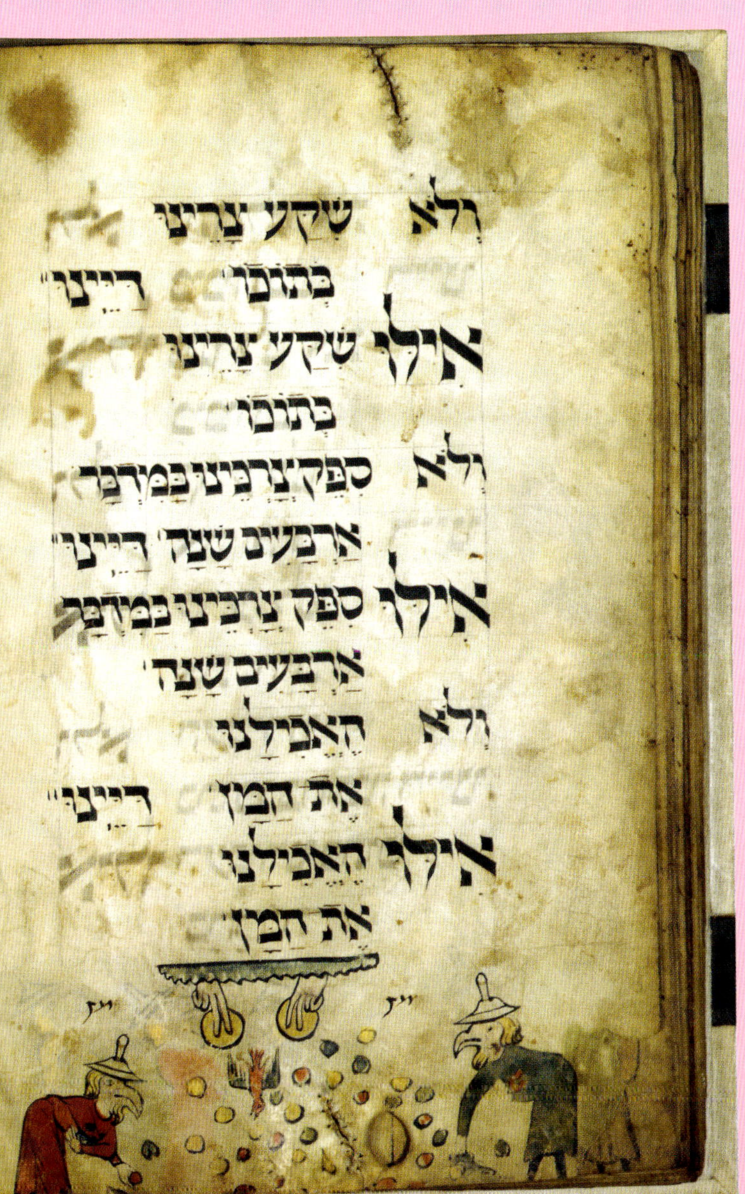

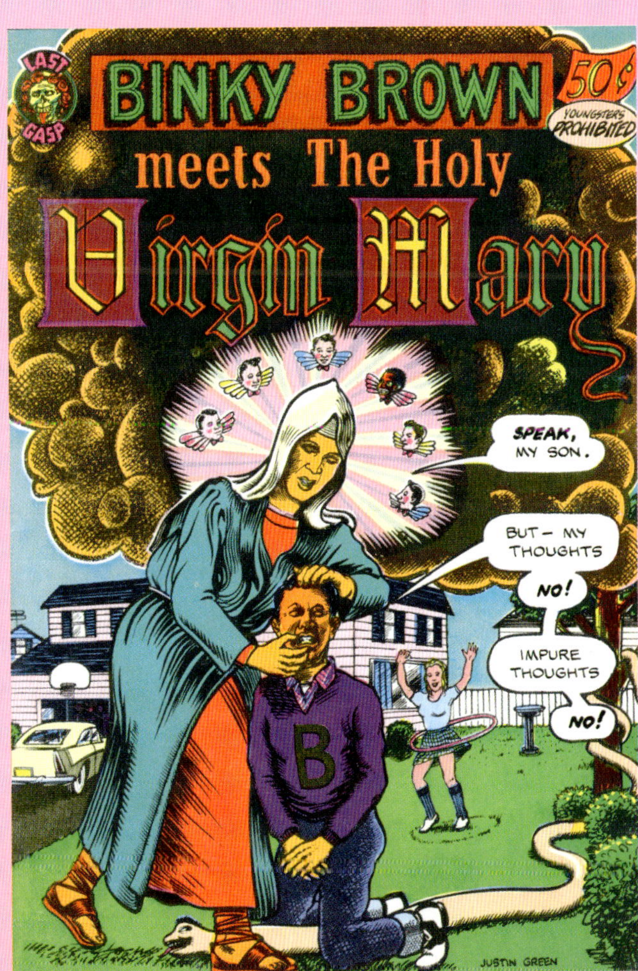

Justin Green, cover art from his autobiographical comic *Binky Brown Meets the Holy Virgin Mary*, 1972

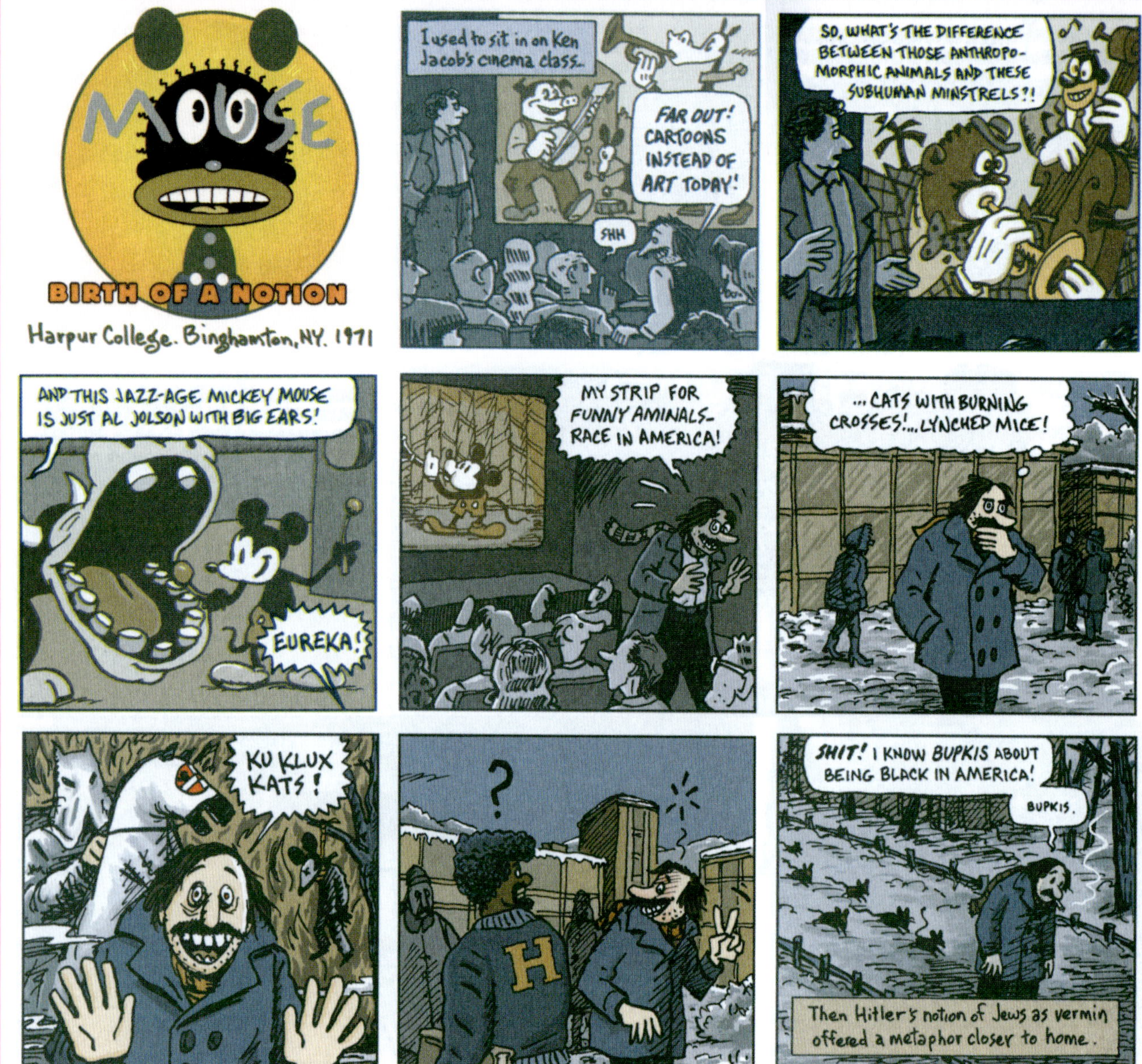

Art Spiegelman, excerpt from "Birth of a Notion," from his graphic novel *Breakdowns: Portrait of the Artist as a Young %@&*!*, 2006

autobiographical relationship to what it means to be a Black person under a hood.

TDH: Yeah, I definitely see representative roots in Justin Green and Crumb. In the 1990s there seemed to be a renaissance of artist-driven work, both in comics and in animation, which was exciting to come of age with. I was just getting to the point where I was starting to think for myself and to question who I was away from home. I was reading [Carl] Jung and Joseph Campbell and all these thinkers who were saying that [the Bible] was just stories, that we were all drawing from the same pool. That was great but hard to hear, because it meant that my folks had been lying to me for so many years.

AS: But the Protestants were right about one thing: pictures *are* dangerous.

TDH: They are! I was happy my folks didn't understand that in a real way, because they supported my becoming an artist. Once I realized that art is weaponry, I thought, Oh my goodness, they sent me to art school and didn't know that I was going to come out the other side as some kind of revolutionary. I don't think they understood that art could do that.

RS: Let's talk more about the autobiographical aspect of your work and the interaction between historical trauma and horror, particularly as expressed in cartoons.

AS: *Maus* was a really long project. It took thirteen years to figure it out, not even knowing fully what I'd dived into. After *Maus*, I kept trying to find another place to stand. It wasn't obvious, because *Maus* loomed over everything else I had done before and after.

I can't help but have a vestigial resentment over what's gone down recently [with *Maus* being banned]. Because I never made *Maus* to teach anything to anybody but me. I was just trying to figure out how I got born when both my parents were supposed to have been murdered years before I was conceived. I was just trying to understand what happened to them.

RS: Trenton, that sounds a lot like how you came to make *Step and Screw!*

TDH: *Step and Screw!* came from several different directions. I was working with the curator Valerie Cassel Oliver on [an exhibition called] *Radical Presence*, about Black performance art. I was happy to be included, because a lot of my work is based in performance. If I can become a character, then I feel great about painting or drawing that character. Sometimes the drawing comes first and the performance later, and vice versa.

For my undergrad thesis show, I did a Mound performance. I was up on a chair with drapery over me and my head sticking out the top. I sat up there and I slept. A year later, in my first gallery show, I did that performance again, but I timed an alarm clock to go off every thirty minutes. The gallery director would come in then and give me a bowl of Jell-O. Over two hours, there were four Jell-O feedings, each a different color. The assistant gallery director was underneath my outfit, hidden from everyone, blowing up balloons that corresponded to the color of Jell-O I ate, and she shoved them out the butthole of the creature. It became a commentary on the nature of the gallery system. They feed you, you feed them shit—it's this cyclical thing that keeps the machine moving.

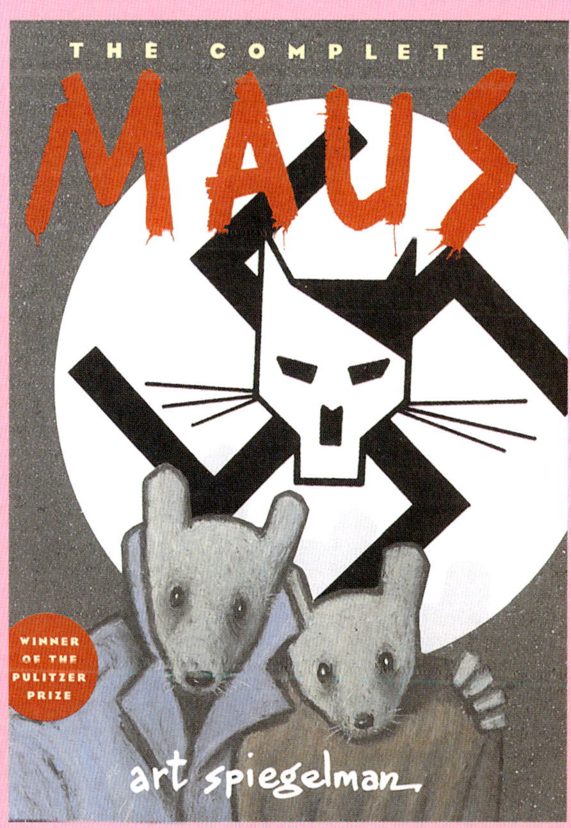

Art Spiegelman, cover art from his autobiographical graphic novel *The Complete Maus*, 1994

Valerie suggested that I do that performance again, but I don't do anything the same way twice. I wanted to change the performance to fit where I was at that point in my life, and I wanted to use the space of the museum in a way I hadn't before. My stepfather and his mother (my grandmother) both passed away in 2010. This exhibition offered a perfect moment to interpret my relationship as an artist to the museum system, but it was also a moment to commemorate things I had learned from my grandmother and stepfather, these hymns they taught me in church that, as a junior deacon, I had to sing or lead in devotional services every Sunday.

So I turned the museum into a chapel for a ritual or service. It was a call-and-response thing, where one person would sing a verse and then the congregation would sing it back. We did it as a Mound (see p. 124). And all of it made me want to know more about what my folks had gone through before I was born, the harder realities of being Black in the South—like you, Art, with what you were doing when you made *Maus*.

Around that same time, I went home to Paris, Texas, to give a talk for the local NAACP. By then I had started doing some research about the town's lynching history. A lot of terrible things, unfortunately and weirdly, happened right there in Paris.

AS: When did your family get to Paris, Texas?

TDH: In the late 1800s. So they were there for it all. They breathed it. All these things that happened, they either saw them firsthand or they were passed down as cautionary tales. *This is what they will do to you if you step outside the boundaries*. I got a very emotional version [of the story] from my mom and my grandma. They were sharing with me in a way they hadn't shared before. And I thought, I got to do something. That started the *Step and Screw!* project.

AS: [If I can return to your *Moundverse* comic I mentioned earlier, Trenton, which is also autobiographical,] one thing I find even more interesting than the Klan masks in *Step and Screw!* are the black-and-white-striped figures. It's a strong symbol! These characters, they're not black and they're not white. They're an amalgam of what it means to be living in America in the twenty-first century (see pp. 136, 139).

TDH: Yes, that's the Mound character. That started in the 1990s. I was reducing a lot of what was going on in my head into that form, and thinking of the black and the white, the code switching. If you're Black in America, just to exist, you have to think white but live Black. The images also speak to my love of all things black and white, just on a formal level, how text looks on a page. I love it.

AS: Going between words and pictures—that's a kind of code switching, too.

TDH: I think for me—for everyone—we're multifaceted beings, but everyone wants to think of a person as just one thing. We all oscillate from one mindset to the other quite naturally. Identity is never fixed—especially right now, when identity is being promoted as a monolith.

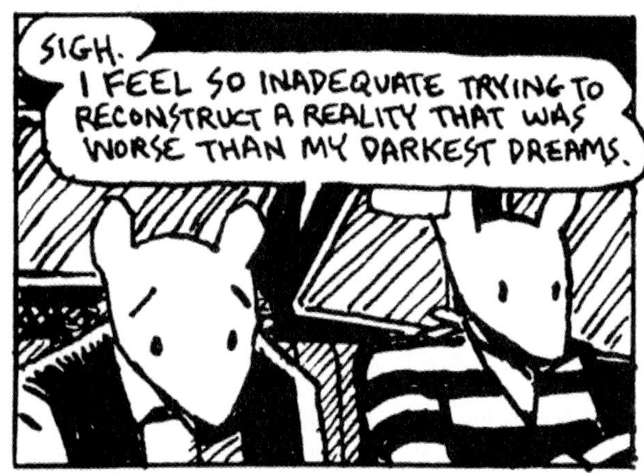

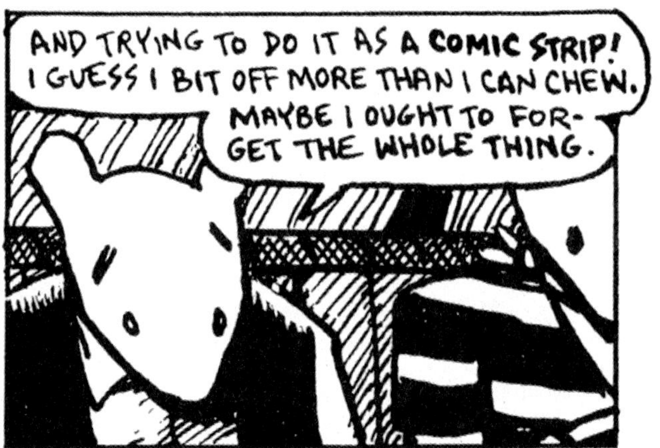

Art Spiegelman, excerpt from *Maus*

If you're Black, you must think this way. Or if you're Jewish, you must be just this one thing.

AS: That's been a problem for me ever since we got into this project. It's touchy, but I don't like being the poster boy for the Holocaust. I've never wanted to be the Elie Wiesel of comic books. But it's imposed on you because it's easy and it fits the moment. On your behalf, Trenton, I got offended when I read that you were going to do this show, even though I understand why, I really do. But it's so fucking reductive to invite this work into the Jewish Museum because of the link-up between Guston's Klan and Trenton's Klan.

TDH: Rebecca and I have actually talked about this at length. I think when you're trying to introduce an idea to a public that may not have a total, holistic understanding of the

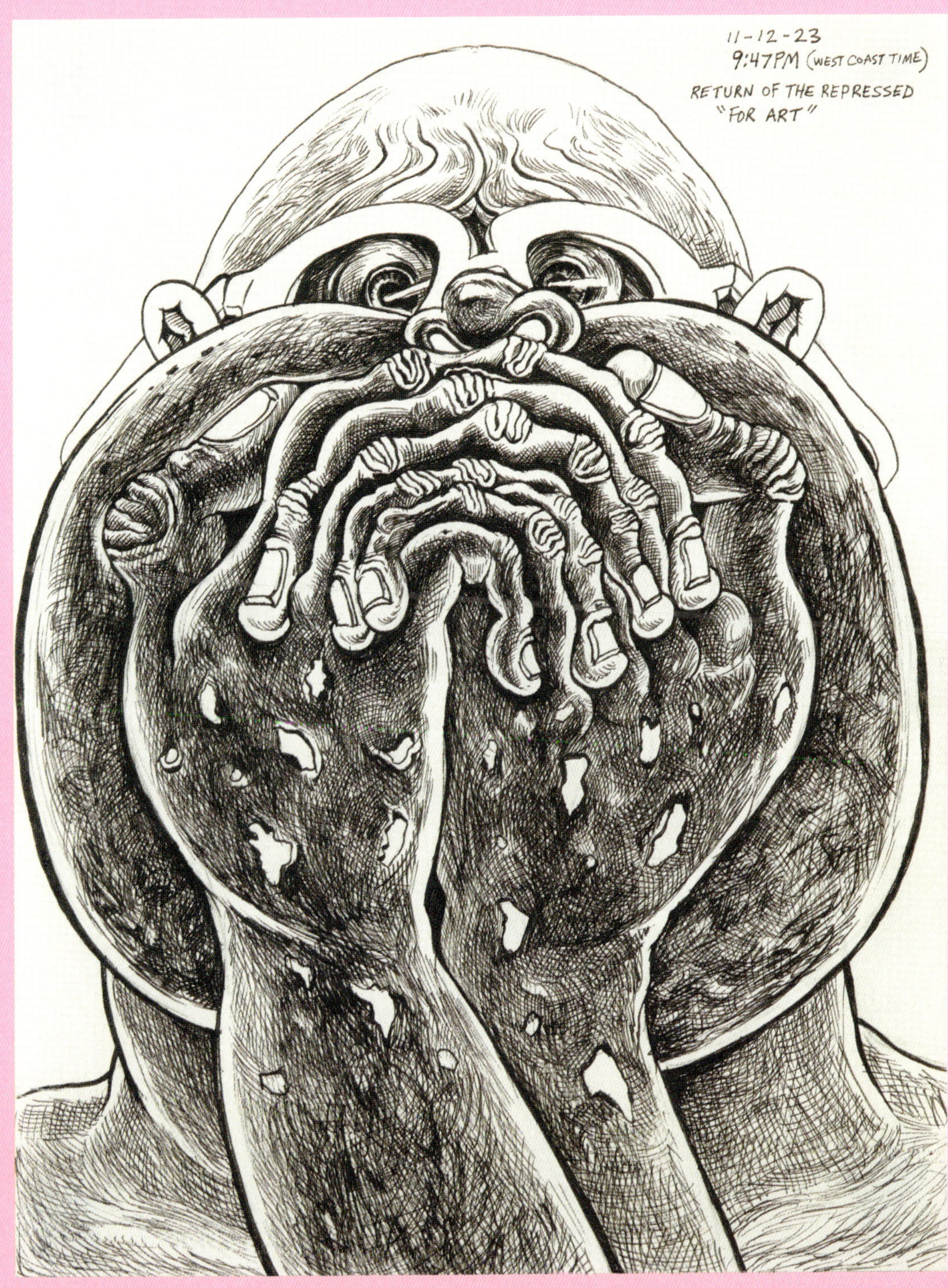

Trenton Doyle Hancock, *Return of the Repressed, "For Art,"* 2023, ink on paper, 11 × 8½ in. (27.9 × 21.6 cm). Collection of the artist

155

whole picture, you have to take it slow. That's what we're trying to do. I've come to the conclusion that, with this very focused show, people will be able to enter into both my work and Guston's work—a kind of hyphenated "Trenton-Guston" hybrid—and then do research beyond that.

AS: That makes perfect sense. But it's an issue, because everything now is so reductive. It's important to explore that reductiveness if we're ever going to get to a place where we can think again.

   As a First Amendment fundamentalist, I feel obligated to be able to say something and not be pilloried and shamed for it, but to have a fully breathing conversation about it, so one can actually master it and internalize it. That's an important project. To have to squeeze our understanding of something into a narrow funnel, to be able to see aspects of Trenton move through cinema and animation and toys and whiteness and Blackness and art from different eras—that is a very narrow needle to have to thread it through, to then allow it to expand again and become a living organism. But right now, it's what needs to happen, because the conversation has become so stultified and suppressed that we have to go through this to get anywhere meaningful.

TDH: Yup, which is why I do keep an open mind about work that is difficult. I ask questions like, Well, if the Klan—not Guston, but a Klan member or an actual racist person—made artwork, what would it look like as an expression? Do objectively evil people even *have* creative impulses? I'd like to see that and not have a knee-jerk reaction of, Well, just burn it.

   Like we were saying, there's an empathy for Guston's Klan characters. You could get very angry that those images exist, but I don't approach them from that sort of place. I try to look at *why* someone does what they do, especially when it comes to painting. There are so many other things a person can do with their life. They don't have to sit in front of a canvas and work it out there. Why would someone do that? I know that for myself, I go through a similar role-play where I enter into a character and I lose myself. I end up being influenced by the character within the picture. It's the craziest thing, but sometimes that line becomes blurred. And I see some of that blurriness with

Guston. There must have been some psychological reason for him to want to experiment like that, one that rests outside words, logic, or explanation. It's why these paintings ultimately exist. And it's why you and I do what we do, too.

Trenton Doyle Hancock, panel no. 19 from
Epidemic! Presents: Step and Screw!, 2014
(detail; see p. 86)

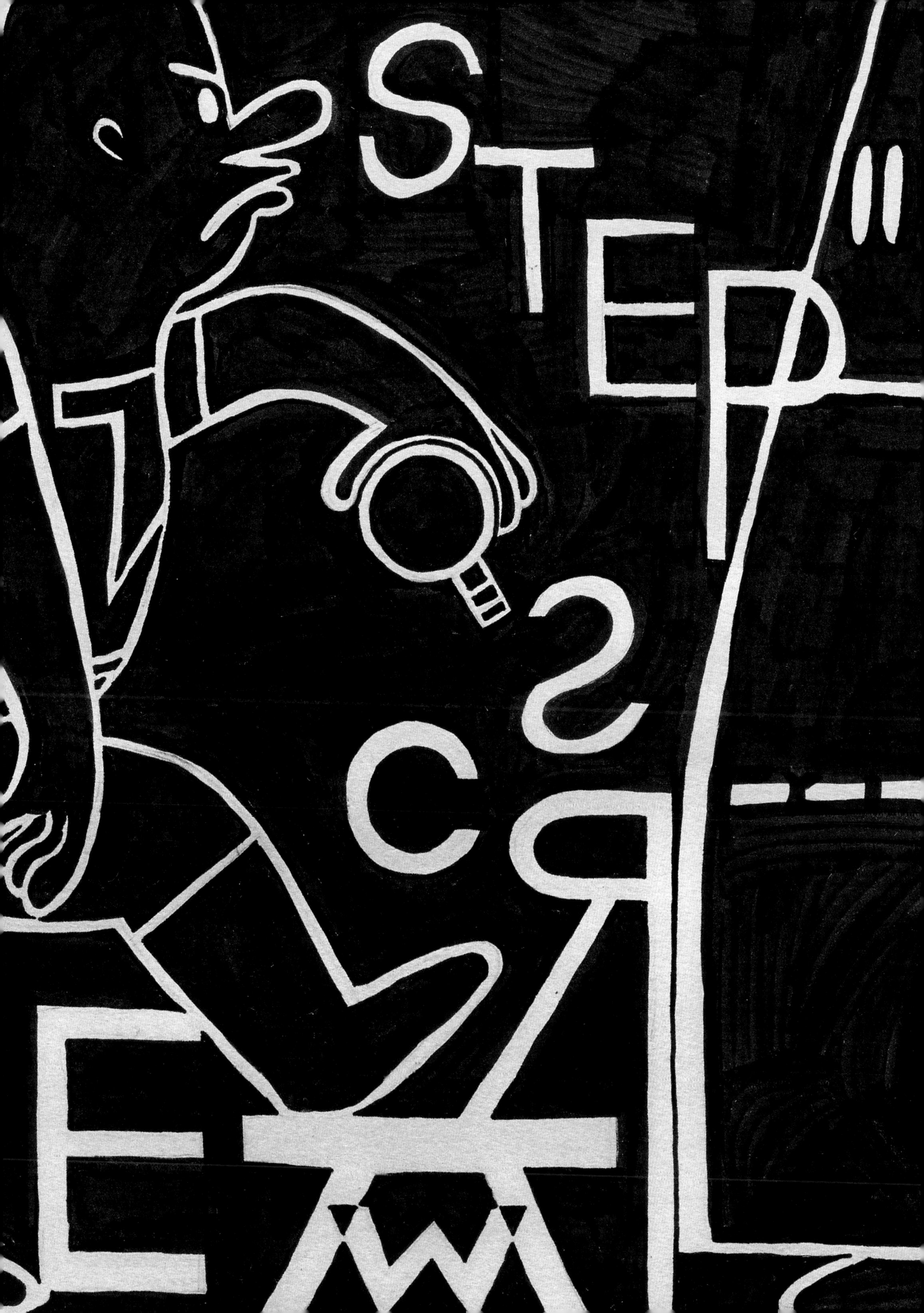

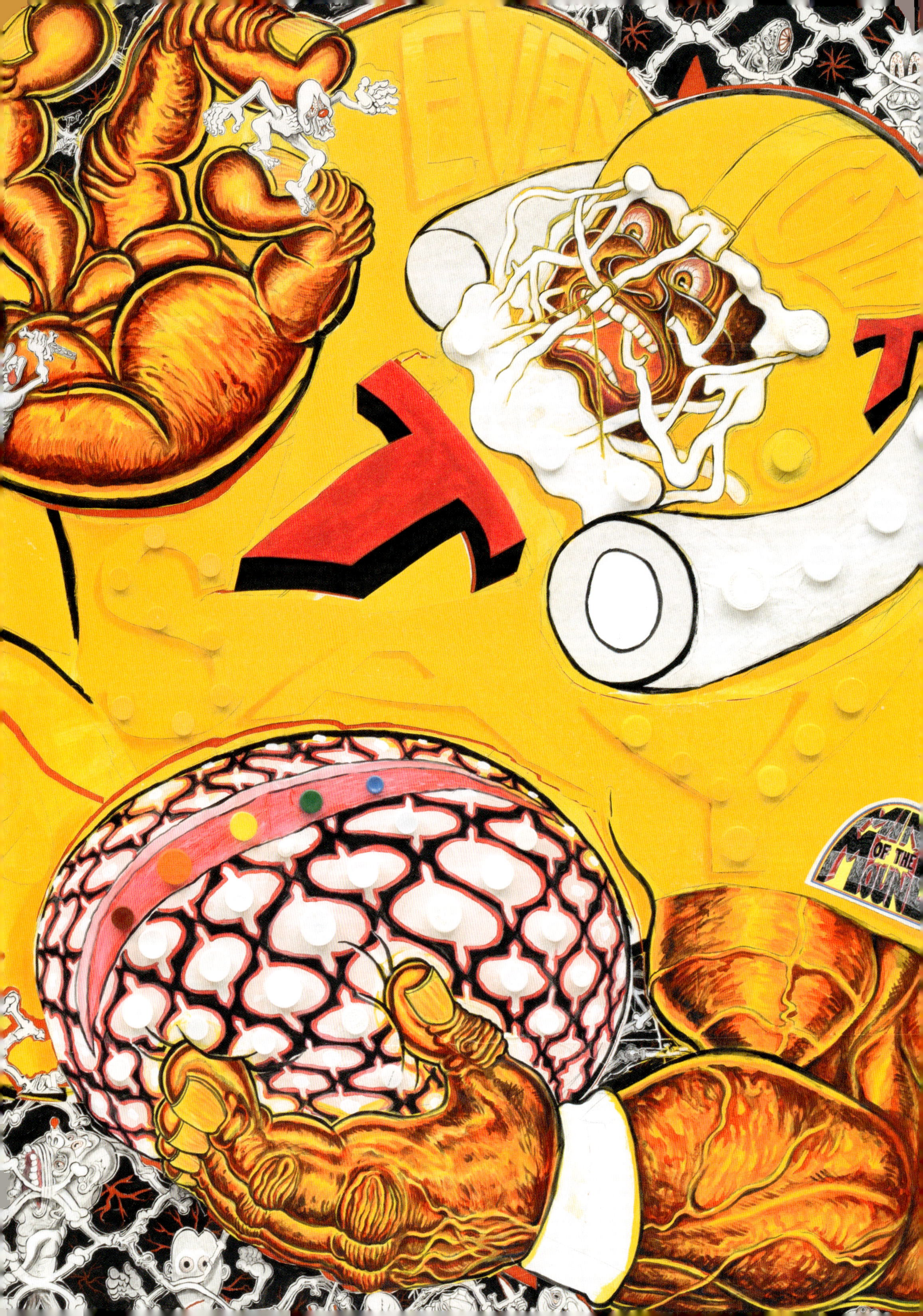
SEVEN
OF THE
MOUND

Trenton Doyle Hancock, *I Didn't Even Get to Say Goodbye*, 2021 (detail; see p. 113)

This book has been published in conjunction with the exhibition *Draw Them In, Paint Them Out: Trenton Doyle Hancock Confronts Philip Guston*, organized by the Jewish Museum, New York, November 8, 2024–March 30, 2025.

JEWISH MUSEUM, NEW YORK
DIRECTOR OF PUBLICATIONS
Eve Sinaiko

PROJECT EDITOR
Marcie M. Muscat

YALE UNIVERSITY PRESS
EDITOR, ART AND ARCHITECTURE
Amy Canonico

ASSISTANT MANAGING EDITOR
Alison Hagge

PRODUCTION MANAGER
Sarah Henry

EDITORIAL ASSISTANT
Elizabeth Searcy

DESIGN
Morcos Key (Jon Key, Chuck Gonzales)

TYPOGRAPHY
Helveesti by Dinamo
Self Modern by Bretagne

PRINTED IN MALAYSIA BY
1010 Printing International Limited

FRONT COVER
Trenton Doyle Hancock, *Schlep and Screw, Knowledge Rental Pawn Exchange Service*, 2017 (see p. 103)

BACK COVER
Philip Guston, *The Studio*, 1969 (see p. 59)

ENDPAPERS
Trenton Doyle Hancock, panel nos. 2 and 30 from *Epidemic! Presents: Step and Screw!*, 2014 (details; see pp. 69, 97)

Jewish Museum
1109 Fifth Avenue
New York, New York 10128
thejewishmuseum.org

Yale University Press
P.O. Box 209040
New Haven, Connecticut 06520–9040
yalebooks.com/art

Library of Congress Control Number: 2024936244
ISBN 978-0-300-27820-0

A catalogue record for this book is available from the British Library.

The paper in this book meets the requirements of ANSI/NISO Z 39.48-1992 (Permanence of Paper).

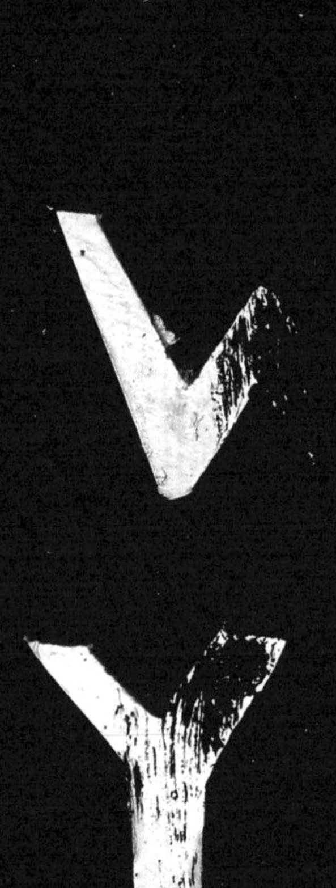
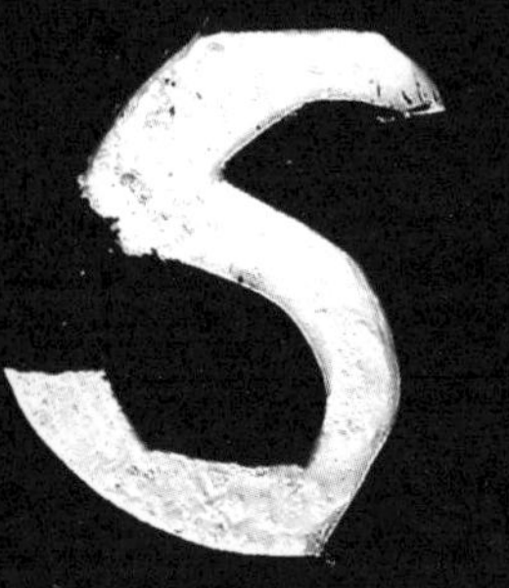

WILL OUR H
HIMS
OUR
OU
O
V
Y
S